Grab Their Belts
To Fight Them

WARREN WILKINS

Grab Their Belts
THE VIET CONG'S BIG-UNIT WAR AGAINST THE U.S., 1965–1966
To Fight Them

NAVAL INSTITUTE PRESS
Annapolis, Maryland

Naval Institute Press
291 Wood Road
Annapolis, MD 21402

© 2011 by Warren Wilkins

All rights reserved. No part of this book may be reproduced or utilized in any form or by any means, electronic or mechanical, including photocopying and recording, or by any information storage and retrieval system, without permission in writing from the publisher.

Library of Congress Cataloging-in-Publication Data
Wilkins, Warren.
  Grab their belts to fight them : the Viet Cong's big-unit war against the U.S., 1965-1966 / Warren Wilkins.
     p. cm.
  Includes bibliographical references and index.
  ISBN 978-1-59114-961-3 (hardcover : acid-free paper) 1. Vietnam War, 1961-1975—Campaigns. 2. Mat trân dân tôc giai phóng miên nam Viêt Nam. 3. Mat trân dân tôc giai phóng miên nam Viêt Nam—Regimental histories. 4. Military art and science—Vietnam (Democratic Republic)—History—20th century. 5. Vietnam (Democratic Republic)—Military policy. 6. Strategy—History—20th century. I. Title.
  DS557.7.W546 2011
  959.704'3322—dc22
                                                    2010046866

Printed in the United States of America.

19 18 17 16 15 14 13 12 11   9 8 7 6 5 4 3 2 1
First printing

To my mother, Lois,
for a lifetime of love and support

Contents

List of Maps	ix
Foreword	xi
Acknowledgments	xv
Introduction	1

PART I. THE VIET CONG
1	Origins, Infrastructure, and Organization	7
2	On the Field of Battle	21
3	Generating Friction	41

PART II. THE BIG-UNIT WAR: 1965
4	Strategic Debates and Decisions	51
5	Van Tuong	64
6	An Ninh and the Ia Drang Valley	82
7	The B2 Front	96
8	Cong Truong 9 Enters the Fray	105
9	The Die Is Cast	127

PART III. THE BIG-UNIT WAR: 1966
10	An Inauspicious Beginning	143
11	Winter–Spring Battles: Region 5	159
12	Winter–Spring Battles: The B2 Front	175

PART IV. EPILOGUE
13	The Big-Unit War and the Road to Tet	197
14	Attitudes and Adversaries	213

Notes	229
Bibliography	261
Index	275

Maps

1	South Vietnam, 1965–66	3
2	Operation Starlite, August 18–19, 1965	69
3	Communist command and administrative areas in South Vietnam, July 1965	97
4	III Corps Operations, October–December 1965	107
5	Battle of Ap Bau Bang, November 12, 1965	114
6	Battle of Ap Nha Mat, December 5, 1965	122
7	Operation Masher/White Wing, January 25–March 6, 1966	152
8	Operation Texas, March 1966	169
9	III Corps Operations, January–April 1966	182

Foreword

The Vietnam War, which the United States joined in the early 1960s and abandoned in 1973, was and remains the most controversial struggle the country ever fought. The war had an even more searing effect in terms of its consequences and, most importantly, how the United States would act militarily to protect its perceived national security in the future. When the United States decided to enter the struggle, the country was engulfed in a wave of optimism, a spirit of "Camelot" produced by the electoral triumph of President John F. Kennedy. By the time the United States decided to withdraw from the conflict in 1973, the political careers of two presidents had been demolished and, in sharp contrast with the Kennedy era, the country was gripped by introspection, pessimism, massive protests over what many considered ten years of cruel and unjust war, and virtual paralysis in military thought generated by the country's failure to prevail militarily in what most perceived as the new realm of unconventional warfare.

It is indeed ironic that when it reached its decision to intervene in Vietnam, the Kennedy administration did so at least in part because of a new military strategy it articulated to overcome frustrations produced by a previous war—in this case the local but still bloody struggle in Korea from 1950 to 1953. Specifically, the strategy of "Flexible Response," which the Kennedy administration implemented to replace the previous one of "Massive Retaliation," which the administration believed contributed to the four-year stalemate in Korea, received its first test in Vietnam.

The Vietnam War, in addition to producing striking changes in the political landscape in the United States, also represented a watershed in American military thought. At the beginning of the 1960s the subject of conventional war, albeit in a nuclear context, dominated U.S. military thought. Unlike the strategy of "Massive Retaliation," which deterred global nuclear war but left the United States clearly vulnerable to defeat in limited conventional war, "Flexible Response" seemed to promise victory in limited war. Thus, in part, President Kennedy's decision to intervene in Vietnam resulted from the articulation of a new military strategy. In short, the Vietnam War became a testing ground for "Flexible Response" and for the new force structure of the U.S. armed forces.

When it became clear in 1973 that victory had eluded the United States in Vietnam, military analysts quickly concluded it was due to the U.S. military establishment's failure to appreciate and prepare for a new type of struggle they termed unconventional or guerilla war. Supporting this analysis, political and military leaders in the Soviet Union, Cuba, and other people's "democracies" bombarded the world with bold proclamations concerning the new realm of what they deemed partisan, unconventional, guerilla, or revolutionary wars.

In the wake of the Vietnam War, most U.S. and Western military and political pundits and historians concluded that the United States had suffered defeat because American armed forces failed to understand or cope with these new types of struggles. Citing the British army's experiences in Malaysia after World War II and many other instances, they generally agreed that the United States applied a strategy and tactics in the war suited to conventional limited or local war—that is, those suited to the newly articulated national military strategy of "Flexible Response"—to what was clearly an unconventional war.

Unlike virtually all existing books about the Vietnam War, this one challenges previous studies by asserting that the conflict in Vietnam was not simply a "classic" unconventional clash of arms. Although it was always a *hybrid* armed struggle, Warren Wilkins demonstrates that during 1965–1966 the Communist Vietnamese forces emphasized a traditional "big-unit" approach to war with the United States and ARVN in an effort to achieve a quick and decisive victory.

This fresh approach, based on careful and extensive research, study, and analysis of North Vietnamese strategy and tactics, as well as the course of military operations in South Vietnam, presents an altogether different mosaic of the war. In short, it provides a new perspective and balance to a subject that, largely because it has been politicized, has sorely lacked both. It should be required reading for all interested in military history and past, present, and future military affairs.

David M. Glantz, Colonel, USA (Ret.)

Carlisle, Pennsylvania

Acknowledgments

First and foremost, I would like to thank God, for without Him I could never have negotiated the trials and tribulations this odyssey invariably entailed. While not *divine*, the support I received from my family, most notably my mother and my sister Andrea, also warrants my enduring gratitude. Indeed, no one championed this project more than Andrea.

As is customarily the case in most literary endeavors, this project profited immeasurably from the tangible support of numerous individuals. I am, for example, eternally indebted to Merle Pribbenow. Encyclopedic in his knowledge of our Communist adversary in Vietnam yet extraordinarily magnanimous with both his time and his resources, Merle translated and furnished scores of Communist Vietnamese histories, documents, and other research materials for use in this project. Merle, moreover, patiently answered question after question with remarkable specificity and thoroughness, and through our conversations and correspondences, succeeded in enhancing my understanding of Communist Vietnamese strategy and strategic thinking. Indeed, Merle served as a de facto mentor to me on this project.

Sgt. Maj. Dan Cragg, USA (Ret.), coauthor of the landmark tome *Inside the VC and the NVA: The Real Story of North Vietnam's Armed Forces*, reviewed an early draft and provided invaluable editorial advice and much needed encouragement. Similarly, Lieutenant Colonel Otto Lehrack, USMC (Ret.), reviewed excerpts of subsequent drafts and dutifully embodied his daunting

Marine Corps nickname of "No Slack Lehrack," leaving this work the richer for it. Colonel Tom Faley, USA (Ret.), meanwhile, searched for and retrieved pivotal research material. And I would be shamefully remiss if I failed to acknowledge the profound impact and influence of Colonel David M. Glantz, USA (Ret.) on my development as a student of history in general and armed conflict in particular.

Additionally, many others deserve my heartfelt gratitude as well, including General P. X. Kelley, USMC (Ret.); Captain Ken Sympson, USMC (Ret.); Colonel Bill Haponski, USA (Ret.); Gary Hutchinson, USMC (Ret.); Tom "Doc" Stubbs, USN (Ret.); Gary Ball, USA (Ret.); Will Parish, USA (Ret.); Bill Baty, USA (Ret.); James Tobias, Center of Military History; Ashley Ekins, Head, Military History Section (Australian War Memorial); and Amy Mondt at Texas Tech University. I would also like to extend my thanks to Mark Moyar, Eric Bergerud, Martin Loicano, Marissa Sestito, Kil J. Yi, Lien-Hang Nguyen, Stephane Moutin-Luyat, and of course my intrepid editor at the Naval Institute Press, Adam Kane.

I would, furthermore, like to thank America's Vietnam veterans. Your service and sacrifice have not been forgotten.

Finally, I and I alone shoulder the responsibilities for any and all errors.

Grab Their Belts
To Fight Them

Introduction

The subject of books, articles, and documentaries, not to mention a veritable fixture in the global pop culture lexicon, few armed forces have captivated the world as much or been more fondly romanticized than the Viet Cong. Regrettably, few armed forces have ever been so woefully misunderstood, and aspects of their military campaign so neglected, as the Viet Cong and the "big-unit" war they waged against the U.S. military in Vietnam. How the Viet Cong shaped up as a military entity and big-unit adversary of the U.S. military in Vietnam is, therefore, a major objective of the chapters that follow.

If so inclined one might mention the matrimony of political *dau tranh* (struggle movement) and armed *dau tranh* at the heart of the Vietnamese Communist brand of warfare. Renowned Vietnamese communism expert Douglass Pike once averred, "The dualism of *dau tranh* is bedrock dogma. Neither can be successful alone, only when combined—the marriage of violence to politics—can victory be achieved."[1] General William Westmoreland spoke to this synthesis when he admitted, "Their [Viet Cong] integration of efforts surpasses ours by a large order of magnitude."[2] Consequently some might judge any effort to divorce one from the other as fatal to a lucid understanding of the Viet Cong *on war* and *at war* against the armed forces of the United States.

In addressing the big-unit war, a thorough investigation of political *dau tranh* need not be included so long as its incestuous relationship with armed *dau tranh* is readily acknowledged and addressed when patently necessary.

Thus "pacification," an issue in which political *dau tranh* deserves as much if not more attention than armed *dau tranh*, and those aspects of armed *dau tranh* not typically associated with the big-unit war (kidnappings, assassinations, and so on), exceed the objectives of this work and have been excluded. Several wonderful tomes are available on the *other war*, not the least of which is Bing West's classic *The Village*. On the other hand, the occasionally forgotten political forces, and the enduring mistruths about those forces, animating the Viet Cong big-unit war warrant—and receive—substantial coverage.

Laymen, however, generally care little about political *dau tranh*, no matter how instrumental it was in the Viet Cong concept of war.[3] They want to know if, as pop culture maintains, peasants from a jungle nation seemingly without any of the trappings of modernity bested the mighty U.S. military on the field of battle. And if so, how—exactly—were they able to accomplish the feat? The actual fighting itself and whether they "kicked America's ass," to put it inelegantly, weighs most heavily on the curiosities of the general public. This curiosity can be partially sated by examining the Communist big-unit war in South Vietnam.

For several years early on, the Viet Cong and the North Vietnamese Army, the official army of the North Vietnamese state, fought a big-unit war against the U.S. military. "During 1965 and 1966, the Communists fought the Americans toe to toe, making little effort to act like guerillas," wrote Dale Andrade, a historian at the U.S. Army Center of Military History. "Those years saw the largest percentage of attacks by battalion-sized enemy units or larger—even greater than in the years of the two biggest enemy offensives of the war, 1968 and 1972."[4] Accordingly, this work will focus on the opening months of that big-unit war, namely, August 1965 to May 1966 and the activities related to it.

Author and Marine Corps veteran David Sherman once admitted: "For the most part, when I was in the 1st Marines we never wanted to fight them [Viet Cong]. But when we did we wanted them to stand and fight so we could kick ass on them."[5] The following examines within the big-unit war context the tactical framework and doctrine, noteworthy engagements, strategic objectives, and profound strategic consequences that resulted when the Viet Cong did just that.

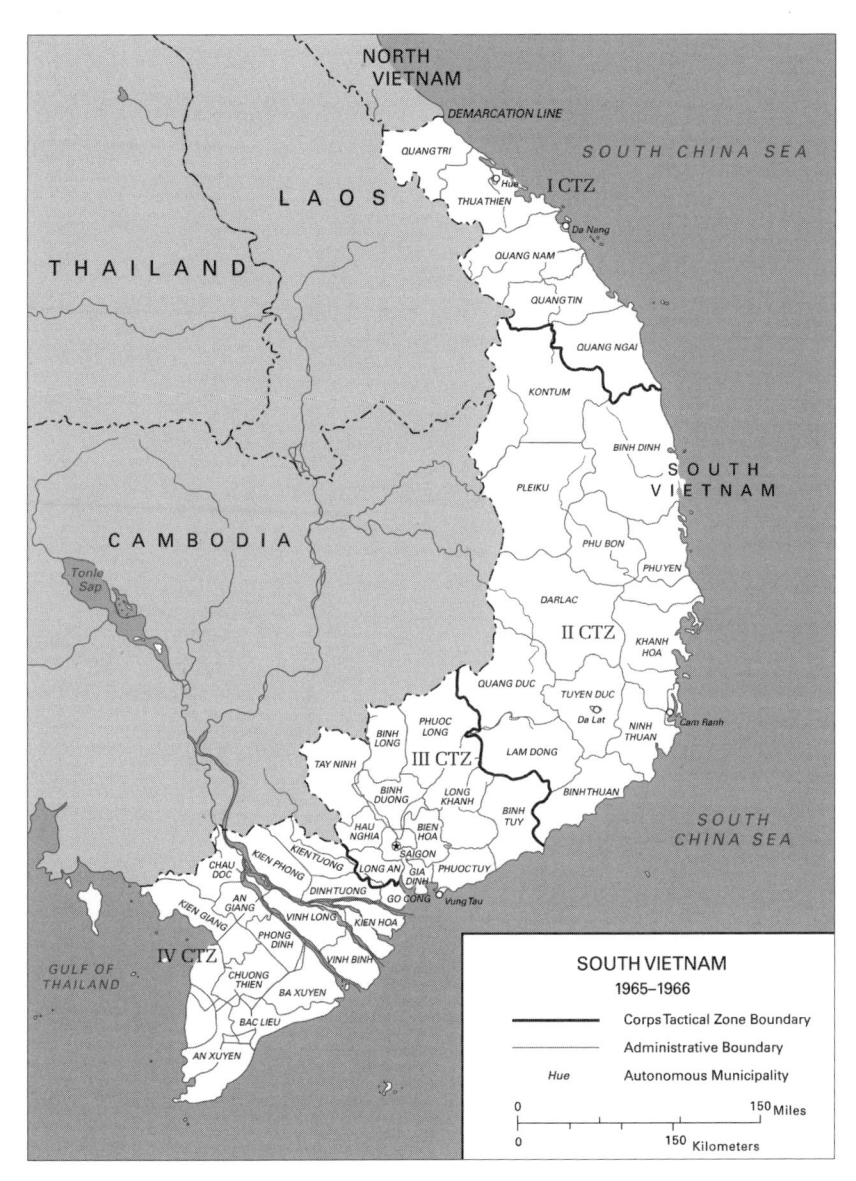

Map 1. *South Vietnam, 1965–66 (From Carland,* United States Army in Vietnam)

PART I
THE VIET CONG

1

Origins, Infrastructure, and Organization

Central to the Viet Cong (VC) mystique is a dubious appreciation of its origins, architects, and organization. Rather than a spontaneous uprising of heroic if manifestly ill-equipped and -trained indigenous farmers, the Viet Cong armed movement to overthrow the South Vietnamese government and reunify the country was formally approved by North Vietnam's Communist Party Central Committee.

During the second session of the Fifteenth Plenum of the Central Committee, held in July 1959, North Vietnam's Communist leadership ratified a resolution "affirming," in the words of a Communist Vietnamese source, that "the Vietnamese revolution was led by the Party and that it had two strategic missions to be carried out in parallel: the socialist revolution in North Vietnam and the people's national democratic revolution in South Vietnam. Although these two missions were different in nature, they were intimately connected with one another, because they affected, influenced, and supported one another."[1] The plenum also pronounced that "the fundamental path for the advancement of the Vietnamese revolution in South Vietnam is an insurrection to place the reins of the government into the hands of the people. . . . Based on the specific situation and the current requirements of the revolution, that path is to use the power of the masses, relying primarily on mass political forces supported by armed forces, to overthrow imperialist and feudalist rule in order to establish a popular revolutionary government."[2]

The North's political establishment, not apolitical rice farmers rebelling against governmental oppression, had ultimately chosen the path of political agitation and armed revolt in South Vietnam. So disposed, the Central Committee avowed: "Our Party must make active preparations in all fields" for "staging an insurrection to overthrow the U.S.-Diem regime" and "to unify the nation."[3] The die had thus been fatefully cast, and it had been cast in North Vietnam.

Following what some in the Communist leadership viewed as an imprudent course of action chartered at the plenum, North Vietnam began the process of infiltrating South Vietnam with men and supplies. For such an endeavor to succeed on a grand scale, a reliable access way to the South had to be established. In May 1959 the Military Commission of the Central Committee submitted a resolution creating Group 559, "which had the missions of, along with the liaison route of the Unification Committee, creating the first foot-travel route connecting the North and South, and organizing the sending of people, weapons, and supplies to the revolution in the South, first of all to Interzone 5."[4] From these humble beginnings and through the remarkable labors of Truong Son troops (Group 559 personnel), the "Ho Chi Minh Trail" germinated into a war-winning strategic route for Hanoi.

The first infiltrators to go south were southern-born insurgents siphoned from a pool of approximately 100,000 ethnic South Vietnamese who had regrouped to North Vietnam in the aftermath of the North-South division. These "regroupees" jettisoned all personal belongings before departing, and some were even asked to change their names.[5] Extensive military training, including expert instruction in guerrilla warfare, ambush tactics, and the building of fortified positions, accompanied the infiltrators' political indoctrination prior to their journey south along the then-embryonic Ho Chi Minh Trail. To accommodate their training, Hanoi established facilities like the Xuan Mai Infiltration Training Center and the "special training base" site located at a North Vietnamese Army (NVA) base in Son Tay. The NVA also tasked at least one division, the 324th in Nghe An Province, with training infiltrators.[6]

These surreptitiously dispatched infiltrators had a major impact on the Viet Cong, both politically and militarily. First and foremost they possessed excellent training, experience, and, quite often, ideological fidelity. Because of those attributes, regrouped infiltrators formed the original nucleus of the "Viet Cong" (southern Communist) armed movement. A wartime paper documenting the roots and progression of the Vietnam conflict thoroughly addressed the makeup, qualifications, and imprint of the infiltrator: "Until late 1963, most of these infiltrators were ethnic southerners, veterans of the Viet Minh with years of military experience and training, who had regrouped to the North. They were preponderantly officers or senior noncommissioned officers; through 1961, a high proportion of them were members of the Lao Dong Party. They assumed command positions in the Viet Cong forces and also carried out a wide range of political assignments. The provided, in sum, the core of the Viet Cong military and political apparatus."[7]

Liberating the South from neocolonial tyranny may have sounded noble and adventurous, but for the infiltrator the journey was fraught with hardship. Homesick and beset by fatigue and hunger, the men sent south experienced untold privation. The following verse from a young infiltrator's diary captured their plight:

> In this, my youth, my life should blossom like a flower,
> But gladly, I bore hardship and danger,
> For they told me it was in the name of Peace.
> Month after month I marched by day and tried to rest by night.
> My shoes wore out, my jacket is so thin the cold easily cuts through.
> Evening finds me
> Here in the heart of the Truong Son range,
> O Mother I yearn for home.[8]

Hanoi also sent down a high-ranking military and political cadre to assist with the southern insurrection. Headed up by Major General Tran Van Quang, alternate member of the Communist Party Central Committee and deputy chief of the General Staff, one particularly large delegation arrived in Binh Long Province in July 1961, fully prepared to impart their revolutionary know-how.[9] An earlier grouping of North Vietnamese military cadres allegedly had set off for the swampland areas near Ben Tre in South Vietnam's Mekong Delta and by early 1961 had succeeded in raising the first two Viet Cong battalions from locally obtained recruits. Individuals from the northern cadre, rather than local candidates, were said to have filled the two battalions' officer corps.[10]

In conjunction with the mechanics of infiltration, North Vietnam quietly presided over a subordinate apparatus that administered to the political complexities of the Viet Cong revolution in South Vietnam. North Vietnam's political leadership deduced early on that the hydraulics of internal political opposition in South Vietnam, including a failed 1960 coup against South Vietnamese president Ngo Dinh Diem, presented an opportunity to erect a broadly based, anti-Diem national coalition. On November 11, 1960, Hanoi's Politburo cabled its party apparatus in South Vietnam (the Cochin China Region Party Committee, and so on) and decreed:

a) Our policy at this time is to exploit the contradictions, disruptions, and confusion in the enemy's ranks to the maximum in order to incite a large mass struggle movement aimed at overthrowing the entire reactionary clique, and especially the Diem government. . . .

b) Because of this new situation, we must shift to new forms of struggle using new and appropriate slogans and demands to gain further support and isolate and topple our enemies. In order to accomplish these goals, we must publicly issue the program of the National Liberation Front for South Vietnam.[11]

Not much more than a month later, on December 20, 1960, officials from the "southern branch" of the Communist Party headquartered in Hanoi convened in Cambodia and established the National Liberation Front (NLF), which publicly espoused the goal of overthrowing the "dictatorial Ngo Dinh Diem administration." Ostensibly a sovereign South Vietnamese political invention, the NLF was little more than a North Vietnamese contrivance designed to deflect suspicions and put an "independent," ideologically neutral southern face on the movement to unseat Diem's anti-Communist government.

The party branch in South Vietnam complied with Hanoi's wishes by announcing, aiding the buildup of, and then dominating the NLF. There was, admittedly, a non-Communist NLF constituency, but party members retained all of the important positions within the organization.[12] "The Central Committee," said one Communist defector, "could hardly permit the International Control Commission to say that there was an invasion from the North, so it was necessary to have some name . . . to clothe these forces with some political organization."[13] The National Liberation Front provided exactly that.

Despite the elaborate lengths employed by North Vietnam to conceal its involvement, often enlisting the incredulously uncritical advocacy of influential Westerners, internal Communist memoranda betray the extent of Hanoi's management of the Viet Cong insurrection. The Central Office for South Vietnam (COSVN) issued a November 1961 directive reiterating Hanoi's instructions to change the name of the southern branch of the party, formerly referred to as the Party Chapter for South Vietnam, to the People's Revolutionary Party. If the change produced a name that sounded more homegrown and self-determining—and hence more palatable for domestic and especially foreign consumption—it did not free the People's Revolutionary Party, and by extension the NLF, from Hanoi's direction. The COSVN directive went on to clarify:

1. The first thing that everyone must understand is that it is only a name change. Although the overt name will be different than that used in North Vietnam, secretly, internally and from the organizational standpoint, the Party Chapter for South Vietnam will still be a part of the Vietnam Labor Party [Dang Lao Dong Viet Nam] and will be under the leadership of the Party Central Committee, headed by Chairman Ho Chi Minh. This means that except for the name change, the Party Chapter for South Vietnam will not change in any other way.
2. Why is it necessary to have a separate name for the Party Chapter for South Vietnam?

    Under the current conditions of ferocious political and armed struggle, if the Party Chapter for South Vietnam openly kept its old name, identifying it as a Party Chapter of the Labor Party of Vietnam under the leadership of the Party Central Committee in North Vietnam, then our enemies, both domestic and foreign, could utilize that to spread distortions and accusations that North Vietnam was intervening to overthrow South Vietnam.[14]

Likewise the People's Liberation Armed Forces (PLAF), or the more general Liberation Army of South Vietnam, was the official name of the Viet Cong armed forces. Established in early 1961, the PLAF acted as the military wing of the National Liberation Front. As with the NLF, the PLAF was designed to convey the appearance of independence, in this case military independence. In Hanoi, however, the terms PLAF and PAVN (People's Army of Vietnam, the official name of the NVA) represented a distinction without appreciable difference. All Communist forces fighting to "liberate" South Vietnam were regarded as the logical extension of the latter (PAVN/NVA), and all were to answer to the party in Hanoi. Hanoi's General Military Party Committee, in fact, privately acknowledged the interrelationship of Communist forces in the opening of a January 1961 communication. It read: "The Liberation Army of South Vietnam is part of the People's Army of Vietnam, having been organized, developed, educated, and led by the Party."[15]

As for COSVN, its origins dated back to 1951 and the First Indochina War. With the conclusion of 1954 and the resettlement of Viet Minh forces from South Vietnam to North Vietnam per the Geneva Agreements, COSVN gave way to a new command body, the Cochin China (Nam Bo) Party Committee, or Xu Uy Nam Bo, and disbanded. Established in October 1954, the Cochin China Party Committee assumed responsibility for the southern half of South Vietnam. The Region 5 Party Committee, incidentally, managed the northern half of South Vietnam. COSVN then reemerged on January 23, 1961, when the Third Plenum of the Central Committee in Hanoi authorized its "creation." COSVN was subsequently activated in October 1961.[16] August in name though in actuality nothing more than a roving leadership group for Hanoi's Central Committee, COSVN had a host of responsibilities but a straightforward mandate:

1. The Central Office for South Vietnam is an element of the Party Central Committee made up of a number of members of the Party Central Committee whom the Central Committee has chosen and has authorized to direct all Party activities in South Vietnam.
2. The Central Office for South Vietnam is under the leadership of the Party Central Committee, and the Politburo, acting on behalf of the

Central Committee, will provide constant direction and guidance to COSVN.
3. The Central Office for South Vietnam has the following missions and responsibilities—Based on resolutions passed by Party Congresses and on Central Committee and Politburo directives and resolutions regarding the revolution in South Vietnam, the Central Office for South Vietnam will establish concrete guidelines, policies, formulas, operating plans, and guidance to implement those Party resolutions and directives in South Vietnam.[17]

For the sake of clarity, it may also be instructive to consider COSVN the "central committee" of the People's Revolutionary Party in South Vietnam. And while it can be a bit much to digest all at once, an allied military intelligence officer intimately familiar with the Viet Cong explained how the two entities, COSVN and the People's Revolutionary Party, interacted:

> COSVN receives political instruction from the DRV [North Vietnam] Politburo and passes them on in its own resolutions which are referred to as a *nghi quyet* [resolution]. These instructions go to a senior PRP [People's Revolutionary Party] organizational group of party members within the Liberation Army Headquarters called the *"Quan uy Trung uong Cuc."* That's the COSVN Military Committee which includes all the senior commanders within the Liberation Army Headquarters. They take the broad instructions from Hanoi and reissue them through two channels. On the strictly military side, they issue the instructions as orders from the Liberation Army Headquarters, often referring to such and such a resolution of COSVN as the basis for a specific order. Within the party chain of command, COSVN issues sensitive implementing instructions through the PRP organization to both staff and the party and youth group members at each echelon.[18]

Militarily COSVN helped manage the revolution for Hanoi through its control of the PLAF or Viet Cong armed forces. COSVN Military Headquarters, at the risk of overgeneralizing the often confusing Communist military command structure in South Vietnam, commanded Viet Cong and NVA forces in the southern half of South Vietnam. Viet Cong and NVA units deployed in the northern half of South Vietnam were directed operationally by North Vietnam.

While General Nguyen Chi Thanh, who was transferred to South Vietnam by Hanoi in late 1964, accepted overall responsibility for the Viet Cong war in the South as COSVN party secretary and "political commissar" until his death in 1967, he was not the head of COSVN Military Headquarters. That distinction belonged to General Tran Van Tra. "Tran Van Tra was the 'Commander of the South Vietnamese Liberation Army,' which was supposedly the NLF's military arm," said Merle Pribbenow, a former CIA veteran of the conflict and a highly respected expert. "General Tran Van Tra was also, from 1964 to 1967, the Commander of the COSVN Military Headquarters (*Bo Tu Lenh Mien*), also called the 'Regional Headquarters for South Vietnam,' and the Commander of the B2 Front. The B2 Front was the Communist military command for the southern half of South Vietnam. Military command of Communist forces in the northern half of South Vietnam came directly from North Vietnam."[19]

General Tra was born in 1918 in Quang Ngai Province, one of the more northerly provinces of what would become South Vietnam.[20] Tra had served with the Viet Minh during the war against the French, and in the years 1956–58 he traveled to the Soviet Union for military instruction at the Soviet High-Level Academy [Study Institute], becoming one of the first Vietnamese to do so. Feeling ill, he eventually left the Soviet Union but returned in 1960–61 to continue his studies. In 1963 Tra infiltrated South Vietnam to, in his words, "replace Brother [Tran Van] Quang and to establish the Headquarters of the Liberation Armed Forces of South Vietnam"[21]

General Thanh, meanwhile, was not a member of the General Staff in Hanoi despite his membership in the Politburo and rank as a four-star general. A "very extremist and Leftist" *political* general, Thanh led the General Political Department branch of the High Command, Hanoi's "supreme military headquarters," from the early 1950s to the late 1950s and perhaps until the early 1960s.[22] He then spent a brief stint dealing with agricultural affairs in North Vietnam. After his agricultural assignment, Thanh returned to the armed forces and was ordered to South Vietnam to head up COSVN.[23]

Before leaving, Thanh and his colleagues received a stern farewell from Ho Chi Minh: "Fighting the French was hard, but fighting the Americans will be even harder. The Party and the Government are sending you down there to join our compatriots in South Vietnam in fighting the Americans until victory is achieved. When you see our compatriots down there, tell them that the people of South Vietnam are constantly in Uncle Ho's thoughts."[24] In time Thanh would appreciate the enormity of the task for which he had been sent.

Fashioned along the lines of the Chinese Revolutionary Armed Forces, the Viet Cong forces operating under the auspices of General Thanh and General Tran Van Tra at COSVN or in military areas controlled directly by Hanoi consisted of three distinct factions: part-time village guerrillas or militia VC; full-time, tolerably trained, and provincially/regionally based local-force VC; and full-time, well-trained, and geographically more autonomous main-force VC. Whereas the village guerrillas or militia detachments resembled the Westernized caricature of a Viet Cong combatant—a shoddily armed, "farmer by day, guerrilla by night" fighter engaged in setting booby traps and picking off weary American infantrymen—main-force Viet Cong most assuredly did not.

Main-force units were subordinate to military regions or "fronts," and their organization mirrored the battalion-regiment-division configuration present in conventional armies. Generically speaking a Viet Cong division possessed an operating strength of 7,350 men; a Viet Cong regiment, 1,750; and a Viet Cong battalion, 350.[25] An average main-force regiment consisted of between two and four infantry battalions and a heavy weapons/"artillery" battalion. Battalions were usually composed of three infantry companies and a heavy-weapons company, though some battalions featured a fourth infantry company. Party membership, literacy, advanced military training, and very high esprit de corps characterized the makeup of most main-force units.

Although frequently thought of as operating exclusively at the company level, the local-force VC also fielded battalion-sized formations. Every province was expected to contribute at least one local-force battalion for operations within that province.[26] Local-force units soldiered full time, like their main-force comrades, but they were not as well trained and educated or as likely to hold party membership. Additionally these units responded to authority at the district and provincial levels.

A hodgepodge amalgamation of village/hamlet–centered part-timers, the guerrilla-militia force usually included those who were either too old or too young to join the main- or local-force branches.[27] Guerrilla units ranged from a three-man cell to a platoon in size. Guerrilla platoons, while rare, served under village/hamlet front leaders. Much of the guerrillas' time, beyond asymmetrical insurgency warfare, was devoted to intelligence gathering for and logistical support of main- and local-force formations as they waged big-unit battle against American and South Vietnamese forces.

Below the squad level, Viet Cong organization revolved around the three-man cell. A harmonious three-man cooperative, the cell fought, ate, and quartered together.[28] Conversely the "triad system" governed the formation of larger units as well. Three three-man cells equaled a squad, three squads a platoon, three platoons (plus a weapons platoon) a company, and so forth.

Of the three previously discussed VC classifications, main-force units comprised the cream of the Viet Cong armed crop. Envisaged as a companion force to the "main force fist" of the NVA, main-force units were transformed to reflect the force structure and firepower capability commensurate with the task of partnering up with the NVA to destroy the Army of the Republic of Vietnam (ARVN). General Vo Nguyen Giap disapproved initially of the push for a rapid intensification to overt, conventional-style war against South Vietnam, but he faithfully prosecuted his duties as minister of defense nonetheless. Since those included logistical and administrative obligations to Communist forces in South Vietnam, Giap gradually moved the logistically untenable mishmash of Viet Cong small arms into a standard family of weapons using a single caliber (AK-47, 7.62-mm). He also oversaw, in a manner of speaking, the export of thousands of NVA soldiers that were ultimately incorporated into Viet Cong formations in the South.[29] In spite of the chastening cultural effects of integrating northern-born NVA regulars into southern VC units, the presence of skilled and well-armed professional soldiers undoubtedly enabled the main-force structure to expand sufficiently enough to meet conventional battle dimensions without a concomitant reduction in quality.

Communist bloc weapons procurement, not captured relics from a bygone era, enabled Hanoi to equip main-force formations with lethally effective modern armaments such as the AK-47 family of assault rifles, Soviet Degtayrev

7.62-mm light machine guns, and rocket-propelled grenade launchers (RPG-2s and RPG-7s). Soviet DKZ-B 122-mm rockets, 75-mm and 57-mm recoilless rifles, 82-mm and 60-mm mortars, and flamethrowers enhanced the firepower of the Viet Cong arsenal. Former Navy petty officer third class medic F. C. Brown, a solemn witness to the bodily damage wrought by Communist firepower, noted acerbically, "The generally accepted image of a black pajama clad guerrilla with an antiquated weapon, defending his paddy against a huge mechanized American force, is simply not true. Many VC units were well armed and well supplied."[30]

Michael Lee Lanning and Dan Cragg echoed Brown's sentiments. Writing on the often contentious subject of Viet Cong weaponry, the two Vietnam veterans and subsequent authors of *Inside the VC and the NVA: The Real Story of North Vietnam's Armed Forces* intoned, "By the mid-1960s, when the war escalated upon the commitment of US ground troops, the VC and infiltrating NVA units were equipped and armed with the most modern weapons and supplies Communist nations could provide."[31] Some of these weapons, like the AK-47 assault rifle, were on par with and sometimes superior to their American equivalents.

Lest anyone accuse Cragg and Lanning of disingenuously exaggerating the weaponry of the better-armed Viet Cong units out of a misplaced sense of loyalty to fellow American servicemen, others who have studied the subject reached similar conclusions. "The image of the PLAF soldier as a barefoot farmer fighting with only a home-made shotgun was as fanciful as the view that American planes bombed a North Vietnam lying helpless like Ethiopia in 1938," wrote area specialist Douglas Pike. "PAVN and the PLAF received adequate quantities of the best military equipment that the Communist world could produce."[32] The most battle ready of the PLAF—the main-force VC units—quite naturally derived the greatest benefit from the largesse of the Communist world, particularly as the war wore on. It is not surprising, then, that 94 percent of main-force soldiers polled in a 1965 survey of Viet Cong POWs maintained that their weapons were good enough to accomplish their missions.[33] Advanced firepower trickled down more slowly to the guerrilla and local-force units.

Regarding field dress, the Viet Cong had a certain standardization borne of convenience. All types of Viet Cong, but especially the guerrillas, wore the black pants (or shorts) and jackets common to the Vietnamese peasantry. Comfortable and cost effective, the Viet Cong could fight in this "black pajama" outfit and blend in with the civilian populace. However, Viet Cong units were also seen wearing khaki, black, green, and light blue uniforms. Head dress ran the gambit from "bush" hats to the occasional helmet, though the conical hat of the Vietnamese peasant or farmer was fairly typical of the Viet Cong soldier. Footwear frequently consisted of sandals or rubber/plastic "shower shoes" or "flip flops."

What the Communist world would not procure for the Viet Cong was the requisite cannon fodder to fight the war. The Communist Vietnamese would have to hurdle the manpower stumbling block on their own. In North Vietnam the recruiting program for units raised to infiltrate into South Vietnam was efficiently managed and deliberately discriminating, as a report based on the interrogation of an officer from the 1st Viet Cong Regiment confirmed:

> In order to recruit well-qualified cadres and soldiers for Group 34 [initial designation for 60th Battalion of the 1st VC Regiment] as well as other infiltration units, the General Staff sent recruiting teams to contact the directorial boards of agricultural farms, factories, and business establishments and to study the individual files of employees and interview them personally.
>
> Those who fit the following standards and lived near Hanoi were summoned by the General Staff to assemble at the Central Re-Unification Board in Hoang Van Thu Street: (1) No civil convictions, (2) Good physical condition, (3) Belief in NVN [North Vietnam] liberating SVN [South Vietnam], (4) Willingness to infiltrate SVN. Those selected were briefed on the situation in SVN and their future assignments.[34]

Group 34 was comprised mainly of men recalled from farms and other business establishments, and of those most had been "regrouped" to North Vietnam between 1954 and 1955. A smaller percentage, perhaps 10 percent and with the majority of them holding the rank of an officer, came from the standing North Vietnamese Army. Interestingly enough, the interrogation report also indicates that Group 34 was "organized as an independent battalion" and directly subordinate to the General Staff.[35] This revelation indicates that a battalion from one of the signature formations of the Viet Cong—the 1st Viet Cong Regiment—answered to North Vietnam from its earliest days.

Not surprisingly Group 34 had been formed and trained at Xuan Mai. While there the group would have been exposed to a curriculum of propaganda, tactical military training, and socialist indoctrination. "Study," wrote a later alumnus of the training facility, "consists of these subjects: Policies of the Lao Dong Party; Nature of People's War; Nature of People's Army; Military tactics; Ten Principles of Leadership, Use of the Ambush and the Surprise attack; How to React Quickly to Opportunities; Use of Explosive; Social Classes in Socialist and Capitalist Societies; Proselyting Efforts; Guerrilla Warfare."[36] With respect to "military tactics," trainees at the facility studied raids, offensive actions against fortified military posts, and mobile attacks. For entertainment and heightened ideological awareness, some recruits at Xuan Mai watched *Heroic Soldiers*, a movie recapping the life of a revolutionary soldier.

When the time came for the voyage South, infiltrators, whether alums of Xuan Mai or not, left with an equipment allotment befitting a Spartan. One infiltrator listed only a hammock, a pack, a pair of sandals, one set of uniforms, a sweater and cap, a mosquito net, one canteen, two sets of underwear, one can of fish paste, three cans of salt, and one "shelter half."[37] Reports from other infiltrators revealed that bandages, vitamin pills, and rice were also apportioned.

Although NVA regulars and southern-born infiltrators trained at Xuan Mai alleviated some of the demand for troops, additional manpower was needed to flesh out the developing Viet Cong force and furnish replacements. Exhaustive manpower drives were instituted by Viet Cong political cadre (the Viet Cong infrastructure, or VCI) in succeeding years to attract the local South Vietnamese recruits required to sustain the armed movement. Often the "pitch" delivered appealed to the recruit's innate sense of fraternity with the peasant class. Remarkably this "class-centric" charm offensive even managed to seduce the offspring of Viet Cong murder victims. "In the beginning, I was very hurt and angry with them for killing my father," conceded one Viet Cong volunteer. "I quarreled with them. Then they told me that because my father had done wrong in serving as hamlet chief and thereby 'working against his own class interests, against the poor classes', he had to be punished. . . . They talked to a point where I felt that they were right. I no longer felt hurt."[38]

Alternatively the Viet Cong also practiced involuntary methods for culling suitable recruits from the South Vietnamese population. Compelled by the exigencies of an expanding war, the Viet Cong after 1963 imposed a levy on draft eligible male villagers, with precious few exemptions afforded for disability or other extenuating circumstances. Discernibly draconian, this program of compulsory enlistment nonetheless bore considerable fruit. "In Bin Tre province the VC are militarily very strong this year," remembered one former VC platoon leader, "because everywhere they force the population to yield a proportionate number of men for their troops and they no longer use propaganda to get men to enlist."[39] A 1967 survey in which an astounding 66 percent of former Viet Cong respondents claimed to have been drafted seems to affirm, at least anecdotally, the platoon leader's observation.[40] Albeit somewhat lower than the 1967 survey results, the percentage of Viet Cong soldiers pressed into service in the opinion of Marine Lieutenant Colonel and pacification advocate William R. Corson, somewhere in the neighborhood of 40–42 percent, was nevertheless substantial.[41]

The exact figure of South Vietnamese impressed into military service for the Viet Cong will undoubtedly remain a mystery. Moreover, the advent of fully intact NVA regiments in South Vietnam only exacerbated an already muddled and often contradictory portrait of the average Viet Cong soldier and how or why he came to fight. Still wedded in late 1964 to the implausible notion of "deniability," Hanoi sent complete NVA regiments disguised in the black pajama garb customarily associated with the VC into South Vietnam. The invading NVA units—principally regiments from the 325th NVA Division, the 320th Infantry Regiment, and the 545th Viet Bac Battalion—received Viet Cong unit designations and weapons from China and Eastern Europe without identifying markings.[42] Though the North would steadfastly deny the presence of its army in South Vietnam for years, the sheer scope of NVA intervention eventually made the use of such precautions a moot point.

2

On the Field of Battle

Inconsistent with the perception of sandal-wearing warriors innately skilled in the ways of war, the Viet Cong in actuality adhered to carefully considered philosophies for waging war in either an offensive or defensive capacity. Easy-to-remember and -recite slogans often reinforced these philosophies, aiding officer and soldier alike, and well-rehearsed tactics and techniques applied them to the offensive and defensive battlefield. Every so often, however, slogan and tactic merged into a phenomenon universal to all battlefields, as was the case with *Grab the enemy's belts to fight them*.

OFFENSIVE WARFARE

> We resolutely chose the other tactic: to strike surely and advance surely. In taking this correct decision, we strictly followed this fundamental principle of the conduct of a revolutionary war; strike to win, strike only when success is certain; if it is not, then don't strike.
>
> —General Giap, in McCoy, *Secrets of the Viet Cong*

Authored by none other than Giap himself, the passage above enunciates VC/NVA offensive philosophy with eloquent simplicity.[1] General Thanh, after studying the battles fought in the Ia Drang Valley in November 1965 and the battles fought north of Saigon in the fall of 1965, as well as major American offensives such as Operations Attleboro (1966) and Cedar Falls (1967), helped refine Giap's raw philosophical blueprint. Thanh dictated a handful of lengthy essays based on his studies, and from these essays he distilled five "important lessons" on how the VC and NVA should fight:

> Always take control, pick the best location and the most propitious time for battle; force the enemy to fight *our* battle *our* way; always attack and move, concentrate and disperse rhythmically, cover, camouflage, hide, and disguise well, using subterfuge to fool the enemy; fight in close range and fast, fight ferociously, terminate the fight quickly (a battle should last only 15 to 20 minutes, a campaign should last only from three to five days); and the commander should understand the topography of the battlefield well, he should go to the exact location to study the terrain and understand his enemy's modus operandi, he should anticipate the conduct of the battle using different plans, concentrate his firepower, and open fire from a high elevation to overwhelm the enemy.[2]

Overlapping Thanh's lessons in certain respects, the simplistic yet incredibly functional "One slow, four quicks" credo guided the Viet Cong with regard to the planning and carrying out of military operations. Slow planning or preparation, quick advance, quick attack, quick battlefield clearance or "mop up," and quick withdrawal comprised the credo. Irrespective of its physical expression, all Viet Cong offensive operations adhered to these principles.

Attack planning for these operations—the slow phase—was a fascinating study in bureaucratic process and military choreography. Permission to conduct an attack, at least prior to the disastrous Tet Offensive, rested with the appropriate military and party committees. Attacking units first submitted proposals to a provincial military affairs committee, whose chief in turn referred the plan and his approval (or not, whereupon the matter advanced no further) to the secretary of the provincial party committee.

If the party committee backed the proposal, the military affairs committee arranged for additional staff work. "Once the proposal is approved by the Province Committee," the Military Assistance Command, Vietnam (MACV) intelligence section investigation stated, "the Military Affairs Committee divides the preliminary tasks among its three staffs. The Military Staff sends a reconnaissance unit to study the objective from a military point of view, and to prepare a sand table mock-up. The Political staff sends a cadre to contact the civilians in the area, to learn of their reaction to the proposed attack. It also studies the morale of the troops to see if they are mentally and emotionally prepared. If they are not, the Political staff must take the necessary measures to prepare them. The Rear Services Staff determines whether civilians can furnish food and labor, including that needed for removal of the dead and booty."[3]

Reconnaissance operations then informed the final round of committee referrals and approvals. Continuous surveillance of the projected target, a key component of the recon mission, documented enemy troop strength and corresponding weaponry, possible routes of approach and withdrawal, and the overall lay of the land. Area guerrillas were queried for relevant intelligence on the target, and when conspiring to attack an enemy base, the Viet Cong at times mobilized elite reconnaissance units to infiltrate the target and collect more information. These daring incursions helped determine the locations of crew-served weapons, munitions depots, and communications stations inside the enemy base. The Viet Cong also estimated the response times of American fire support and reinforcements. Afterward the military affairs committee, which included among the attendees the commanders of all the attacking units, met and determined whether to recommend the attack plan to the province committee for final approval.[4]

Once granted permission to strike, the Viet Cong indulged in elaborate battlefield preparations and rehearsals. The assaulting VC forces rehearsed the forthcoming attack on sand table mockups and on land similar to the objective area. Dry runs lasted anywhere from three days to about a month. Additionally stores of ammunition, foodstuffs, and other sundry military supplies were cached near the battle zone (to be used by the attack force) in observance of a Communist military phenomenon known as "preparing the battlefield." American commanders likened the practice to having a logistical "nose," as opposed to an American or Western logistical "tail."

Since slow planning called for repeated reconnaissance of the objective area, rigorous intelligence gathering, intricate combat rehearsal, and logistical prioritization, the VC required sufficient time to implement and conclude the planning process. In tandem with that most precious of commodities—time—the Viet Cong also needed patience and the self-restraint to wait for numerical superiority. "We usually carried out an attack operation only when we had obtained reliable information as to the number of enemy troops, their weapons, and their positions," a Viet Cong soldier said. "And we always ensured that we were absolutely superior in numbers before starting the attack. If not, we preferred to avoid contact with the enemy."[5] The soldier's words coincide with the Viet Cong mantra of pitting "ten against one."[6]

Upon completion of the planning process, and after conditions proved conducive for action, the Viet Cong would strike. Heading into battle, every member of an attacking unit understood his individual mission. He knew, for the most part, when to go, where to go, and for how long. Conditioned to stick to the script, he would hopefully go into battle and, as if by rote, perform reliably under the stressors of actual combat. His exact mission in the forthcoming attack thoroughly articulated, the VC soldier learned of the operation's importance and of the importance of his own upcoming tactical missions to the struggle overall and to the party's political and ideological goals. The operation and the soldier's mission were also dutifully connected to the party's political and ideological goals. "It has been said that the Viet Cong soldier probably is told the reason for everything that he does more frequently and in greater detail than any other soldier in the world," stated one American study of the Viet Cong. "Almost certainly he is required to explain the reasons for his actions more than any other soldier."[7] If nothing else, such political and ideological enlightenment instilled in the average Viet Cong soldier some measure of why and for what he had been asked to fight.

Trade-offs were of course inevitable. In exchange for better command and control, which the fairly scripted Viet Cong system promoted, the VC sacrificed a degree of operational flexibility. "The Viet Cong might have had a 'Plan B' to fall back on," said a former Marine Corps company commander, "but as far as a 'Plan C' or 'Plan D'? Forget about it."[8] A glaring shortage of radios only compounded the problem. Indeed, although discussing the net effect of a lack of radios in Soviet tanks for much of the war against Nazi Germany, author George Nipe Jr. might just as easily have been describing some of the

VC's communication and attack inadequacies when he wrote that "this deficiency resulted in delayed or nonexistent response to the changing events of battle, a shortcoming that was exacerbated by tactics often characterized by rigid adherence to orders regardless of losses and conditions."[9] When deprived of these technological assets, the Viet Cong had to improvise with outdated methods of communication such as human couriers and the transmitting of messages/instructions through gunshots.

Nonetheless, the Viet Cong managed to integrate four basic attack methods into a coherent offensive repertoire: the infantry raid, ambush, sapper raid, and stand-off attack. Each will be examined in turn.

The Infantry Raid

Initiated most frequently under cover of darkness, an infantry raid was often categorized as either a "surprise raid" or "power raid." A U.S. military handbook defined the larger and typically more violent of the two: "The 'power raid' is one in which the VC employ overwhelming strength and fire power in order to annihilate a defending unit. The time the raid begins is often a clue to its nature. Raids begun after 0200 hours are rarely power raids intended to overrun an outpost."[10]

For a power raid against a static allied position, a Viet Cong assault force consisting of sappers, a heavy-weapons section, and a main assault unit would leave their bases and safe havens (usually after sundown) and advance *quickly* to staging areas close to the intended target. Normally an attack would commence without preparatory fire and under the cover of darkness, more often than not between the hours of midnight and 2:00 AM. Sapper infiltration to clear avenues of advance through minefields and other defensive obstacles preceded, and covering fire from the heavy-weapons section deployed outside the enemy base, supported the *quick* infantry attack by the main assault unit. Diversionary attacks could also be launched in connection with the primary assault. Thereafter, the attacking force transitioned to the recovery of redeemable battlefield items (weapons, and so on) in accordance with a *quick* "mop up" or battlefield clearance. If possible, the dead and wounded were also recovered. The Viet Cong then withdraw *quickly*, ably abetted by rear-guard activity, along predetermined "exfiltration" routes.[11]

The Ambush

South Vietnamese Colonel Hoang Ngoc Lung proclaimed that the Communist ambush was "a tactical maneuver carried out in accordance with the slogan 'fight a small action to achieve great victory.'"[12] In the same vein, a Viet Cong revolutionary listed "a weak unit attacks a strong one" as one of the guiding principles of the ambush.[13] Both might very well have argued that the ambush rivaled the infantry raid as the Viet Cong's preferred method of offensive maneuver.

Analogous to infantry raid planning, ambush planning also followed the "One slow, four quicks" formula, starting with tactical reconnaissance. Sneaking undetected through the jungle, Viet Cong reconnaissance teams began recording American movement routines and unit strengths. Other teams scouted the terrain of the proposed ambush site for suitability. To warrant selection the land had to provide the ambushing unit with cover at the site and concealment when moving into and out of the ambush area, positions for the deployment of heavy weapons, and areas for the establishment of observation posts to track enemy movement. The land also had to facilitate to some degree the VC's ability to move, encircle, and split up the enemy force. In addition proposed sites would ideally bear a resemblance to other areas along the enemy's route and would not be the first potential ambush site along the way. Prospective sites were also evaluated for their capacity to hamper enemy movement, countermeasures, and the employment of his supporting fires.[14]

Having settled on an acceptable site, Viet Cong planners concentrated next on the shape of the ambush and the actions to be taken before opening fire, upon opening fire, and during withdrawal from the ambush site. As one might expect, terrain features and the expected size and composition of the enemy force influenced shape design. The rudimentary flank or linear ambush with its ambushing position placed parallel to the target for flanking fire was the most convenient and probably the most commonly used. Yet the L-shaped ambush, with the "base" providing enfilading fire and the "leg" flanking fire against an enemy force, may have been the preferred choice. Several other shapes (Z and V ambushes) and schemes ("bloody nose" and "maneuver" ambushes) were employed as well. Regardless of the shape or arrangement, the

Viet Cong practiced with professional thoroughness every sequence of the proposed ambush on sand table models and on terrain similar to the ambush site.

Force structure for an ambush depended on the scope and complexity of the operation, as many were nothing more than hastily put together and/or small unit affairs stemming from chance meetings with American forces. The most intricate force packages featured five interdependent components: observation posts, command posts (CPs), lead blocking element, main assault element, and rear blocking element. The lead blocking element had the responsibility of disorganizing and stopping the enemy force with sudden, unannounced fire. A machine gun was often utilized to accomplish this. If the lead block succeeded in halting the enemy, the main assault element would then move to encircle, break up, and destroy the enemy force with all available firepower. At times the Viet Cong would commit some of their ambushing force to a close-in assault against the besieged enemy unit. The main assault element usually performed this task. If the entire enemy force had wandered into the ambush zone, the rear blocking element would join the main assault effort with an attack against the rear of the enemy force. If the rear of the enemy force remained outside of the ambush zone, the rear blocking element worked to cut it off and engage any enemy reinforcements.

The final two components of the five-element ambush played a critical role as well. An extended set of eyes and ears, observation posts (OPs) monitored the movement of the targeted enemy unit and the movement of enemy reinforcements. The OPs then relayed this tactical intelligence to the ambush command post via wire communication or runner. The CP, meanwhile, exercised control over the other four ambush elements, generally from a location in which the ambush zone could be observed.[15]

Irrespective of the force structure for or the shape of the ambush, the ambushers themselves would presumably possess certain attributes capable of contributing to its success. According to one Viet Cong veteran, the "ideal ambusher" was "courageous, decisive and firm . . . able to think and act quickly, kill quickly and withdraw quickly." Necessarily close-mouthed, he was likewise adept at keeping a secret.[16]

Innumerable examples of Viet Cong ambushes exist from every year of the war, but for an excellent example from 1965, one need only look at the

August 18 ambush of a Marine supply convoy during Operation Starlite. This ambush exhibited a near textbook illustration of the lead block, main assault, and rear block force structure. The results of the ambush, moreover, were reasonably good. Comparatively speaking the 80th Viet Cong Battalion's ambush of a Marine battalion four months later achieved measurably less success. In fact, the Marines of 2nd Battalion/7th Regiment counterattacked the Viet Cong ambush so swiftly and decisively that they disrupted the VC enterprise altogether.

As a participating element of Operation Harvest Moon/Lien Ket, a joint Marine-ARVN initiative aimed at the 1st Viet Cong Regiment, the 2/7 Marines had moved from the northern banks of the Khang River eastward, toward Tam Ky, in search of Viet Cong forces. Intelligence estimates had pointed to a Viet Cong battalion in the Ky Phu area, and on December 18, 1965, the Marines trudged through rice paddies framed by hedgerows and approached the village of Ky Phu. Company G, the 2nd Battalion's forwardmost unit, had advanced through Ky Phu when the 80th Viet Cong Battalion suddenly opened fire. Attacking first from the southeast, the Viet Cong hit Company G with sniper, automatic weapons, and mortar fire. Ambushing VC elements also mortared the Headquarters and Service (H&S) Company, then in the open rice paddies west of Ky Phu. Two VC infantry companies were then dispatched to penetrate the gap separating the H&S Company and Company F. This thrust was intended to encircle and annihilate H&S Company.

Lieutenant Colonel Leon Utter, commanding officer of the 2/7, responded swiftly. Utter instructed Company F, which had barely exited the eastern end of Ky Phu when the mortaring of the H&S Company started, to attack the "main VC positions on the H&S right flank."[17] The counterattack routed the Viet Cong. Subjected to Marine artillery fire, marauding Huey gunships, and Company F's infantry counterstroke from the rear, the Viet Cong assault disintegrated and many of the VC dispersed. "Once we got them going, the VC just broke and ran," said a Marine officer who joined Company F in the counterattack. "It was just like a turkey shoot."[18]

A ways down, toward the end of the Marine column, the VC infantry attacks demonstrated greater determination. One company from the 80th Viet Cong Battalion, for example, assaulted Company H (2nd Battalion/9th

Marines, attached to 2nd/7th Marines) from each flank and from the rear with great fortitude. But after a grueling four-hour fight, the VC realized that they could not defeat the Marine unit nor prevent it from reaching Ky Phu and reuniting with the 2/7 Marines. With night fast approaching, the VC began to disengage. The fighting eventually slackened, but not before 104 VC had been killed in the ambush attempt. Fewer than a dozen Marines were killed, though more than seventy were wounded.[19]

After the battle, the Americans noted the tactics the VC had used at Ky Phu. In a "lessons learned" report produced by MACV, the Americans observed: "(1) VC units attacked the center of the column from positions previously traversed by the flank security elements of the advance guard, moving into these positions during the time and space interval between the flankers of the advance and rear guards (estimated as 3–045 minutes)."[20] The report also cited the Viet Cong's deliberate targeting of American commanders and radio operators with their initial fire. This VC tactic would continue with some success until the Americans became more acclimated to combat conditions in South Vietnam.

The Sapper Raid

Another preferred offensive maneuver, the sapper raid embodied the minimum cost, maximum benefit mentality of the Viet Cong. For a relatively minor monetary investment, and a small contingent of specialists, a sapper raid could infiltrate a U.S. military installation and kill a number of American servicemen and damage or destroy expensive American war machines.[21] Neither the ambush nor the infantry raid/assault possessed as much "bang for the buck" appeal. To illustrate the point, by the close of 1969, and despite heightened allied awareness of the sapper "phenomenon," the monetary damage incurred in an average sapper raid against an allied target had mushroomed to more than $1 million.[22]

Sapper raids plagued both Marine and Army facilities. MAG-12 (Marine Aircraft Group) commander Colonel Leslie E. Brown recounted the scene at the Chu Lai SATS field, site of a VC sapper raid, on the night of October 27–28, 1965: "A couple of the airplanes were on fire, and the sappers had gotten through intact. . . . They were barefooted and had on a loin cloth and it was kind of a John Wayne dramatic effect. They had Thompson submachineguns and they were spraying the airplanes with the Tommy guns and . . . throwing satchel charges into tail pipes."[23]

The Chu Lai sapper raid destroyed two A-4 Douglas Skyhawks and damaged six others. The very same evening, October 27–28, another Viet Cong sapper operation hit the Marines' Marble Mountain helicopter facility located on the Tiensha Peninsula. Sappers armed with fragmentation, concussion, and thermite grenades, along with RPGs and several Bangalore torpedoes, infiltrated the Marine aviation complex and destroyed nineteen helicopters. Thirty-five others suffered notable damage. Added up, the raid wrecked or damaged approximately one-third of the helicopters at Marble Mountain. The helicopter losses, while severe, could be recouped; the deaths of three American servicemen (ninety-one wounded) could not. Colonel Thomas J. O'Connor, the MAG-16 commanding officer, alleged that the devastation inflicted on the Marble Mountain fleet "put a crimp in division plans for several months afterward."[24]

Spectacular raids such as the one at Marble Mountain notwithstanding, sappers excelled in the more mundane role of opening avenues of advance for the main assault element of an infantry raid. Brandishing wire cutters, a metal rod to poke about for mines, small pins for the disarmament of mine fuses, and explosive charges, sappers inched forward through barbed wire, minefields, and other defensive obstacles erected to protect enemy targets from assault.[25] Every foot the sappers cleared brought them one step closer to breaching the protective barrier surrounding the target or, if they were discovered or guilty of the slightest miscalculation, death. "We have the responsibility of being the forward group in any attack, of opening the way for the other elements, and of removing obstacles, erected by the enemy to stop our advance, with explosives," said a sapper platoon leader from the 514th Viet Cong Regiment, operating in the Mekong Delta.[26] Though mindful of the peril involved, most sappers still accepted the mission of creating corridors through defensive obstacles, and attacking targets once inside the objective, with a great deal of dedication and élan.

General Thanh was an avid supporter of the VC/NVA sapper corps. In March 1966 Thanh implored his troops to "attack the Achilles heel"—airfields, communications posts, depots, and so on—of the American presence in Vietnam. Ideally suited for such an undertaking, the sapper, General Thanh believed, would be a "determining" factor in the war.[27] With this enhanced import came greater appreciation for the independent sapper raid and an expansion of the sapper force, from VC/NVA sapper companies early on to eventual sapper battalions.

Force expansion, in fact, may very well have spurred the scheduled conversions of large conventional VC formations, like the V-25 Local Force Battalion in Quang Nam Province, into operationally viable sapper units.[28] Diversification of the force followed as well, and by 1969 the Viet Cong had founded a Swimmer Sapper School in Kien Hoa, South Vietnam. In time the effects of organizational commitment, training, and individual initiative turned the sapper into a "bridge between warfare and terror, with a foot in each camp."[29]

Again, much like the composition and organization of a Viet Cong ambush force, the dimensions and force structure of a sapper party differed depending on the specifications of the mission. In theory a VC/NVA sapper raid fielded an assault element to breach the enemy perimeter and assail selected targets within the enemy position, a fire-support element usually consisting of 60-mm or 82-mm mortars, a security element to attend to enemy reinforcements, and a reserve element. Sapper raiding forces in practice rarely featured a reserve element.[30] Success, nevertheless, was not dependent on the four-element paradigm. The Chu Lai SATS raid in October, for instance, apparently employed very little in the way of a reserve or fire-support element.

Certainly the exclusion or inclusion of ordinary infantry had an influence on the operational conduct of a sapper raid and, presumptively, its effects. "Assaults without the infantry required fullest use of the fire support or reserve elements, either separately or in combination," wrote Major General David Ewing Ott, author of a 1975 volume on American field artillery. Ott continued: "Sapper attacks with the infantry were either with the sappers in support of the infantry or the infantry in support of the sappers. Sapper units considered supporting the infantry a misuse of their tactical abilities. Attached to a large unit, they tended to lose the advantages of secrecy and surprise. Nevertheless, sappers continued to be employed as reinforcements to the infantry.

The second mode of sapper operation—using the infantry as a reserve, security, or secondary assault element—seemed more effective. The greatest threat to allied positions was an attack spearheaded by sappers with explosive charges, followed by the infantry some 100 to 200 meters behind."[31]

No exposé on the Viet Cong sapper and his raids would be complete without referencing the training involved. Although the length and location of sapper training lacked true standardization, agreement on the need for strenuous demolitions instruction was widespread. Sapper recruits learned, among other skills, how to arm and disarm conventional explosives, defeat and convert enemy mines, and the recommended placement and quantity of explosives for destroying various enemy targets and obstacles. Instruction on stealth, reconnaissance, and infiltration techniques was provided as well.[32] Sapper training, as with the training for any other specialized operational discipline, was but one predicator of future success along with individual student aptitude and good fortune on the battlefield.

How did sapper raids contribute to the big-unit war effort? The most obvious contribution was of course the destruction of American war materials and personnel, both of which sustained either directly or indirectly the American big-unit war. American firebases supported the big-unit war directly by delivering firepower to American maneuver units in the field. Successful sapper raids against the former would weaken the firepower umbrella available to the latter.[33]

The Stand-off Attack

In addition to sapper raids, the Viet Cong resorted to indirect attacks by fire or "stand-off attacks."[34] Stand-off attacks, as the name implies, consisted mostly of firing rockets and mortar rounds into enemy installations from a distance. While not an especially imaginative or novel idea, the stand-off attack nonetheless solved the problem of having to "mass" for an attack against a high valued target. The stand-off attack also increased the likelihood of evading return fire. Small groups of Viet Cong could launch Soviet-made 122-mm rockets, which possessed far greater range and lethality than 82-mm mortar rounds, at an intended target and disperse with less chance of being identified and killed by enemy defensive fire than if they had attempted an infantry raid.

A U.S. Marine Corps operations report later in the war reaffirmed that basic point: "On 9 September, Danang received its second attack as the enemy fired three rockets, killing one US airman and wounding eleven others. One F-4C, one A-1E and barracks were damaged. An air observer detected the launch, and soon thereafter Marine ground forces located eight abandoned rockets, four miles southwest of the airfield. These abandoned weapons gave testimony of the enemy's hasty departure."[35] The report, furthermore, summarized the enduring threat of the stand-off attack: "Nevertheless, it remains clear that indirect fire attacks against the fixed major air fields in I CTZ will continue to remain an enemy capability, despite the intensive preventive efforts. In no other type of engagement can the enemy hope to achieve such dramatic results, with the commitment of so small a force."[36]

Over the course of the war, the U.S. military stepped up patrolling around installations, increased aerial overflights, and fired off thousands of rounds of harassment and interdiction (H&I) fire. But in the end, as the September 1967 Marine operations report admitted, the stand-off attack remained a viable Viet Cong and NVA capability.

Despite the success of sapper raids and stand-off attacks, from an offensive standpoint the Viet Cong typically generated big-unit battle against American forces via the infantry raid or ambush. Meeting engagements, which were not intrinsically offensive or defensive in nature, and encounters in which the VC engaged American units while ensconced in fortified defensive positions account for the remainder. Still, sapper raids and stand-off attacks were resource-draining distractions for the American military. Indeed, they were the quintessential "guerrilla warfare" complement to the Viet Cong's big-unit war.

DEFENSIVE WAR

The more sweat on digging defensive positions, the less blood in fighting.
—Lanning and Cragg, *Inside the VC and the NVA*

Notwithstanding the ambush, and even an ambush includes some aspects of dug-in defensive warfare, the most auspicious occasion for engaging American forces on the battlefield occurred when Viet Cong forces had the luxury of assuming a position of defensive strength. More often than not this entailed accepting combat from the relative safety of bunkers, fighting holes, and other defensive fortifications.

Excluding ambush zones and "prepared battlefields" situated near VC/NVA campsites, the VC's elaborately constructed defensive works were most frequently found guarding the campsites themselves. Not surprisingly all camps shared critical characteristics. Principal among them were the availability of dense overhead vegetation to obscure aerial observation and the lack of any outstanding feature like a river or vast open expanse that might complicate a swift and safe getaway. Selecting terrain with scant natural protections for would-be attackers was also regarded as crucially important.

Well versed in the excruciatingly monotonous art of "digging in," Viet Cong soldiers were capable of quickly converting a chosen campsite into a veritable stronghold bristling with belts of defensive positions. Anywhere from fifty to two hundred meters typically separated the belts defending the less permanent campsites, and they were often patterned in the shape of an L, V, or U to promote crossfire potential. Connecting trenches linked individual fighting positions within the belts.[37]

Relatively permanent base camps were usually established in jungle sanctuaries outside of allied artillery range and the normal operating reach of allied sweeps, sometimes even beyond the territorial borders of South Vietnam. Dense jungles, however, were rejected as a potential area to locate base camps by some Viet Cong formations because of the American penchant for subjecting those areas to B-52 bombing runs.[38] Wherever sited, the base camp provided a training, supply, and rear services area for the VC/NVA war effort. Base camps were also more intricately defended than the more temporary "safe harbor" camps:

> Defended base camps present a formidable obstacle to the attacker. They are normally somewhat circular in form with an outer rim of bunkers, automatic weapons firing positions, alarm systems and foxholes. Within the circle there is a rather complex system of command bunkers, kitchens, and living quarters constructed above the ground from a wide variety of materials. . . . Even though natural terrain features may cause

a camp to resemble a cul-de-sac there will be at least one prepared exit or escape route opposite the anticipated direction(s) of attack. Tunnels connect the bunkers and firing positions, enabling the defenders to move from one point to another. This technique enhances the effect of their firepower and gives them a significant advantage over the attacker. An unfordable river may parallel one flank of a typical camp while open paddy land borders the other.[39]

Base camps with a triangular layout were constructed as well. If occupied by a Viet Cong regiment, one battalion would deploy on each side of the triangle. Battalions were often located approximately three kilometers apart, while companies were spaced about a kilometer from one another. Elsewhere in the camp, support companies typically enclosed the regimental command post.[40]

Irrespective of the shape, Viet Cong base camps possessed tremendous defensive potential. To counteract that potential, American forces developed a "surround and pound" strategy—cordon off or surround the base with American infantry, and then pound it with air and artillery. For American commanders the cost of the alternative, a classic "close with and destroy the enemy" infantry assault, was much too prohibitive. "As an infantry commander," recalled an American officer with the 25th Infantry Division, "I have assaulted fortified base camps both ways: the traditional closing with the enemy and the let-the-artillery-and-air-do-it, and believe me, the latter is better."[41] Ideally base camps were to remain inviolate, but if they were attacked by American ground forces, the Viet Cong at the very least had the advantage of fighting the subsequent battle from a position of defensive strength.

The VC/NVA also moved continuously through a network of less permanent campsites with each one acting as a fortified defensive stronghold from which to engage American forces when in between moves. VC/NVA battalions could reportedly control as many as twenty to twenty-five temporary camps apiece, and temporary camps were found throughout South Vietnam. However, since habitual movement was the norm, the VC/NVA never inhabited any one location for more than four days at any one time.[42]

South Vietnamese villages were prime locations for temporary camps. Troops from the laagering Viet Cong unit, often in collaboration with coerced civilian labor, would simply settle down and shovel out the requisite camp defensive belts and positions within the village. To conserve time and sweat, the Viet Cong commandeered bunkers and other positions that were already a part of civilian houses in the war zone.[43] Occasionally peasant labor prepared all of the village fortifications. Efficiently dug and systematically arranged, such defensive fortifications and positions ensured that the Viet Cong would not be easily destroyed or expelled from their village camp:

> One of the enemy's favorite battlegrounds was the fortified village. This usually consisted of several hamlets prepared with extensive fighting positions, trenchworks, connected tunnels, and spider holes. The fighting bunkers often had five to seven feet of overhead cover and could take a direct hit from a 155-mm howitzer round. The bunkers were placed to cover avenues of approach and were interspersed throughout the village, with tunnels connecting the bunkers and trenches, thereby allowing the enemy to disappear and reappear firing from another location. Trees, shrubs, and even the earth itself were reshaped to conceal these positions.[44]

In part because they were so nomadically predisposed, the Viet Cong established and generally adhered to a set of movement procedures when moving between camps. Preceding any scheduled departure, reconnaissance elements from the relocating VC unit rendezvoused with district or village cadre to obtain guides and provisions and to reconnoiter the proposed route. Commanders of the parent unit were then briefed by the returning recon detachments on the nature of the terrain, enemy activity, and other pertinent factors. If circumstances dictated daytime movement, the Viet Cong concealed themselves in camouflage consisting of area vegetation and sought routes beneath the jungle canopy. Approaching aircraft, naturally, compelled the VC to hide motionless until the danger passed. For the most part, though, the Viet Cong preferred nighttime movements. Moving at night served to accentuate the Viet Cong's seemingly innate ability to move swiftly in the dark.

Measures aimed at inhibiting American intelligence collection were assiduously enforced as well. Viet Cong units camouflaged battle positions for future use and cleaned the temporary bivouac sites of incriminating evidence.

Upon arrival at the next camp, the Viet Cong prevented villagers, if that site fell within the confines of a village, from departing lest an "imperialist puppet" slip out and inform American or South Vietnamese forces of their presence.[45]

An informative American intelligence study of the 273rd Viet Cong Regiment examined how a specific Viet Cong unit moved. The third in a series of three enemy regimental histories, the study charted the 273rd's standard movement protocol:

> The regiment will normally build a new base camp when it moves. Sometimes, however, it will use an old base camp, even moving into a partially destroyed one and rebuilding it. The regiment normally does not move back to a base camp which has been discovered. In the rainy season, the unit usually stays in a base camp for about one month. In the dry season, it moves about every 10 to 15 days. Prior to leaving an area which has served as a base area, personnel destroy huts or bunkers and fill in trenches and foxholes.
>
> The 273 VC Regiment normally marches in the following order: 2 Battalion, 1 Battalion, Regimental Headquarters, and 3 Battalion. Its new artillery battalion may attach its companies to the maneuver battalions. While moving, units always march in a single file. There is no flank security but the troops are trained to encircle any ambush position when they are fired upon. A reconnaissance element leads each battalion by 250 meters and is followed by an infantry company. The fire support company and the two other infantry companies follow in order.
>
> Companies are separated by 150 meters in daylight and 50 meters at night. The battalion command element is positioned throughout the battalion, and the commanding officer is always with the last company. Battalions march about two hours apart. Although the regiment has marched during the day in jungle areas, all almost movement is at night. Before resting during the day, the unit digs uncovered foxholes. The unit has moved up to 20 kilometers in a day, and 10 to 15 kilometers is normal.[46]

When not moving or fighting, the VC/NVA sometimes prepared battlefields on land within striking distance of their camps in the hopes of fighting future engagements on familiar and well-fortified terrain. Maximizing any and all topographical advantages provided by the locations of these preselected battlegrounds, the VC/NVA dug or constructed bunkers, trenches, fighting holes, and sites for heavy-weapons emplacements. Notoriously well constructed, some Communist bunkers had withstood 8-inch artillery fire until hit with a direct strike.[47] Mines and booby traps were also planted, and routes of withdrawal were established. Later, when an enemy unit ventured inside an area containing two to three prepared battlefields, the VC/NVA had the option of initiating a battle on favorable terrain.

Assuming the conditions were conducive for an assault, the VC/NVA would dispatch a forward detachment to make contact and maneuver the enemy force into one of the prepared battlefields. While the forward detachment delayed and maneuvered the enemy, the main body of the assault force deployed to the designated battlefield. This force would then seek to destroy or savage the ensnared enemy unit.[48]

GRAB THE ENEMY'S BELTS

The rationale behind the Viet Cong's preference for fighting from prepared positions was both obvious and sensible. Pitted against an American foe with unchallenged air and supporting fire supremacy, the Viet Cong wished to shape or manipulate the tactical environment so that they could mete out maximum punishment while minimizing friendly casualties. In essence the Viet Cong strived to even the odds as often as possible against American firepower until the time came to disengage and withdraw. With more pragmatic imperatives like survival, killing some Americans, and registering a few victories guiding the military agenda of the average Viet Cong soldier, accepting or initiating battle from fortified camps and other defensive positions leveled the playing field and theoretically placed these imperatives within reach.

Prior to the inevitable withdrawal phase, however, the Viet Cong were known to hug American infantry as a means of reducing the effectiveness of American supporting arms. To the Viet Cong, the practice of hugging American troops evolved into a battlefield credo immortalized by the slogan "Grab the enemy's belts to fight them." The slogan has been associated with General Nguyen Chi Thanh, but Thanh was not the man who coined it according to General Dang Vu Hiep. Hiep, who was the chief of political affairs for the Central Highlands Front at the time, recorded an exchange in September 1965 that he had had with General Chu Huy Man, commander and political commissar of the Central Highlands Front, and in that exchange the origins of the phrase are revealed:

> Then, as if having just thought of something, Chu Huy Man asked me, "Hiep, do you remember the battle of Vinh Huy in early 1965, near Tam Ky City?"
> "I remember it," I replied.
> "During that battle, a squad leader from our Military Region's 1st Regiment shouted something that I thought was very good while pursuing the enemy. He shouted, 'Grab the enemy's belts to fight them!' When I heard that, I reported this statement to Nguyen Chi Thanh by telephone. When he heard it, Thanh exclaimed, 'That's great, Man! This is something that applies not just to one regiment or one military region; it can be applied to our entire army, to all of South Vietnam!' I learned later that Comrade Nguyen Chi Thanh ordered all battlefield's throughout our nation to use the phrase, "Grab the enemy's belts to fight them" as our slogan when fighting against U.S. forces."[49]

Hiep's account thus ascribes the slogan to a soldier from the 1st Viet Cong Regiment during the Battle of Vinh Huy, an engagement fought south of Da Nang between the 1st Viet Cong Regiment and South Vietnamese forces on February 17, 1965. Thanh simply popularized it by dint of executive order.[50]

When dug in or otherwise defensively postured, the Viet Cong would frequently attempt to grab American infantry "by the belt" after contact had been made. Frequently, upon making contact with enemy forces, American ground troops would disengage or form a defensive perimeter in order to pound enemy units and positions with artillery fire and air strikes. Following these supporting arms strikes, American infantry would attempt to mop up holdouts and other areas of resistance with methods that were virtually indistinguishable from many previous American conflicts. The Viet Cong, though, understood all too well the dangers of giving American infantry the tactical space required for the effective delivery of supporting fires. "But in order to fight the Americans, you had to get close to them," insisted one battled-hardened southern regroupee. "You couldn't fight them from a distance."[51] To avoid fighting from a distance, the Viet Cong would pursue American infantry as the latter fell back to allow input from air and artillery assets. By remaining in close proximity, the Viet Cong and NVA hoped they could prevent American infantry from disengaging enough to permit the safe and effective intervention of American supporting arms. At the very least, the VC and NVA hoped to delay that intervention as long as possible.

Fundamentally the notion of grabbing the enemy by the belt was little more than a means of separating the American infantryman from his firepower, as the Viet Minh had attempted to do years earlier to the French. General Vuong Thua Vu of the NVA General Staff expounded on the importance of the concept in his "Three cuts, one destroy" approach to fighting. In Vu's mind the VC/NVA had to fight the Americans at close quarters, and to do that they needed to cut American infantry off from artillery, tanks, and airpower. Since the two opposing infantry forces were reasonably well matched in terms of basic soldierly competence and courage, Communist units would invariably find the odds of defeating American infantry that had been cut off from their fire support more favorable than the odds of defeating those that were able to harness the frighteningly destructive power of American support arms.

Decidedly utilitarian, the "Grab the enemy's belts" maxim was employed in offensive situations as well. Veteran American commanders noted that the Viet Cong would spend the opening minutes of an infantry assault striving to hug American forces.[52] That American firepower averted disaster here and there despite this Communist tactic and numerous instances of VC/NVA numerical superiority testifies to the unflappable disposition of American forward observers and to the American military's unparalleled aptitude for putting firepower on target. On other occasions, however, the tactic reduced the battlefield impact of American supporting arms.

3

Generating Friction

British military historian Anthony Beevor authored a riveting tome on the epic battle waged between German and Soviet troops in the urban ruins of Stalingrad: "In such a concentrated area, a soldier had to become more conscious of war in three dimensions, with the dangers of snipers in tall buildings. He also needed to watch the sky."[1] In Vietnam the ubiquitous Viet Cong mine or booby trap prompted the American soldier to watch the ground. Constant downward glances, much like the incessant skyward glances of German and Soviet heads at Stalingrad, had replaced the American infantryman's normal spatial awareness with an all-consuming fear of what lay at or beneath his feet.

Mines and booby traps were by no means a Viet Cong innovation. In fact, both had been used extensively throughout the twentieth century. Wars of the twentieth century were frequently linear, however, and in linear wars, mines and booby traps are generally laid in relation to the front lines. Vietnam was a decidedly nonlinear war. With no clear demarcation to mark the front lines, and in a war frequently waged with guerrilla or unconventional means, the battlefield could be anywhere and *clearing* territory replaced *possession of* territory. Correspondingly the Viet Cong sowed mines and booby traps anywhere and everywhere American infantry might stroll or American military vehicles might roll.

Against American infantry the Viet Cong fielded a myriad of antipersonnel mines, especially as the availability of "regular" antipersonnel mines increased following the infiltration of NVA units into South Vietnam.[2] A particularly insidious Viet Cong mine, the aptly named "Bouncing Betty," featured a three-prong design that protruded up from the soil. If one of the prongs was struck, a charge would detonate and propel the mine a yard or so into the air, whereupon an explosion would discharge the shrapnel. Another mine used quite often, the directional fragmentation mine or DH-10, was routinely called the Viet Cong Claymore mine after the highly effective American antipersonnel mine.[3] Finally the VC utilized the cast-iron fragmentation mine, which resembled a stick grenade with a short handle, and numerous other explosive charges in an antipersonnel capacity.

Mines improvised from artillery shells, mortar shells, and other war materials were prevalent as well. "The guerrillas were known to dig such shells out of the soil and unscrew their detonating fuses," reads an account of VC/NVA salvage operations involving fired but unexploded American shells. "They would cut the shell in half with a hacksaw to remove the TNT or other explosive 'filler.' Knowing that a blast rather than heat detonates the explosive, the guerrillas would liquefy the TNT by cooking it over a fire and then pour it into Coca Cola cans salvaged from an American dump. Finally the cans were capped and topped with pull-string detonators to form deadly hand grenades or satchel charges."[4] Constructed out of cartridge cases or sections of pipe filled with a charge of black powder, a primer, and fragmentary material, the toe-popper mine was another excellent example of VC mine improvisation.

Written in May 1967, a U.S. Department of the Army Training Circular outlined the full tactical spectrum of Viet Cong antipersonnel mine employment:

> As a general rule, the Viet Cong can be expected to employ antipersonnel mines anywhere that troops might walk. No area can be assumed to be clear simply because it had been at some previous time. Some of the more likely places of employment are: along trails, in high grass, in front of defensive positions, in and around likely helicopter landing sites, near shaded areas where troops may congregate, at bridges and fording sites over streams and drainage ditches, on rice paddy dikes, along roads at ambush sites, in what appears to be the *easy* way through dense vegetation, in the vicinity of cave and tunnel entrances, and in and around

villages. . . . Tripwires and electrical command firing systems are the most prevalent methods of initiating antipersonnel mines."[5]

In addition to American infantry, the Viet Cong faced the reality of American military motorization. The VC, consequently, resorted to antitank mines such as the Soviet model TMB-2 and TM-41, the Chinese Communist take off the U.S. M-1 series antitank mine, as well as homemade anti-"vehicle" mines refashioned from rigged American artillery shells and bombs that had failed to detonate. Dirt or paved, any road was subject to being mined if it was used by American vehicles. When mining dirt roads, the Viet Cong would commonly dig down, plant the mine, and then disappear from sight. The more ingenious would add a deceptive twist by digging up areas of the road without implanting any mines at all. Awhile later, after allied forces had filled in the dug up segments, the VC would reappear and mine those very same segments of road. For paved surfaces, the Viet Cong would simply tunnel beneath the shoulders of the road. Other times, the VC placed mines directly on the road and concealed them with straw, dung, or any other substance that might ordinarily be found there.[6]

Regardless of the road surface, the Viet Cong favored command-detonated antivehicle mines over those stimulated by pressure initiation systems. The term "command detonated" connotes a certain technological sophistication, but in actuality it could mean nothing more than a wire running from an emplaced mine to a concealed Viet Cong position. From this concealed position, the mine could then be detonated "on command" against a target of opportunity.[7] Command-detonation systems, even the relatively rudimentary, afforded the Viet Cong user control over time and target.

Prodded by the omnipresent threat of Communist roadside mines, the U.S. military began committing M48 tanks and M113 armored personnel carriers (APCs) to road security.[8] As a matter of fact, some American histories of the war contend that road and convoy security was the reason for introducing Army mechanized and armor units into the country in 1966.[9] Road security required American armor to rumble back and forth along the roads and thoroughfares of South Vietnam, clearing routes of advance and escorting softer skinned supply vehicles. Sometimes these security measures succeeded in neutralizing the threat, and sometimes they did not. "We did a lot of road security," said APC crewman Lee Reynolds. Nevertheless Reynolds remembered seeing an American track "demolished by a huge mine. Eight of our people were blown to bits. Shreds of their tissue hung from the trees, and birds came to feed on it."[10] Reynolds' recollection reflects the cold truth that about 75 percent of the losses the U.S. military sustained in tanks and armored personnel carriers over the course of the war were attributed to VC/NVA mines.[11]

The Viet Cong booby trap, however, may have achieved a level of variation that surpassed both the antipersonnel and antiarmor mine. Explosive booby traps, for instance, were limited only by the designer's imagination. Though the Viet Cong exploited all kinds of explosive material, the hand grenade was probably utilized most frequently in the making of explosive traps. A paragon of simplicity and functionality, the hand grenade booby trap employed hand grenades of every description, including homemade models fabricated in jungle workshops out of discarded American beer and C-Ration cans. In constructing the trap, the Viet Cong would attach a tripwire to the safety pin of the grenade and then place it along a route with ample foot traffic. Any subsequent "tripping" of the wire pulled the safety pin, setting in motion the grenade's "firing chain." For variety the VC would also leave grenades under objects. The safety pins in the grenades were then removed so that any action that moved the object would initiate the grenade.

Explosive booby traps, regardless of the type, were often arranged in "multiple." The success of the multiple arrangement depended on an initial explosive event acting as a catalyst for a second, and preferably more deadly, event. The latter event, in turn, depended on the intrinsic urge of an American soldier or Marine to assist a comrade in distress. When an American infantryman tripped a wire or otherwise triggered the first booby trap blast (the initial explosive event), the hope was that his comrades would come to his aid. As these troops converged on the location of the initial blast, the Viet Cong would then detonate another concealed explosive device and inflict casualties on the first responders.[12]

Ingenious in their ability to exploit the mundane, the Viet Cong booby-trapped any object an American soldier or Marine might handle or any seemingly safe place he might wish to sit or repose. Viet Cong flags, banners, and other war souvenirs were frequently booby-trapped, as were everyday items such as bicycles, knapsacks, pens, and cigarette lighters. And while well-traversed trails were obvious targets for VC booby traps, an American soldier and Marine could not simply assume that the paddy dike on which he wished to sit was devoid of booby traps.

Antiquated, nonexplosive Viet Cong booby traps like the nail-festooned "swinging logs" or *punji* pits—camouflaged pits with sharpened bamboo stakes, or *punjis*, lining the bottom—attracted substantial Western coverage at the time and have since become almost synonymous with the Vietnam War. In reality they were responsible for far less damage than their coverage would intimate. *Punjis*, contrary to popular belief, caused a mere 2 percent of U.S. Army casualties between January 1965 and June 1970 and not one fatality. Over that same time period, over half of the U.S. Army's killed in action (KIA) died from enemy small-arms and machine-gun fire. Another 36 percent were killed by enemy grenades, mortars, and artillery.[13] No impartial student of the war would dispute that many aspects of the Viet Cong or NVA soldier's existence would have been deemed positively prehistoric by American standards. The weapons he utilized most often to kill and wound his American counterpart, on the other hand, were not.

While mines were sown with abandon by main- and local-force Viet Cong, the village guerrilla was perhaps the foremost practitioner of the booby trap. Since the Communist Vietnamese way of war endorsed guerrilla war along with big-unit war, with the only variable being one of emphasis and not exclusivity, the guerrilla and his brand of booby trapping, low intensity, asymmetrical war never fell out of favor. Northwest of Saigon, for example, Cu Chi district's congress of "Hero Killers of Americans" went so far as to transcribe ten ways to defeat U.S. forces in guerrilla warfare. Numbers 2 and 7 read, respectively: "any weapon can be used to fight the Americans" and "we can fight the Americans both from the front and from the rear."[14] The village guerrilla certainly fit the profile of a "rear" combatant, just as his homemade booby trap qualified as "any weapon."

Obviously the Viet Cong planted mines and booby traps to inflict casualties and in that regard they were no different than any other warring party.

They were, of course, exceedingly effective at the craft. Casualty estimates for 1966 alone credited booby traps with the deaths of more than one thousand American soldiers.[15] Such casualty figures are indicative of how profligate the Viet Cong were with mine and booby trap emplacement. An enterprising lot, the VC used mines and booby traps to spring ambushes along roads and jungle paths, protect base areas, strengthen defensive areas, confine and channel enemy movement, and hinder American pursuit. Physically and emotionally drained from the exhausting chore of stalking an elusive enemy day in and day out, American infantry units were especially susceptible to this kind of warfare.

Beyond the killing and maiming of American soldiery and the destruction of American military vehicles, VC mines and booby traps fostered a climate symptomatic of a central condition that occurs in all wars. According to Eric Bergerud, a military historian and author of *Red Thunder, Tropic Lightning: The World of a Combat Division in Vietnam*, the presence of so many Communist mines and booby traps "just added to what Clausewitz would call *friction*. Tanks had to escort convoys, and roads were patrolled up and down constantly. The Americans were always doing sweeps. And for the infantry, it didn't matter how good you were because there was always this element of chance as far as stepping on something and getting your head, or more likely your feet, blown off. The situation just made for a huge pain in the butt."[16] Unfortunately for American troops, that pain would endure for the duration of American ground combat in Vietnam.

Michael Call may not have been conversant with Clausewitz, but the Vietnam combat veteran understood the agonizing mental duress that even the routine act of placing one foot in front of the other created. Call remembered:

> We begin to walk with our eyes fixed on the ground, looking for some telltale sign we should avoid. I ask myself: 'Is that little thing ahead the three prongs of a Bouncing Betty or just three blades of grass? As my right foot moves in front of my left foot, I carry on a debate within my mind if I should place it down on that rock just ahead, or behind it . . . or in front of it . . . or to the side of it.

But now I face another dilemma. If I choose to step to the side of the rock, which side do I choose? These gooks are very clever. They must figure that I will want to place my foot on hard ground, so maybe they put the mine under the rock. Maybe I shouldn't place my right foot anywhere near that rock. Maybe I should move over to the left a little or to the right. Then again, why not place my foot in the step of the guy ahead of me? But he is already too far ahead. And if you walk too close to him, he will get pissed off because if I trip a mine, he'll get blown away, too. What to do with my right foot? I say: 'I can't stand on my left foot forever.' I finally put my right foot down and nothing happens. My next decision is what to do with my left foot, which, in the act of walking, comes up when the right foot goes down.[17]

Multiply Call's "to step or not to step" dilemma by a factor of several thousand strides per infantry "sweep" operation—or imagine the grinding daily tedium of awaiting the OK from minesweeping combat engineers to begin motorized road travel again—and the ability of Viet Cong mines and booby traps to tie down/slow down American forces and create friction becomes eminently clear. Such friction served the big-unit war by grinding the gears of the American war machine.

PART II
THE BIG-UNIT WAR: 1965

4

Strategic Debates and Decisions

Scholars have said, quite reasonably, that Hanoi and the Viet Cong harbored parallel if not identical goals, and that mutual self-identification, and a certain degree of distrust, colored the participants' perception of their relationship. "There were two communist-led armed forces in the Vietnam War—PAVN and PLAF," Douglas Pike observed, "—if for no other reason than because of a sense of separate identity among their rank and file. Whatever monolithism may have existed at the generals' level, the perception by those who fought was of a sharp difference, especially in purpose."[1] In truth Hanoi would probably have been elated to consummate victory and reunification solely through the supply of northern military technicians, strategists, and war-waging essentials to the Viet Cong. Instead, the ever increasing burden shouldered by the NVA resulted in a severe hemorrhaging of Hanoi's military forces and ultimately a diminution of Viet Cong contributions to the "liberation" of South Vietnam.

Hanoi's turning on of the strategic spigot—the dispatch of men and material to South Vietnam—reinforced its commitment to, and its strategic command and control over, the Communist military effort against South Vietnam. From the beginning, however, acrimonious debate raged in Hanoi regarding the proper role of Communist military forces in the South. Over the ensuing years of conflict, the debate simmered between the proponents of a more measured acceleration in the intensity of combat, represented early on by North Vietnamese defense minister Vo Nguyen Giap, and the big-unit battle clique, represented by southern-bred party luminaries Le Duan, then first secretary of the Central Committee, and General Nguyen Chi Thanh.

Hoang Cam, the first commander of the famed 9th Viet Cong Division, was privy to arguments on each side of this grand strategic divide.[2] Inside a small hut doubling as the COSVN Headquarters, in the jungles of War Zone C northwest of Saigon, Cam listened to COSVN party secretary General Nguyen Chi Thanh, General Tran Van Tra, and others discuss these divergent viewpoints. Of that early 1965 conference, Cam recalled the following spirited exchange:

> [Thanh speaking:] "We must be prepared to defeat the enemy's 'special war,' but if we want to defeat this type of war we must commit regular main force units to the battle, and we must begin to build main force fists powerful enough to break the backbone of the enemy's 'special war'—the puppet government's regular army units."
>
> He suddenly turned and looked directly at Tran Do and I, as if this was a conversation with us personally. He said, "We are all, even me, just raw recruits who have just arrived in the South. We have an understanding and viewpoint of the situation based on the conferences and the training courses we attended up North. The Central Committee and the Politburo has equipped us with this knowledge, but the actual situation and developments on the battlefield are extremely changeable, like a living creature, so we need to study the situation in depth, building forces and organizing combat operations and using those activities to gain an understanding of the enemy's modus operandi, his pattern of operations, because our current opponent is the United States—the puppets have been built and propped up by the Americans, after all. We also have to study the particular, special characteristics and nature of our own Eastern Cochin China cadres and soldiers. We share the same heritage, we are all the children of the Fatherland, but they have their own special nature and character."
>
> At that point Tran Van Tra, the Commander of the Liberation of South Vietnam, jumped into the discussion. "You two have arrived at a time when the Center [Hanoi] and the COSVN Military Command are discussing the decision of whether to push ahead with the policy of build-

ing main force units. You got here at just the right time. Down here there are currently two different opinions on this matter. The political cadres down here agree with the Center, with the Politburo, that we must build up a powerful main force army."

"Correct!" Nguyen Chi Thanh thundered. "During our nation's long history of fighting against outside aggression, there has never been an instance in our history when we secured victory and won the war by fighting small battles. Without the first battle of Bach Dang River, fought under the command of Emperor Ngo Quyen, the Southern Han armies [the army of China's southern Han Dynasty] would never have accepted defeat and ended the period of our nation's colonization by our northern neighbor, a period that lasted for more than a millennium. That battle opened up the era of our nation's independence and sovereignty. Without the strategic counteroffensive conducted by our Tran Dynasty on the Bach Dang River, how could we have possibly had defeated the third invasion by the Mongol aggressor armies?"

General Tra, according to Cam's recollections, then defended the use of main-force units and argued for the creation of a more powerful main-force army:

"They argue that in Algeria France was defeated even though the resistance did not possess even one single regiment. For that reason, they say, we should not build main force units. The effort will be too costly, they say, and they say that we already have a few regiments but these units have not been able to accomplish anything in battle?! It is true that in Cochin China, throughout the entire resistance war against the French, and on until just before the Binh Gia Campaign was fought, our largest main force unit was the regiment, and we have very few of those. For that reason, in reality we have never fought a truly regimental-sized action, and we operate almost exclusively at the battalion level in combat, which is why the Glorious 307th Battalion has become so famous."

At this point Tra turned to me, tapped on my shoulder, and asked, "Up North did you guys hear about our victories at Ap Bac and Duong Long?"

"Yes!" I answered. "We received timely reports on both these actions, although the information we received on the Battle of Ap Bac was more concrete and detailed."

"It is true that both these victories were tactically significant," Tra continued. "Our success in both battles was very clear, but internally, between ourselves, we must acknowledge the fact that even though they were victories, because we did not have powerful main force units we were unable to totally annihilate the opposing enemy force. The results of recent actions, such as the Binh Gia Campaign, have been the same. In that campaign, for the first time in the history of Eastern Cochin China we fought a regimental-sized action and were able to kill many enemy troops, but still we were unable to gain the upper hand, the superior posture, because our main force army is still too small and weak.... After the Binh Gia Campaign everyone is filled with joy at our great victory, and that battle has made even clearer the necessity for us to build up main force units."[3]

Each of these schools of strategic thought enjoyed intervals of predominance, rendering the Viet Cong's strategic orientation virtually hostage to the shifting winds of deliberation in Hanoi and to military organizations like COSVN that were subservient to Hanoi. General Tra maintained that the idea of building up and using main-force units early on was not unanimously accepted because "at that time, many of our people in South Vietnam continued to cling to the concept of guerrilla warfare and armed insurrection by the civilian populations and said there was no need for a regular army, even though the U.S. had already started full-scale war." Tra, moreover, claimed that he had asked COSVN to "recruit youths primarily from the Mekong Delta and to send weapons up from the Delta to Song Be and northern Tay Ninh" for the express purpose of building up main-force units.[4]

Lieutenant General Le Van Tuong, formerly the deputy commissar of Liberation Armed Forces in the B2 theater, insists that General Thanh ultimately persuaded COSVN on the divisive issue of establishing main-force units. Describing the process, General Tuong wrote:

In 1964, a COSVN conference to study a resolution for the Center [a Politburo resolution] dragged out for 21 days arguing about our strategic formula, especially regarding the building up of our forces. Many attendees suggested that we continue to intensify our guerrilla warfare operations and said we should not concentrate our efforts on building up COSVN main force units. Some of the arguments became rather heated. However, with an attitude of patient persuasion, and by focusing his leadership efforts on building main force units and fighting large-scale battles of annihilation at Binh Gia, Dong Xoai, Dau Tieng, Bau Bang, etc., he [Thanh] gradually was able to build a high level of unanimity from COSVN and the COSVN Military Party Committee down through each individual military region down to each individual province and to successfully build powerful main force "fists" to fight on the battlefields of B2.[5]

According to Tra the philosophical struggle over building up and deploying powerful main-force units did not conclude until 1967. "The struggle over this military concept continued," he explained, "and it was not until 1967 that our people finally completely accepted it, even though as far back as 1963 we had won a resounding victory in the battle of Ap Bac by using main force battle tactics, by combining military, political, and military proselytizing efforts, by combining regular and guerrilla tactics."[6]

In retrospect it is doubtful that the Communist leadership ever attained the degree of unanimity in 1967, or any other year for that matter, that Tra suggested. Although the ratification of Resolution 15 at the Fifteenth Plenum in 1959 sanctioned armed struggle and North Vietnamese support for the revolution to overthrow the regime of Ngo Dinh Diem in the South, domestic and international politics moderated its implementation to one of political agitation and "limited" armed struggle. Domestically "southern-firsters" in the North Vietnamese Politburo like Le Duan and similarly minded "militants" had yet to consolidate their increasing clout on military and political matters into "absolute power."[7] Many in the party still preferred to concentrate on socialist economic development in North Vietnam and, over time, to defeat the South through economic competition. Meanwhile, on the international front,

North Vietnam's principle patrons, China and the Soviet Union, urged Hanoi to pursue reunification through *political* and not armed struggle.[8]

It was not until the Ninth Plenum of the Central Committee in late 1963, and the passage of Resolution 9, that the southern-firsters and their accelerated-armed-struggle compatriots were able to register a more gratifying policy triumph. Internationally the situation had changed somewhat since 1959. China, unlike the Soviet Union, now appeared more amenable to a more aggressive military approach. Taking care to avoid overtly offending Soviet sensibilities, Le Duan and his fellow hardliners exploited this emergent Sino-Soviet fissure at the Ninth Plenum to steer through a resolution authorizing a concerted attempt to "seize a favorable opportunity by massing our forces to resolutely seek to win decisive victories during the next few years."[9] Massed, conventionally organized Communist forces, according to the strategy espoused by the resolution, were to fight big-unit battles and smash the ARVN. Thereafter a "General Offensive–General Insurrection" would collapse the South Vietnamese state quickly and decisively.

Resolution 9 asserted that limited armed struggle coupled with political agitation would no longer suffice to topple the Saigon regime and effect reunification, particularly in light of the growing American stake in the fortunes of South Vietnam. Opposition to the measure ran deep, however. Hoang Minh Chinh, director of the Nguyen Ai Quoc Party School at the time, alleges that approximately half of the Politburo favored continued peaceable "coexistence" with South Vietnam during the Ninth Plenum. Chinh, in fact, had apparently authored a report advocating neutrality in the Sino-Soviet rift and peaceable "coexistence." Others, including Ung Van Khiem, then foreign minister, objected to Resolution 9's implicit embrace of the Chinese line (that is, more aggressive armed struggle) as well.[10]

If the adoption of a more aggressive military policy at the Ninth Plenum implied something of an emerging philosophical alignment with the Chinese, the denunciation of "modern revisionism" at the same conference must have been similarly disquieting to the Sino-Soviet "neutralists" like Hoang Minh Chinh, Ung Van Khiem, and Lieutenant General Dang Kim Giang. Increasingly more militant in its international outlook than the Soviet Union, the Chinese had made use of the phrase "modern revisionism" in reference to

Khrushchev's guiding policy of coexistence with the West.[11] Mao, in fact, had even taken the rather extraordinary step of condemning Khrushchev as a revisionist. For the Ninth Plenum to then pass a resolution in opposition to modern revisionism indicated the hardliners in the Politburo were more in league with the Chinese in late 1963.

Opposition to the "modern revisionism" measure and the apparent pro-China philosophical tilt attracted, perhaps not unexpectedly, the attention of North Vietnam's "public security apparatus." Branded the perpetuators of "propaganda distorting Marxism-Leninism" by a Communist Vietnamese security history published after the war, some elements of the neutralist camp were accused of "using revisionist concepts as the subject of propaganda that opposed the policies of our party." These party policies included "the resolution of the Ninth Plenum of the Party Central Committee in 1963, the basic thrust of which was a critique and denunciation of modern revisionism."[12]

The consequences for such transgressions, beyond heightened scrutiny from the domestic security apparatus, were tangible if reasonably mild by the standards of a totalitarian police state. Hoang Minh Chinh, for instance, had his report derided as "revisionist" at the plenum, and he and a few other neutralist officials endured the ignominy of either being demoted or sacked altogether.[13] More important, however, the reprisals clearly demonstrate that the hardliners considered the neutralist opposition a security risk as early as 1963, even if they were as yet unwilling to entirely neutralize it.

Nuanced and highly fluid, the debates over how to maintain strategic equilibrium in the Sino-Soviet rift and how best to conduct the wider war—emphasize guerrilla war/protracted struggle complemented by big-unit war or emphasize big-unit war/quick ending complemented by guerrilla war—persisted for years. Indeed, to the extent that unanimity was ever achieved even in the run-up to the momentous Tet Offensive of 1968, mechanisms to suppress if not silence domestic dissent were conspicuously employed by the hardliners in Hanoi.

■ ■ ■

On March 23, 1965, a disenchanted soldier from the 101st Regiment, 325th NVA Division in Kontum Province defected to an ARVN unit. The "bully boys," General Westmoreland's name for Communist main-force units, had come to demolish what Westmoreland had dubbed the "house": South Vietnam. Hanoi, it could now be said, had been pushed by the hardliners through the first stage of Giap's Maoist-influenced formula for revolutionary war.

In ascending order of escalation, Giap's "Revolutionary Guerrilla War" featured an initial phase of guerrilla war followed by a second phase that combined guerrilla war and conventional war as revolutionary forces approached parity with government forces. The final phase, the General Offensive–General Insurrection, envisioned revolutionary forces defeating government forces in conventional battle, and that defeat, when coupled with a general uprising of the civilian population, would topple the State. Hardliners such as General Thanh and Le Duan had lobbied for a wider armed struggle in the South and for the attendant big-unit buildup and big-unit battle associated with a more expansive war. Both the buildup of large conventional forces and the commitment of those forces to large-scale battles were necessary, they believed, to fulfill a key prerequisite of the General Offensive–General Insurrection: smashing the South Vietnamese armed forces.

No doubt reflecting on the administrative inadequacies in the South Vietnamese countryside, the enduring political instability in coup plagued Saigon, and the crippling attenuation of the South Vietnamese armed forces, the hardliners in Hanoi considered South Vietnam ripe for the picking by 1964. During high-level strategy sessions in September of that year, the North Vietnamese leadership discussed moving quickly "to seize this opportunity to strive to completely defeat the puppet army before the U.S. armed forces have time to intervene."[14] Accordingly the Politburo dispatched the first grouping of complete NVA regiments to South Vietnam, where they were to participate in big-unit campaigns designed to shatter the ARVN. With ARVN incapacitated the Communists then planned to mount a General Offensive–General Insurrection campaign against the city of Saigon.[15]

The Politburo's "militant" decision, ironically, also prompted the disclosure of an assessment of Viet Cong strength that supported the misgivings of those who worried about escalating the war too quickly: "Our main force army in South Vietnam is still weak and is not yet ready to mount massed combat operations to destroy the puppet regular army."[16] The hardliners, in deciding to reinforce the existing Viet Cong units with NVA regiments, had evidently reasoned that the participation of well-trained and -equipped North Vietnamese regulars would ameliorate the situation and enable the "main force army in South Vietnam" to crush ARVN and open the door for the General Offensive–General Insurrection. "To the North Vietnamese Politburo," wrote former MACV staffer General Phillip Davidson, "the extra push which the North Vietnamese Main Force units could furnish would bring about a 'general uprising' and victory."[17] South Vietnam's day of reckoning was now close at hand.

Yet one critical question remained: Could Communist forces destroy ARVN, and with it the "puppet" regime in Saigon, before the United States intervened decisively? Le Duan, in correspondence with General Thanh in early 1965, addressed that very question. "Can we defeat the Americans before they have time to change their strategy?" he asked. "I believe our opportunity has arrived and I believe there is still a possibility we can restrict the enemy enough to defeat them in the 'special war.'"[18] If "special war" conditions prevailed, VC/NVA forces would continue to face a South Vietnamese military buttressed by American advisors and support, as had been the case since the very infancy of the armed Communist insurgency in the South, not thousands of American combat troops. Le Duan was certainly optimistic and with good reason about the prospects for defeating the "puppet army"—the derisive Communist term most often used to describe ARVN—under those circumstances.

Le Duan's combination of political clout (as first secretary of the Central Committee) and his acknowledged revolutionary bona fides lent persuasive power to his optimism. Born in Quang Tri in 1908, Le Duan completed his high school studies and eventually joined the Indochinese Communist Party. When Japanese forces invaded Indochina in September 1940, the resident French colonial administrators cooperated with the invaders and arrested a number of Indochinese Communist Party Central Committee members, including Le Duan. Handed a lengthy sentence, he was imprisoned at the Poulo Condore island penitentiary off the southern coast of Vietnam until his confinement ended in August 1945.

Le Duan operated in the South during the war against the French. A committed ideologue, he served as an Indochinese Communist Party (later changed to the Vietnamese Workers' Party or Lao Dong Party) political commissar with the "people's army" and in the original COSVN. Le Duan remained in the South following the French defeat and the 1954 partition of Vietnam, serving, for example, as secretary of the Cochin China Communist Party Committee, before he was summoned to North Vietnam in April 1957. Eight months later, in December 1957, he ascended to the post of acting secretary general of the party's Central Committee. Le Duan then held the title of secretary general until it was replaced in 1960 with the new title, first secretary of the Central Committee.[19]

The daunting political power and revolutionary credentials of Le Duan notwithstanding, President's Johnson's authorization of a punitive bombing campaign, code named Rolling Thunder and slated to begin in March 1965 against targets in North Vietnam, together with his February approval of a request by General William Westmoreland for U.S. Marine battalions to protect the air base at Da Nang, reminded the hardliners of the danger of a dramatic expansion of American involvement. That same March the Central Committee convened at the Eleventh Plenum and again chose the path of big-unit war and rapid conquest of the non-Communist South: "The faster we score a decisive victory in South Vietnam, the better chance we have of preventing the enemy from switching from a 'special war' in South Vietnam into a 'limited war' and of preventing the enemy from expanding his 'limited war' into North Vietnam."[20] "Limited war" would of course include the introduction of large numbers of American combat troops on the battlefield, the concussive effects of concentrated American firepower, and increased aerial bombardment of North Vietnam's war nourishing logistical apparatus. If at all possible Hanoi wished to avoid that strategically undesirable scenario.

Corresponding with General Thanh in February 1965, Le Duan outlined once more the strategy for averting American "limited war" and achieving a quick victory over the South. First, Viet Cong and NVA forces would attack and destroy "three or four puppet regular divisions in battle in the course of wave after wave of attacks by our forces." Subsequently, according to Le Duan, the Communists were to "launch a general insurrection in coordination with a general military offensive aimed straight at the heart of the enemy to seize control of the government. This will shatter the morale of the puppet army.

Taking advantage of this opportunity, we will make strong military attacks combined with powerful political and military attacks conducted by the masses to incite military mutinies and in this way create the possibility of causing the collapse of the remaining units of the puppet army."[21] Once again the recipe for victory in Le Duan's mind consisted of big units, big-unit war, and a General Offensive–General Insurrection.

Le Duan's words indicate rather strongly that the hardliners in Hanoi were, in the late winter and early spring of 1965, seeking a quick victory through the employment of big units and big-unit war. Viet Cong forces, in conjunction with the NVA, would disperse and then defeat ARVN in South Vietnam in a grand strategic offensive. Thereafter the axis of the offensive would shift to the capture of Saigon, the fomentation of a popular uprising throughout South Vietnam, the creation of a Communist dominated "neutral" regime, and the negotiated withdrawal of American forces from South Vietnam.

Curiously neither Le Duan nor the resolution passed at the Eleventh Plenum in March 1965 discounted entirely the possibility of fighting a protracted conflict or of fighting against an American "limited war." As a matter of fact, although the resolution announced that the "basic mission" was to "positively restrain and defeat the enemy in the 'special war' at its highest level in the South," it also advised the undertaking of preparations "to cope with and defeat the 'limited war' if waged by the enemy in the South."[22] Just how much of this call for preparations to defeat limited war was sincere foresight and how much was lip service remains unanswered, particularly when the professed goal of the hardliner clique was to knock out South Vietnam *before* the American special war escalated to limited war.

To clarify, it is beyond the purview of this work to chronicle the deployment of American military advisors, equipment, and aerial assets in support of South Vietnam's war against the Viet Cong prior to 1965 or to examine in depth the political rationalizations underlying President Lyndon Johnson's decision to commit large numbers of American combat troops to defend and preserve South Vietnam. Volumes have been devoted to each of the aforementioned topics. Nor will independent combat between American forces and the NVA, insofar as one can parse VC from NVA engagements in the interwoven fabric of Communist combat operations and directives, receive coverage other than that which is essential to preserve the context and continuity of the big-unit war the *Viet Cong* fought against American forces.

If the Eleventh Plenum pushed the Viet Cong and NVA to the precipice of a potential big-unit war against the United States, how did Washington ensure that American troops would be there to oblige? Overtly invested in the military welfare of South Vietnam since the establishment of MACV (Military Assistance Command, Vietnam) under President Kennedy in 1962, the United States and its civilian and military policy makers understood all too well the gravity of the military situation in the summer of 1965. Beginning in May Hanoi's momentous offensive had severely damaged South Vietnam's continued capacity to prosecute the war. Bloody battles at Song Be, Ba Gia, and Dong Xoai, as well as a spiraling desertion rate among South Vietnamese units, thoroughly depleted Saigon's reserves and foretold of an imminent defeat. General William Westmoreland, the commander of MACV, issued a dire report on June 7 warning that without adequate reinforcement from American and third country troops, ARVN "would be unable to stand up to the pressure."[23]

Sufficiently alarmed and after much rumination, President Johnson took action. Heeding the advice of Secretary of Defense Robert McNamara and others, Johnson delegated the authority to commit elements of the U.S. 173rd Airborne Brigade to Westmoreland during the intense fighting around Dong Xoai in June. American airpower ultimately tipped the scales in favor of the hard-pressed South Vietnamese before Westmoreland could commit the paratroop brigade, but further postponements in committing American ground forces to staunch the Communist tide risked more South Vietnamese military defeats and eventually the outright collapse of the Saigon regime.

President Johnson responded to the rapidly deteriorating situation with a drastic escalation in American involvement. During a televised speech on July 28, 1965, Johnson informed the American public, "I have today ordered to Vietnam the Airmobile Division and certain other forces which will raise our fighting strength from 75,000 to 125,000 men almost immediately. Additional forces will be needed later, and they will be sent as requested." Fittingly Johnson then accused North Vietnam of directing the Viet Cong insurgency before pronouncing that "most of the non Communist nations of Asia cannot, by themselves and alone, resist the growing might and the grasping ambition of Asian Communism. Our power, therefore, is a very vital shield."[24] If General Thanh and his allies in Hanoi were to remain implacable on the issue of toppling South Vietnam through military escalation and big-unit war, a massive infusion of American combat power would soon stand in their way.

5

Van Tuong

Operation Starlite in August 1965 occasioned perhaps the most significant encounter between the Viet Cong and American ground forces in the period immediately following President Johnson's July 28 speech. Launched on August 18 by Marines from the III Marine Amphibious Force to protect the critical Marine enclave at Chu Lai from a suspected Viet Cong attack, the operation targeted elements of the 1st Viet Cong Regiment laagering in the Van Tuong area. General Thanh had opined that the "Southern Liberation Army is fully capable of defeating U.S. troops under any circumstances."[1] Starlite, or what the Communist Vietnamese would call the Battle of Van Tuong, was in many respects a baptism of fire for the Viet Cong and an opportunity to validate Thanh's assertion.

Reconsidered with the benefit of historical hindsight, the timing of the engagement was hardly inevitable. After its attack against the village of Ba Gia in early July, the 1st Viet Cong Regiment had been ordered to rest and regroup in the Van Tuong area of Quang Ngai Province. A 1991 Communist Vietnamese study of the battle paints a general picture of the regiment's activities and dispositions before the battle: "After completing its summer operations with the destruction of the enemy's Go Cao position on 19 July, 1st Infantry Regiment [1st Viet Cong Regiment] was ordered to base itself in the Van Tuong area to consolidate and regroup, to conduct training, and to carry out preparations for a new round of operations in accordance with the Military Region's battle plan. The regiment deployed its forces at many points that formed a line stretching along the coast. The regimental headquarters and command post was located in Van Tuong hamlet."[2]

Not surprisingly Marine intelligence had kept abreast of the 1st's movements. Despite some collegial skepticism from U.S. Army I Corps Advisory Group experts and the South Vietnamese, the Marines believed they had cobbled together enough information to predict where the VC regiment was headed next. "Early in August," wrote Marine intelligence officer Colonel Leo J. Dulacki, "we began receiving countless low-level reports from the numerous intelligence collection organizations concerning the movement of the *1st VC Regiment*. The sources for most of these reports were of doubtful reliability and, indeed, many were contradictory. Regardless, the Marines decided to plot all of the hundreds of reported movements, regardless of credibility, on a map, and an interesting picture developed. When the many 'aberrations' were discounted, it appeared that the *1st VC Regiment* was, in fact, moving towards Chu Lai."[3]

Even more compelling, on August 15, a Viet Cong soldier, seventeen-year-old Vo Thao, deserted to the South Vietnamese. Thao divulged that his unit, the 1st Viet Cong Regiment, had based itself in the Van Tuong village complex and planned to strike the Marines at Chu Lai, some twelve miles farther north. Major General Nguyen Chanh Thi, the South Vietnamese I Corps commander, personally interviewed Thao.[4] Thi then informed the Marines of what he thought of the intelligence he had acquired from the Viet Cong defector. "General Thi thought this was the best information he's had in the corps area throughout the whole Vietnam War," said General Lewis W. Walt, commander of the U.S. III Marine Amphibious Force.[5] In response to Thao's information and some supposedly substantiating intelligence from another source, the Marines began planning Operation Starlite.

A multibattalion, amphibious-air mobile assault designed to preempt, trap, and rout the 1st Viet Cong Regiment, Starlite was an impressively complex feat of military staff work. Marine Lieutenant Colonel Joseph E. Muir's 3rd Battalion, 3rd Marine Regiment was to disembark on the morning of August 18 at "Green" Beach, located southeast of Van Tuong (1) near the hamlet of An Cuong (1). Shortly after Muir's landing, Marine helicopters would deposit Lieutenant Colonel Joseph R. Fisher's 2nd Battalion, 4th Marine Regiment on three landing zones (LZs) situated west-southwest of the Van Tuong complex. From north to south the landing zones were named "Red," "White," and "Blue." The two Marine battalions were then to link up elements near An Cuong (2) and thrust on through the Van Tuong village complex and across Phuoc Thuan Peninsula to the sea.

Retiring to the Van Tuong area did not, however, preclude the 1st Viet Cong Regiment from preparing for the possibility of fending off an enemy attack. Prior to the Marine assault, the Viet Cong had dutifully considered possible combat scenarios, plans for handling them, and a "guidance concept" that advised the massing of forces along with cooperation with local-force troops and area guerrillas.[6] "We had one regiment in the Van Tuong area which was training, consolidating, and preparing to fulfill its missions," a Communist postwar tome published in Hanoi declared. "It had a contingency plan for countering a sweeping operation launched from many directions."[7] Interestingly enough, the measures that the VC devoted their time to were defensive in nature, not offensive as the Marines had anticipated while preparing Operation Starlite. Historian Otto Lehrack, a former Marine Corps officer and probably the most persuasive revisionist authority on the subject, theorizes that the 1st Viet Cong Regiment camped south of Chu Lai without any real intention of mounting a regiment-sized push against the Marine's Chu Lai enclave. And *if* the Viet Cong launched an attack at all, it would most likely have been a sapper incursion, not a full-scale infantry raid.[8]

Several pertinent details substantiate Lehrack's hypothesis. After a lengthy spell of tough campaigning, the 1st Viet Cong Regiment, by August 1965, was in need of a break. Shortfalls in personnel and weaponry had arisen, compromising some of the regiment's combat power.[9] Moreover, only two of its battalions (Duong Ba Loi's 40th and Nguyen Xuan Phung's 60th) plus the regimental headquarters and elements of the 45th Weapons Battalion were prepared and quartered close enough for immediate combat.[10] The balance of the regiment, therefore, was either unprepared or had been garrisoned too far away for effective action on August 18.[11]

Furthermore, most of the 1st Viet Cong Regiment's leaders, including the regimental commander, were absent "preparing the battlefield in another location" and therefore were unable to command the unit in battle during Starlite.[12] Had a major assault against Chu Lai been imminent, the regimental military leaders would probably have been on hand along with the political cadre, deputy military commanders, and troops of the regiment.[13] Vo Thao's interrogation notwithstanding, the 1st Viet Cong Regiment in all likelihood had no intention of striking the Marines at Chu Lai in mid-August.

Though unaccustomed to combat against American forces, the 1st Viet Cong Regiment nevertheless possessed several advantages over the attacking Marines. The Van Tuong area, in keeping with all sites used for Viet Cong bases, boasted an assortment of predug trenches, fortifications, and other fighting positions into which the regiment could quickly deploy. The locale terrain itself was also advantageous for fighting "countersweep" operations. According to the 1991 Communist battle study:

> The terrain in this area consisted of dry, stepped rice-paddies and fields. In a few places there were marshy areas, and there were many dirt embankments and earthen mounds. The villages along the bottoms of the foothills were located near one another, making it easy to create linked, integral positions in battle. Like most of the rest of Binh Son district, the Van Tuong area had long been a liberated zone and the people had built combat villages with fortified fighting positions and communications trenches that were 1.5 meters deep and three meters wide. They had planted many bushes with long, hard, sharp thorns to form natural obstacles and barriers, ready to counter the enemy's sweeps and land-grabbing operations.
>
> The northern and eastern edges of the Van Tuong area were bordered by the ocean. . . . On the west the Van Tuong area was bounded by Pho Tinh and Go Dam Mountains. These were two high-points which dominated the area and from which all activities within the area could be observed. . . . In the western and southwestern parts of the area there were a number of gentle sand dunes and grass-covered hills that were relatively open and exposed, which restricted the movement of forces during daylight hours. There were few roads in the area, and those that did exist were narrow.[14]

In addition to familiar and favorable terrain, the 1st Viet Cong Regiment had a good deal of seasoning and excellent training credentials, dating all the way back to Group 34 and its days at Xuan Mai Training Center in the fall of 1961. The regiment was raised in November 1962, and by the end of 1963 it had abandoned its local obligations to focus on "building up to serve as one of the Military Region's main force mobile [reserve] units."[15] Le Huu Tru, the regimental commander, had previously commanded the 803rd Regiment at Dien Bien Phu. Tru's political officer, Nguyen Dinh Trong, had also served with the Viet Minh against French colonial forces. More recently the regiment had received, in recognition of its May 1965 defeat of ARVN forces at Ba Gia, an honor banner bearing the inscription "Loyal to the Party, Dutiful to the People, and First in the Victory of Ba Gia."[16] Ba Gia had thoroughly blooded the regiment as well; one particularly hard hit company had all but one of its ninety-five officers and men killed or wounded in the operation.[17] Bred for decisive combat and backed up by the 21st Viet Cong Local Force Company and area guerrillas, the Ba Gia Regiment was an outstanding candidate for the first significant battle of the big-unit war.

Over a diverse landscape of beaches and hills, paddy fields, fortified hamlets, and hedgerows, a disjointed but violent battle erupted between the defending 1st Viet Cong Regiment and their inexperienced Marine attackers on the morning of August 18, 1965. Murderous Viet Cong machine-gun fire imperiled 3rd Battalion's passage through the surf and sand at Green Beach. Away from the shoreline, Viet Cong rocket-propelled grenades and heavy mortars set American amphibious tractors ("amtracs") ablaze and the anxious troops within them aground. Intermittent Viet Cong sniping, sometimes from riflemen moored high up in trees, kept the Marines' nerves on edge.[18]

Lieutenant Phan Tan Huan, an excellent and reliable staff officer, rallied the 1st Viet Cong Regiment's defense against the Marine amphibious landing at "Green Beach." Substantially more important than a routine delaying action, Huan's mission was to engage and stall the Marine companies moving inland with his small defense force and screen the potential evacuation of the regimental CP located in Van Tuong (1). When Lieutenant Colonel Muir's troops came ashore at Green Beach around 6:30 AM, fewer than four kilometers separated them and the nascent Marine bridgehead from acting

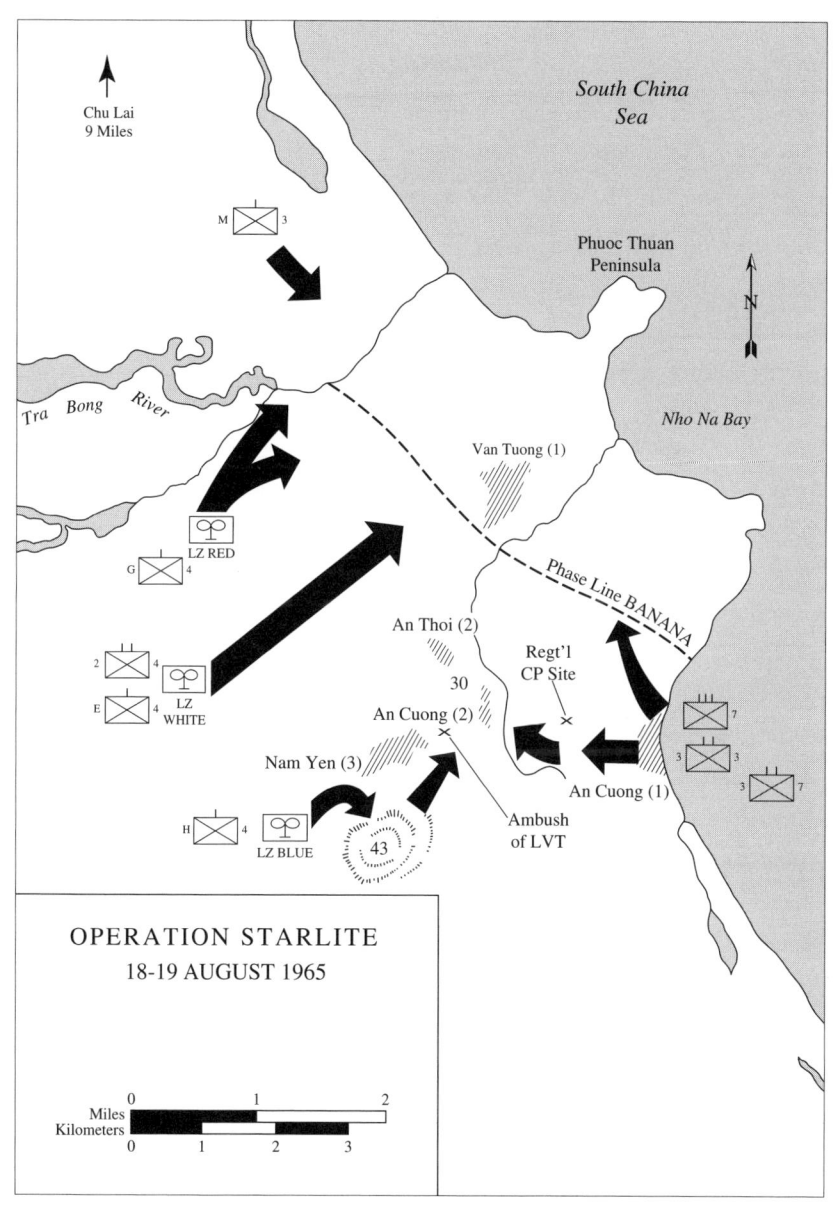

Map 2. *Operation Starlite, August 18–19, 1965 (From Johnson and Shulimson, U.S. Marines in Vietnam)*

regimental commander Nguyen Dinh Trong's CP. And that distance shrunk a little more after Company K (3/3) splashed onto the beach and pushed inland. Earlier, a mine had detonated in front of Company I (3/3) but the explosion had failed to kill a single Marine much less halt the company's forward progress from Green Beach. Huan knew that if Company K, Kilo Company, advanced inland unimpeded, Nguyen Dinh Trong's CP would likely fall into enemy hands.

Perched atop a slope southeast of An Thoi and burrowed into a defensive trench line to the left of the Marines' northerly advance, Huan's delaying force sprayed Company K with automatic weapons fire. Rather intense, this small-arms salvo pinned much of the Marine company down, and had he more than a just a small delaying detachment at his disposal, Huan may have attempted to exploit the situation by flanking the Marines. As the war progressed VC/NVA efforts to outflank a pinned down American unit emerged as a staple of Communist combat tactics. Instead, Huan settled for holding up the Marine advance.

Eventually Huan's defenses crumbled. Silver Star recipient Lieutenant Burt Hinson rounded up a squad, crested a slope, and with his small group of Marines eliminated all Viet Cong resistance on the hill. Nearly in concert with Hinson, another Marine platoon swept the trench line clear of Viet Cong defenders. Huan, however, had achieved his objective. Company K deemed further advance on August 18 inadvisable and began digging in. With Company K anchored a kilometer away, the 1st Viet Cong Regiment CP deserted Van Tuong (1) and moved west-southwest.[19]

Elsewhere, around the fortified village of An Cuong (2), Viet Cong forces attacked Company I, Company K's left flank neighbor. Cradled geographically between a streambed and the village of Nam Yen (3) to the southwest, An Cuong (2) formed an operational fulcrum. From An Cuong (2), the Viet Cong could stage attacks against an enemy unit shadowing the streambed north, or they could pivot and strike an enemy unit wandering through the open rice paddy area between Nam Yen (3) and An Cuong (2). Accordingly, when Company I appeared on the eastern bank of the streambed directly across from An Cuong (2) around 9:00 AM, the roughly platoon-sized force of Viet Cong inside the village opened fire on the Marines. Responding aggressively the

Marines crossed the streambed and scampered down the other slope, silencing VC fire emanating from a line of small trees. Scores of fleeing VC were then slaughtered as they scurried into the scrub brush on the western bank. The battle on the outskirts of the village had gone to the Marines.

Surrounded by woodlands and teeming with camouflaged bunkers, trenches, and fighting holes, An Cuong (2) was still a very heavily defended Viet Cong village strong point wedged between Muir's 3rd Battalion and elements of Fisher's 2nd Battalion. Company I, consequently, edged cautiously onward toward the village. As the Marines advanced, the volume of defensive fire intensified. Three out of a four-man Marine machine-gun team were shot and killed tramping across a rice paddy. Viet Cong mortars then entered the fray, lobbing two 60-mm shells into the Marine ranks.

Predictably the Marines fought back with ardor. Houses inside An Cuong (2) changed hands. Overhead F4 Phantom attack bombers and A4 Skyhawk light-attack bombers tumbled out of the clouds to unburden their deadly cargo on Viet Cong positions. On the eighteenth alone, the 1st Marine Aircraft Wing unloaded sixty-five tons of bombs, four tons of napalm, 523 2.75-inch rockets, and six thousand rounds of 20-mm ammunition.[20] Slowly but surely the Marines secured the restive village, and by early that afternoon, Company I had reached the 3rd Battalion's main line northeast of An Cuong (2). Two Marine squads and three supporting tanks stayed behind to protect a UH-1E gunship that the Viet Cong had downed with small-arms fire northeast of An Cuong (2). During the battle some fifty VC soldiers along with Captain Webb, the commander of Company I, were killed.[21]

Although the small (twenty-five to thirty huts) village of An Cuong (2) had fallen, Viet Cong forces in Nam Yen (3) and on Hill 43 to the east-southeast of Landing Zone Blue would require repeated attacks and a hefty demonstration of Marine firepower to subdue. Shortly after Company H (2/4) touched down at LZ Blue south of Nam Yen (3), Viet Cong fire from Hill 43 lashed the landing zone. Company H's landing happened to lie within the defensive areas of the 60th Viet Cong Battalion, and in addition to the fire from Hill 43, groups of VC soldiers camouflaged to look like bushes crept forward to threaten the Marine company.[22] These leaf-and-branch-bestrewn VC closed on LZ Blue, but the groundswell of Marine return fire beat them back.

Lieutenant Mike Jenkins, Company H's commander, then enjoined one platoon to seize Hill 43 and the rest of his company to secure Nam Yen (3). The Viet Cong stopped both attacks.

Occupying fighting positions atop Hill 43, two platoons from a company belonging to the 60th Viet Cong Battalion were responsible for halting the Marine attack near the bottom of the hill.[23] Meanwhile, at Nam Yen (3), well-entrenched Viet Cong troops led by political commissar Nguyen Ngoc Nhuan parried Jenkins' two-platoon thrust with grenades and heavy infantry fire. Reassessing the situation, Jenkins summoned Marine aviation to bludgeon Nam Yen (3) and Hill 43 before renewing his assault. Hill 43, now grotesquely pockmarked from the impact of multiple bomb blasts, yielded to the cumulative combat power of all three of Jenkins' platoons, Marine armor, and close-in air support.

Surprisingly, even with the loss of Hill 43, Viet Cong defenses around Nam Yen (3) remained every bit as cohesive and obstinate. Advancing anew from the Hill 43 area sometime around 11:00 AM, Company H moved across a rice paddy between Nam Yen (3) and An Cuong (2) and right into a vortex of Viet Cong fire. Without warning, Viet Cong positions in Nam Yen (3) and around Hill 30 to the northeast raked the 1st Platoon, Company H's rearguard formation, with machine-gun fire. Up ahead, to the east of Nam Yen (3), Viet Cong 82-mm and 60-mm mortar shells exploded among Company H's 2nd and 3rd Platoons.

Hill 30, which formed the northern apex of an imaginary triangle encompassing Nam Yen (3) and An Cuong (2), offered an adequate view of Company H's movements. Viet Cong forces in the vicinity of the hill took advantage of the available observation points and leveled their antiarmor weapons at the tracked vehicles supporting the Marine infantry. Aiming accurately the VC struck two of the three Marine Ontos vehicles churning through the area's rice paddy quagmire, while the third suffered a disabled radio. Trained to behave assertively in combat, the Marines regrouped and punched back hard. Lance Corporal Ernie Wallace, for example, single-handedly identified and killed fifteen VC disguised as baby pines. Viet Cong defenses around Nam Yen (3), however, held firm.[24] After requesting air strikes on Hill 30 and an artillery mission against Nam Yen (3), Lieutenant Jenkins authorized a retreat back to LZ Blue.[25]

Northwest of the Nam Yen (3)–An Cuong (2) locus, opposite LZs Red and White, Viet Cong defenders were either oddly nonexistent or simply incapable of stemming the eastward flow of Marine forces. Company G (2/4) landed at LZ Red around 6:45 AM and marched virtually unopposed to the northeast, ultimately making contact with Company M of the 3/3 Marines. To the south, in hilly terrain east and northeast of LZ White, Company E's (2/4) point of departure featured a ridgeline from which the Viet Cong brought mortar, machine-gun, and small-arms fire to bear on the Marines. The defending Viet Cong killed two Marines and wounded three others on the first hill alone, but after a strenuous fight, Company E carried the heights.[26]

Marine artillery unloaded later that morning on a procession of about one hundred uniformed VC moving away from Company E. Salivating at the prospect of finding the enemy out in the open, in obvious violation of normally understood Viet Cong movement protocol, the Marine gunners bombarded the exposed Viet Cong force with abandon. The shellfire killed approximately ninety VC and shattered a potentially dangerous impediment to Marine operations.[27]

In retrospect the Viet Cong's most noteworthy action of the "countersweep" operation, other than Lieutenant Huan's delaying action, was arguably the violent ambush of a Marine supply convoy during the afternoon hours of August 18. Assigned the mission of resupplying Company I (3/3), which had advanced inland after coming ashore in the early stages of Operation Starlite, a platoon of water and ammunition hauling Marine amtracs and their supporting "flame" tanks departed sometime after noon. Along the route, somewhere between Nam Yen (3) and An Cuong (2), a sharp bend leading into a wooded area slowed the Marine column as the lead tank and the first two amtracs negotiated the turn. Farther behind, the rest of the column eased to a halt and waited.

Suddenly two explosions disturbed the previously uneventful advance. The first blast took place near the lead tank rounding the bend. The second occurred near the middle of the Marine supply column. A company of Viet Cong, most likely from the 40th Battalion, had selected a section of trail bounded by a rice paddy on one flank and hedgerows and thicket on the other to ambush the Marine column. While the 1st Platoon of the ambushing VC company crouched in a trench to block the lead elements of the Marine convoy, the 2nd Platoon occupied positions to the right for a flanking assault. Off to the right of 2nd Platoon, the 3rd Platoon prepared to cut off the rear of the mechanized column.[28] From this series of trenches and defensive positions Viet Cong mortar, RPG, and 57-mm recoilless rifle fire descended on the Marine column. Several amtracs were damaged by the concentrated fire, and two Marines who had attempted to evacuate their disabled vehicles were killed.

In time the accurate and unceasing Viet Cong fire suppressed much of the Marines' vehicle-borne firepower. Then, as the barrage of fire gradually lifted, anxious groups of Viet Cong infantry assembled in the smoke and dust for a classic close-in assault against any and all Marine survivors. What began with a torrid volley of RPG and recoilless rifle fire would end with Sergeant Ho Cong Tham and the infantry:

> The company organized three-man cells equipped with sub-machineguns and grenades and sent them to try to climb up on the vehicles in order to destroy them and kill the enemy troops. When 1st Cell charged all of its men were killed. Then 2nd Cell charged, and all of its men were killed as well. 3rd Cell launched its assault and suffered heavy losses. The following cells continued to run up next to the vehicles, but they were unable to climb up onto the vehicles because the enemy vehicles were very tall and very slippery. When some of our men managed to climb up onto an enemy vehicle, they were killed or wounded by machinegun fire from the other enemy vehicles.[29]

Despite bitter fighting the assaulting Viet Cong infantry failed to annihilate the Marine holdouts. Men such as Sergeant James Mulloy, who personally shot down groups of Viet Cong from a rice paddy close to the ambushed column, held the VC at bay throughout the afternoon.[30] Five Marines died and several others were wounded, but most of the convoy survived the harrowing ordeal.[31] Viet Cong losses were decidedly heavier.

Annihilating the ambushed Marines would have been quite a coup for the 1st Viet Cong Regiment. Even so, the ambush on the eighteenth was hardly a failure. For openers, the ambush prevented the supply convoy from fulfilling its assigned mission of resupplying an inland Marine company. Marine relief forces, in fact, did not recover and withdraw the battered convoy until the following day, August 19. That achievement alone represents a measure of tactical success. Additionally, Company I, the unit to whom supplies were to be transported, ended up joining the search *for* the ambushed convoy later on in the day. And though of a purely speculative nature, it is not beyond the pale to presume that higher Viet Cong commands would have gladly exchanged the lives of sixty soldiers—the Marines counted sixty VC bodies on the battlefield—to interdict the resupply of an American combat unit in the field.[32]

Nevertheless, surmounting the combined arms proficiency of naval gunfire, air strikes, artillery, and tough Marine infantrymen in "stand up" conventional battle proved a bit much for the soldiers of the 1st Viet Cong regiment at Van Tuong. A harmonious integration of personnel, weapons platforms, and, at the macro level, armed branches, the American version of "combined arms" was, for the Viet Cong, a bit Byzantine. The Viet Cong understood war as a competition of soldiers in which "combined arms" meant employing mortars and machine guns in tandem, mortars and recoilless rifles in tandem, recoilless rifles and machine guns in tandem, and so on. Though undeniably accomplished in this more provincial definition of combined arms, the 1st Viet Cong Regiment and supporting forces had been defeated at Van Tuong by the American concept of combined arms.

By the early morning hours of August 19, the 1st Viet Cong Regiment had been put to flight and its base in the area temporarily "liberated." Communist forces lost a confirmed 614 dead over the duration of the Marine offensive (August 18–24), but it should not be forgotten that Communist units typically dragged away as many of their dead as possible after battle. This phenomenon might explain the elevated Viet Cong body count of 1,430 given by a Marine intelligence source in early September.[33] The Marines incurred 45 dead and 203 wounded.[34] "In the first major engagement between American and Main Force Viet Cong soldiers, the Americans had been victorious," announced historians Edward Doyle and Samuel Lipsman. "Had the Americans lost—a real possibility given their inexperience—the effects may have been severe indeed."[35]

Troops of the 1st Viet Cong Regiment, and those who fought with them at Van Tuong, were not the Communist Vietnamese supermen of postwar Western lore. They were, by any objective measure, soundly defeated. Yet in defeat, the 1st Viet Cong Regiment had also acquitted itself well. Its troops courageously defended trench lines, hills, and defensive positions at rifle point and for the most part did not cower in the presence of Marine tanks or Ontos.[36] Such resistance exposed many Marines to a heavy dose of combat sobriety about the nature of their opponents, particularly as the adrenaline of battle slowly receded. Communicating a bit of the begrudging admiration that would later become unspoken, Marine Brigadier General Frederick Karch said of the Viet Cong, "I thought that once they ran up against our first team they wouldn't stand and fight. I made a miscalculation."[37] Karch would not be the first or the last American to underestimate the professionalism of the elite Viet Cong units.

VAN TUONG: ONE BATTLE, TWO VICTORS, SEVERAL LESSONS

After the battle both the Marines and the Viet Cong claimed victory at Van Tuong. Starlite certainly raised the confidence of many young, inexperienced Marines and it reassured Marine brass that the latest generation of Leathernecks was cut from the same cloth as their predecessors. Alternatively the Viet Cong also felt reasonably good about having "stood up" to the Americans at Van Tuong. Communist Vietnamese histories of the battle, in fact, offer a different interpretation than those found in American histories of the war. And while the details differ slightly, depending upon the particular Vietnamese source in question, the theme of resounding victory at Van Tuong remains a constant in the Vietnamese accounts. One such source, for example, boasted:

> In one day of ferocious fighting, we had eliminated from the field of battle a total of 919 American troops, had knocked out 22 enemy vehicles and 13 helicopters, and had captured one M-14 rifle. Our victory at Van Tuong illustrated the incredibly heroic fighting spirit of our soldiers and the close coordination between our three types of troops [main force, local force, guerrillas], demonstrated the power of Vietnamese people's war, and marked the beginning of the modern war of aggression waged

by the American imperialists.... The American troops could not claim that they had lost the battle of Van Tuong because they had been taken by surprise. This was a battle in which the Americans were the ones who selected the battlefield, who chose the timing of the attack, and who held absolute superiority in both manpower and firepower, and yet they had been defeated. Our victory at Van Tuong strengthened and firmed up the confidence and the resolve of our soldiers and civilians throughout the country to fight the Americans and to defeat the Americans.[38]

Another, less verbose recap of the 1st Viet Cong Regiment's actions at Van Tuong proclaimed: "When American troops entered the battle, in spite of being outnumbered eight to one, the regiment completely defeated the first major operation by eight U.S. Marine battalions at Van Tuong (18 August 1965). This was the first battle against American forces to be fought by any of our main force units in South Vietnam, and it was also their first victory over the Americans."[39]

Politically inspired aggrandizement of the 1st Viet Cong Regiment's performance notwithstanding, the Viet Cong gained invaluable experience and insights from Van Tuong. First and perhaps foremost, the VC had learned firsthand the dimensions of American force projection capabilities. Prior to the battle the military command of the 1st Viet Cong Regiment had overestimated American dependence on overland travel. This misjudgment led to an inadequately conceived countersweep defensive plan: "Even though we had detected the enemy's planned operation ahead of time and had prepared a plan to counter the enemy operation, perhaps because the regiment was ready to move out of the area to carry out a new mission, the plan that we developed was too simplistic and *failed to anticipate the enemy's ability to conduct an amphibious landing operation from the sea* [emphasis added]."[40]

The same study continued: "The men who commanded this countersweep battle made an assessment of the enemy that was not in accordance with the realities of the battlefield. For instance, they concluded that the enemy's primary effort would be an attack mounted overland, but in fact the enemy's primary effort was helicopter assault landings combined with an amphibious assault from the sea. Because their assessment of the enemy was wrong, their battle plan was too simplistic: 'If the enemy conducts an air landing in any unit's area of responsibility, that unit will be the primary element for the fight against the enemy.'"[41] Such candor was not typically forthcoming in Communist Vietnamese postbattle analyses.

For the Americans some ominous portents of the big-unit campaign ahead also emerged from the fighting at Van Tuong. The Americans learned that the VC had already become somewhat acclimated to ground assaults via helicopter landing and on occasion allowed the first wave of American helicopters to land unmolested. Viet Cong units nearby would then subject the disembarked American infantry, particularly the follow-up forces attempting to land and reinforce the first wave, to a withering fusillade of automatic rifle, machine-gun, and RPG fire.[42] The premise behind the technique—pin down a numerically containable American force and decimate piecemeal the reinforcements—revealed a degree of basic tactical competency that augured well for the future growth and maturation of the Viet Cong as a big-unit fighting force. Company H (2/4), which had the misfortune of landing basically on top of the 60th Viet Cong Battalion, encountered this technique at LZ Blue. Without the aid of offshore naval gunfire, Company H may have found itself in a far more precarious predicament.

Countermeasures like the one used against Company H represented the tactical templates of VC/NVA antiairmobile doctrine. These templates were varied and frequently conditions dependent. When practicable and expedient, the VC/NVA would booby-trap American landing zones with poles, mines, *punji* pits, and trip devices to discourage landings, damage helicopters, and induce preparatory fires. The use of preparatory fires to ease the insertion of American airmobile troops frequently suppressed Communist fire at or near the landing zone but at a steep tactical price: preparatory fires telegraphed American intentions and forfeited the element of surprise. In other instances the VC/NVA would assail incoming enemy helicopters with concentrated small-arms fire from prepared positions around the landing zone. Mounting a close-in assault against just landed and temporarily disorganized American troops was another possibility. Nor were these tactics mutually exclusive in the sense that a close-in assault might *follow* concentrated fire against incoming enemy choppers.

If battlefield conditions called for engaging enemy airmobile troops following a landing and away from the LZ, the Viet Cong at times deployed an ambush force along routes leading to the locations enemy troops might select for an overnight defensive position. Assembly areas for attacks against these potential enemy night defensive positions (NDPs) were also identified and sometimes prepared beforehand.[43] Depending upon the availability of friendly forces, the Viet Cong could then use such an assembly area to facilitate a power raid against a nearby American NDP.

If the VC were aware of the general location of an American NDP but were unwilling for whatever reason to launch a power raid against it, they could instead set up the laagering Americans for future action by building fires and letting off bursts of automatic weapons fire, all from a comfortable distance away. Provoked by the sight of the smoke, the flames of the blaze, or the sound of enemy gunfire, the Americans would frequently reply with artillery fire and then search the area at first light. Expecting just such a reaction, the Viet Cong would booby-trap or place snipers along the routes American troops were most likely to travel when advancing the next morning.

Antiairmobile doctrine was also evolutionary. In September 1968, more than three years after Operation Starlite, the U.S. 9th Infantry Division obtained a letter from a higher VC headquarters to its subordinate regiments. The letter explored American airmobile tactical innovations and the possible responses to them, including the training and deployment of specific landing zone ambush squads. Austerely armed with three or four AK-47 assault rifles and one "automatic rifle," a Claymore mine, and a "sniping rifle," the landing zone ambush teams received the following instructions:

1. If the enemy drops his troops close to the edge of a village and the choppers have not quite landed, we will concentrate maximum firepower to destroy the enemy force immediately. The function of the sniping cell will be to shoot down the CP chopper.
2. If the enemy drops his troops away from the edge of the village, we will deploy in combat formations and wait for them. When they are three or four meters from our positions, we open fire.

3. If the enemy drops troops on our position, our efforts depend on the situation. After we have destroyed the enemy force and cleared the battlefield, we will move to another location 300–500 meters from the contact area and deploy again, ready to fight.[44]

To this day many American helicopter pilots profess wonderment not at the defenses they encountered on or over a landing zone but at how the Viet Cong and NVA were able to consistently and correctly deduce *which* LZs to defend. Robert Mason, who piloted a chopper for the 1st Cavalry Division, penned a memoir after the war in which he mused, "No one ever figured how the VC always knew which clearing we would use for an LZ. There were thousands of possibilities, but Charlie would almost always be waiting for us in the one we picked."[45]

Without overstating the actionable effect, Viet Cong agents and sympathizers within the South Vietnamese government certainly compromised some American military operations. That said, the VC/NVA also stressed field security and emphasized vigilance against the omnipresent threat of American airmobile operations. Patrols and other reconnaissance/security activities canvassed the terrain near VC/NVA base areas and pinpointed every potential American LZ and NDP. Armed with the aforementioned information, the VC/NVA could then decide whether to prepare ambush sites and assembly areas in relation to those locations. Routine patrolling and thorough LZ surveillance, moreover, established an adaptable and dependable early warning system. In sum the VC/NVA catalogued potential enemy LZs and NDPs around their bases and strongholds and conducted contingency planning in response to them. It can be safely assumed that these preparations greatly hastened Communist reaction time to American airmobile activity.

Equally elucidating for the Marines, Viet Cong resilience at Van Tuong despite punishing bombardment foreshadowed future battles in the big-unit war. Marine Sergeant Pat Finton recalled an episode in which an air strike on a village occupied by VC produced a surprising result. "By that time that A-4 would come around and make another pass and the VC would head on into their holes or whatever cover they had there in the village," Finton explained. "After the pass, the VC would come back out again and . . . try to get out of the village."[46]

Brigadier General (Ret.) James Timothy could certainly commiserate. While commanding the 1st Brigade, 101st Airborne Division in September 1965, the then-colonel Timothy watched a Viet Cong battalion operating in the An Khe area (Binh Dinh Province) withstand an inordinate amount of supporting arms punishment. "Despite massive artillery support and overwhelming air support furnished by the brigade, the 1st Cavalry Division, and air units from not only the USAF but also U.S. Navy offshore carriers (luckily we were the only 'show' in country during this battle)," wrote Timothy, "the VC hung in there for three days with no artillery support and little rocket support."[47] Timothy did not overstate the quantity of firepower committed against the Viet Cong force, either; American artillery expended some 11,000 rounds and dozens of tactical air strikes were flown in support of his paratroopers throughout the fierce fighting.[48]

Some attributed the Viet Cong's uncanny durability to a distinctly pedestrian source: good old-fashioned spade work. Remembering the visual effect of American firepower on VC forces embedded along the southern bank of the Kinh Tong Doc Loc canal in March 1969, Colonel David Hackworth nonetheless wondered about the *material* effect of that bombardment: "By 1700 hours, the tree line that ran parallel to the canal and concealed the enemy force started to look like it was hit by a tornado. But I'd learned the hard way how artillery fire and Tac Air could blow an area to smithereens with not a tree left standing—and still the VC or NVA would survive thanks to their amazing shovel-work and deep bunkers."[49]

Whether the result of exquisitely constructed defensive positions, the dissipating effects of terrain on firepower, sheer unadulterated luck, or some combination thereof, the ability of some Viet Cong units to endure the stupefying effects of American firepower only to fight on or escape unscathed made an indelible impression on the U.S. military.

6

An Ninh and the Ia Drang Valley

Composed, not exclusively but at its core, of veterans from the French battalion that had served in the Korean conflict, Groupement Mobile 100 (GM 100) entered service on November 15, 1953. A hard-hitting regimental task force, GM 100 was to solidify French defenses in the Central Highlands area of what would later become South Vietnam. Colonel Barrou's formation contained four truck-mounted infantry battalions, ten light tanks, and an artillery battalion.[1] The men themselves were well rested, equipped, and trained for battle.

In June 1954, after months of grinding attritional combat against the Viet Minh, Groupement Mobile 100 had been ordered to evacuate An Khe and retreat westward to Pleiku. That May, after the fall of Dien Bien Phu, the soldiers of GM 100 had heard the haunting taunts of a Communist loudspeaker. "Soldiers of Mobile Group 100," a sneering voice called out, "your friends in Dien Bien Phu have not been able to resist the victorious onslaught of the Viet-Nam People's Army! You are so much weaker than Dien Bien Phu! You will die Frenchmen, and so will your Vietnamese running-dogs!"[2] Shrugging off these crude attempts at psychological warfare, GM 100 began the evacuation at dawn on June 24. About ten miles to the west of An Khe, along Route 19 near Kilometer 15, the 803rd Viet Minh Regiment intercepted the French force. In the ensuing ambush, Ha Vi Tung's regiment all but annihilated the French force.[3]

Eleven years later, and exactly one month after the 1st Viet Cong Regiment's baptism of fire against Marine forces at Van Tuong, the 101st Airborne Division surprised elements of the 2nd Viet Cong Regiment north of Route 19 but to the east of Groupement Mobile 100's grim ordeal. Though not a battle of annihilation, the resulting engagement at An Ninh would be significant in that it was the first for the 2nd Viet Cong Regiment and its parent formation, the 3rd NVA Division, against the American "expeditionary army."

Hailed as "the soul" of the 3rd NVA Division, the 2nd Viet Cong Regiment was created in May 1962.[4] As such the unit became Military Region 5's first main-force regiment.[5] Thereafter the Military Region Party Current Affairs Committee incorporated the 2nd Viet Cong Regiment into the newly formed 3rd NVA Division, otherwise known as the "Yellow Star" Division (Su Doan Sao Vang). A history of the division written after the war recounted its formation:

> Conditions were ripe to form main force divisions in Region 5. On 9 August 1965 the Military Region Party Current Affairs Committee met and issued a resolution on forming the following main force divisions:
> - 2nd Division, consisting of the 1st and 21st Infantry Regiments plus a number of supporting battalions subordinate to division headquarters;
> - 3rd Division, consisting of the 2nd, 12th, and 22nd Infantry Regiments, one artillery/mortar battalion, one 12.7-mm anti-aircraft machinegun battalion, one combat engineer battalion, one signal battalion, and one reconnaissance company.
>
> 2nd Division would be responsible for the Military Region's primary battle area, from northern Quang Ngai province up to Quang Nam province. 3rd Division's primary area of operations would be southern Quang Ngai and Binh Dinh provinces.[6]

Despite the August resolution, the 3rd NVA Division, and correspondingly the 2nd Viet Cong Regiment's part therein, was not officially created until September 2, 1965 (Vietnam's National Day). The 2nd NVA Division, meanwhile, was officially formed on October 20, 1965. Formally established on December 20, 1965, weeks after the founding of the 2nd and 3rd NVA Divisions, the 1st NVA Division consisted of the veteran 33rd, 66th, and 320th NVA Regiments. All three regiments had taken part in the October–November (1965) Plei Me campaign, a campaign that included the famous Ia Drang Valley battle against the U.S. 1st Cavalry Division.[7] Hanoi appointed two northerners, Nguyen Huu An, who had infiltrated South Vietnam as commanding officer of the 325th Division in 1965, and Nguyen Nang, a veteran of the Dien Bien Phu campaign, as commanders of the newly formed 1st and 2nd NVA Divisions, respectively. Fellow northerner Giap Van Cuong, a native of Ha Bac Province and onetime commander of the 324th Division, became the first commander of the 3rd NVA Division.[8]

Although Cuong's 3rd NVA Division operated primarily in southern Quang Ngai Province and Binh Dinh Province, the 2nd Viet Cong Regiment served in Quang Ngai, Binh Dinh, and Kontum Provinces. The regiment had an initial strength of four infantry battalions (20th, 80th, 90th, and 95th), one artillery/mortar battalion, and one sapper company.[9] Between August 1963 and late 1964, however, three battalions—the 20th, 80th, and 90th—were detached from the regiment and subordinated to the provinces of Quang Nam (90th Battalion) and Quang Ngai (20th and 80th Battalions). But regimental reorganization did not end there. In May 1964 the 93rd and 97th Battalions infiltrated South Vietnam to reinforce the regiment. These two formations, along with the 95th, comprised the three infantry battalions of the 2nd Viet Cong Regiment in September 1965.[10]

Created only weeks before, the 3rd NVA Division began redeploying for battle in mid-September. The movement of divisional forces, the upcoming mission, and the anticipated adversary were clearly articulated in the division history:

> In mid-September [1965], the Yellow Star Division and its attached reinforcing units were ordered to shift gradually toward the area of operations. Columns of soldiers moved through the night. 2nd Regiment moved from Vinh Thanh across the Bo Bo Pass and past Phu Cat and Binh Khe. 22nd Regiment moved from southern Quang Ngai into west-

ern Hoai Nhon district. 12th Regiment shifted from Hoai An down to Phu My. The [Binh Dinh] province 50th and 52nd Local Force Battalions moved from the coast up close to Route 1. A battle posture more than 50 kilometers long took shape stretching from north of Bong Son to south of Phu Cat....

According to the plan that had been carefully and thoroughly discussed, before the Military Region's Winter Campaign began, the Yellow Star Division would launch a wave of attacks against puppet army traffic along Route 1 between Bong Son and Phu Cat. Province local force units would operate from southern Phu Cat district down toward the south. Their mission was to lure the forces of the puppet 22nd Division away from the area that would be the focal point of our attacks. District local force troops and village militia would help the masses surround and besiege the Bong Son district capital, the Military Headquarters at Go Boi (Tuy Phuoc), and the Phu My district capital. During the Winger Campaign the division would move up into southern Quang Ngai province to destroy enemy forces at Mo Duc and Duc Pho, cut Route 1, and then attack and annihilate enemy relief forces. This meant that the primary battlefield opponent of the Yellow Star Division during this period would be puppet regular army units, not U.S. troops.[11]

For Do Phu Dap's 2nd Viet Cong Regiment, the primary battlefield opponent that September turned out to be American, and not South Vietnamese, troops. In September the 1st Brigade of the 101st Airborne Division captured a soldier from the 95th Viet Cong Battalion. The 1st Brigade had been engaged in road security on Route 19, and sweeps to the north and south of the thoroughfare, when it captured the soldier. These road and sweep actions fell within the framework of Operation Highland, a multiphased operation to secure An Khe and open Route 19 from Qui Nhon to An Khe in anticipation of the 1st Cavalry Division basing at the latter. While in custody, the Viet Cong prisoner revealed the location of the 95th.[12] Though only skirmishes with small Communist forces had occurred to that point, the prisoner's intelligence placed a worthwhile target, Commander Luong Van Thu's battalion, in the mountainous terrain east of An Khe and to the north of Route 19.

Regrettably it is not immediately clear what the exact troop strength and firepower capability of the 95th Viet Cong Battalion was in September 1965. Clues of what they may have been, on the other hand, can be gleaned from estimates and captured documents. As of December 1966 intelligence materials indicated that the 95th consisted of approximately 350 men. With respect to weaponry, the battalion possessed one 82-mm mortar, three 60-mm mortars, three 57-mm recoilless rifles, light machine guns, and automatic rifles. Unit personnel were said to have been wearing yellow uniforms. Obviously none of this can be applied arbitrarily to the 95th Viet Cong Battalion of September 18, 1965, to say nothing of the 94th and 97th Viet Cong Battalions. Refitting and rearmament undoubtedly occurred in the 95th over the intervening months. In any event the intelligence report provides an inkling as to what the battalion *might* have looked like in an earlier period.

Ignorant as well with regard to the exact strength and composition of the 95th, Colonel James Timothy, commander of the 1st Brigade, 101st Airborne Division, was nevertheless convinced of the need to act and he directed his forces to remove the potential threat. Under the code name Gibralter, three rifle companies from the 2nd Battalion/502nd Regiment and an attached ARVN Ranger company would stage a heliborne assault east of the suspected location of the 95th Viet Cong Battalion. The assault, which was to take place near the hamlet of An Ninh, would precede a move west against the enemy force. Meanwhile, Task Force Mark, so named after its commanding officer Major Mark Hanson, would advance north from Route 19 to a position west of the 95th before turning east to attack the VC battalion. Hanson's combined-arms force was composed of Company A, 2nd Battalion/327th Infantry Regiment, Troop A, 1st Battalion/17th Cavalry Regiment, B and C Batteries, 2nd Battalion/320th Artillery Regiment, and tanks from the 2nd Battalion/7th Marine Regiment.[13]

Almost from its inception, Operation Gibraltar ran into difficulties. First, nature refused to cooperate. Muddy trails, some virtually impassable to mechanized forces, slowed the advance of Task Force Mark up the narrow valley toward the An Ninh area to a crawl on the morning of September 18. Vehicles sank and had to be hoisted up out of the mud. Operational timetables could not be kept, and frustration levels rose in proportion to the difficulties. Northwest of An Ninh, on a 110-by-400-meter landing zone, the trouble was manmade. Company C, the vanguard of Lieutenant Colonel W. K. G. Smith's jump force, landed on schedule shortly after 7:00 AM. Once on the ground, the 138 men of Captain Robert E. Rawls' company initially noticed only hastily vacated campsites and fleeing Viet Cong troops. Enemy fire was sporadic and light. But the situation would change rather quickly, for Rawls and his men had combat assaulted into a basing area for the 95th Viet Cong Battalion.[14]

Petitioning his regimental commander for permission to postpone the training exercises planned for September 18, Thu, the commander of the 95th, ordered his companies into defensive positions to oppose the enemy air assault. Peering out from their battle positions, Thu's men speculated about the nationality of the troops spilling out of the enemy helicopters. Were they Korean? Were they American? Suddenly the mystery was solved. The troops were American. The 95th had only arrived at the hamlet a mere three days before and were not expecting to fight American forces so soon. Thu's battalion was not alone. The 3rd NVA Division supposed that the Americans would intercede on behalf of the South Vietnamese after the latter had "suffered a painful blow" along Route 1, and only after that did the division expect to do battle with American forces for the very first time. Rather than postpone the first engagement against American troops, however, the Yellow Star Division elected to stand and fight:

> At 8:30 that morning the division headquarters command post received a radio message from 2nd Regiment that said, "2nd Battalion is now fighting American troops at Thuan Ninh." Many questions were raised in the division headquarters. Why had the Americans sent their troops out into battle so soon? . . . After discussion and analysis, the division command group concluded that this was only a lightning-quick raid launched by the Air Cavalry Division in response to some slip-up made by 2nd Battalion. The goal of this raid, the command group concluded, was to protect the right flank of the American troop columns moving up to An Khe. However, no matter what this clash really was, this was the division's best opportunity to deal a powerful initial blow to the American army. The command group decided that we had to concentrate our guidance

and leadership to win this battle—to win a clear and convincing victory. And from this battle we might be able to learn many lessons for use in our future operations.[15]

Luong Van Thu and his 95th Viet Cong Battalion may not have been fighting the "Air Cavalry Division," as surmised at division, but the message resonated just the same. Composed in spite of the unanticipated American air assault, Thu telephoned his subordinates and said, "Stay calm and let them get up close before you open fire."[16] A glut of small-arms, machine-gun, and mortar fire soon engulfed the American paratroopers. "The Viet Cong began pouring deadly fire into us," said an American veteran of the battle. "I jumped into a hole with two of our troops who were firing up a storm. Next thing I knew the guy beside me had been hit right above the left eye. It almost tore his head off and killed him instantly. Before I recovered from that, the guy on my left yelled that he had been hit in the arm."[17] The troops of the 95th had heeded the call to action.

American reinforcements were to have arrived with the second airlift, slated for 7:30 AM, but extraordinarily intense Viet Cong fire prompted Lieutenant Colonel Smith, the commanding officer on the ground, to wave off the rest of the helicopters. As a result only the battalion tactical command group and two platoons from Company B succeeded in landing.[18] Some VC had originally dispersed in confusion, but they were now rapidly regrouping into platoon- and company-sized elements.

The aborted second airlift to the An Ninh landing zone illustrates the effectiveness of Viet Cong antiairmobile activity on September 18. Throughout the day Viet Cong fire would down or damage a total of twenty-six American helicopters.[19] Some of the credit for this impressive tally can be attributed to a vigilant antiairmobile mindset, extensive antiairmobile training, and to the leadership of Luong Van Thu. Home-field advantage figured into the equation as well. During the engagement, American forces collared a Viet Cong prisoner who confessed that the 95th Viet Cong Battalion had trained for antiairmobile operations on the very landing zone upon which the paratroopers had landed that morning.[20]

Back on and around the An Ninh landing zone, the seesaw struggle for survival continued. At approximately 7:50 AM, a Viet Cong machine gun opened fire unexpectedly, killing Captain Rawls and his forward observer, Lieutenant Ed Fox. Rawls had led a small group south along a trail and had been ordering his 3rd Platoon to deploy in a rice paddy southeast of the landing zone when he was fatally wounded. Later in the morning, stiffening Viet Cong resistance pressured elements of the 3rd Platoon. Second Lieutenant George Carter, Rawls' 3rd Platoon commander, tried to shepherd his unit back up the trail leading from the southeastern sector of the landing zone, but VC machine-gun and small-arms fire from the east and west separated Carter and the company command group from the platoon. The Viet Cong had now killed the Company C commander and pared a section of Carter's 3rd Platoon from the main American body.

West of Carter Viet Cong forces warded off an attack by Company C's weapons platoon. Operating near the southwest corner area of the LZ, the weapons platoon had attacked across a hill south of the landing zone to silence a Viet Cong machine gun and mortar emplacement. The Viet Cong answered with a shower of defensive fire that killed one paratrooper. Unable to liquidate the nettlesome Viet Cong stronghold, 1st Lieutenant Gerald Nakashima's platoon retreated back to the relative safety of the LZ. Viet Cong defenders in this sector, like their comrades to the east, had contained the American perimeter.

High drama unfolded elsewhere as well. Sometime after 8:30 AM, Viet Cong forces occupied positions atop a hill to the east of the landing zone. Previously Company C's 1st Platoon had moved onto the slope of the same hill. Now a mere fifteen meters separated the belligerents.[21] Platoon Sergeant Ezra Vaughen summarized the encounter that followed: "They were waiting for us on the hill and dug in. They were wearing a kind of camouflage poncho liner and hard to see. When we got near the top of the hill, a whistle signal blew and they really opened up. I also could see at least 20 of them throwing grenades. We had to pull back."[22] Under intense fire the 1st Platoon redeployed to a rice paddy dike at the base of the hill.

At 9:40 AM Major Hebert Dexter, the operations officer for the 2nd/502nd, spearheaded an assault to seize the hill. Dug-in VC machine-gunned the advancing paratroopers, killing Major Dexter, but the assault carried the hill. Some time afterward, troopers from the 3rd Platoon, Company B spotted Viet

Cong camouflaged as bushes descending down the opposite side of the hill. In Operation Starlite, this camouflage technique had been used to conceal troops approaching for an attack; at An Ninh it masked a withdrawal.

Thirty-six minutes before Dexter's hill assault, F-100 Super Sabres blasted Viet Cong positions in the first of many air strikes to be delivered on the eighteenth.[23] The close tactical air support accidentally killed two paratroopers during the fighting, but without it the entire 224-man force under Smith's command may have been destroyed à la Groupement Mobile 100, outnumbered and surrounded as the Americans were. Yet jet aircraft were not the only American aviation assets to lend a hand to the beleaguered paratroopers. At about 9:20 AM, lift helicopters dropped eight men from Company A and twenty-eight men from Company B off at a landing zone eight hundred meters south of the landing zone at An Ninh. Isolated from one another until noontime, and thus powerless to relieve Smith, the two groups of airlifted paratroopers from Company A and B still tied down enemy forces and fended off three large Viet Cong attacks. If not for this dogged resistance, the attacking VC forces might have massed against the primary American LZ. In addition to transporting the aforementioned troops, American helicopters also inserted an artillery battery opposite An Ninh early that evening. Firing from the word go, the guns brought much needed fire to bear on Viet Cong forces assailing the original landing site.

A ninety-minute window (7:30–9:00 AM) in which to operate without fear of much American tactical air support or artillery fire had presented the 95th Viet Cong Battalion with a golden opportunity to annihilate an American force. Despite the temporary absence of American supporting arms, not to mention a pronounced familiarity with the battlefield, Luong Van Thu's battalion could not wipe out the paratroopers of the 101st. By the evening of September 18, an American–South Vietnamese relief task force had choppered to a landing zone east of An Ninh. All the while, the gunners of the American artillery battery continued to rain death and destruction on the VC. Fighting subsided as the night wore on, and come the following day, September 19, the Viet Cong had for the most part exfiltrated the immediate area. An estimated 226 to 257 Viet Cong soldiers were killed in the engagement. On the American side, 13 paratroopers were killed and 28 were wounded.[24]

After the battle Lieutenant Colonel Smith praised the cadre and soldiers of the 2nd Viet Cong Regiment. "The Viet Cong," Smith said to a *New York Times* reporter, "fought well and were exceptionally well led."[25] Smith also signed his name to an after-action report (AAR) that elaborated on his pithy description to the *Times*: "The enemy was well trained. Enemy tactics included assault line formations and coordinated attacks. Whistles and bugles were used for signal and control during enemy assaults. Enemy command control and discipline were excellent. On several occasions, the enemy advanced aggressively in the open, under the control of small unit leaders. . . . The 2d Bn (Abn), 502nd Infantry, was opposed by a well organized, highly trained, experienced, and well equipped enemy."[26] Smith's men doubtlessly agreed; the 2nd Viet Cong Regiment, 3rd NVA Division had fought well in its first major battle with American forces, particularly since the regiment had not envisioned an encounter at such an early juncture.

Praise must be extended to the 2nd Battalion, 502nd Regiment of the 101st Airborne Division as well. Outnumbered, surrounded, and forced to fight on the enemy's home turf, the paratroopers persevered brilliantly and denied the Viet Cong victory over a highly vulnerable American force. President Lyndon Johnson honored the paratroopers' sacrifice and skill in the Spring of 1967, awarding the 2nd Battalion/502nd Regiment the Presidential Unit Citation for heroism during the engagement.[27] As one Viet Cong private later acknowledged, fighting the Screaming Eagles, the well-deserved nickname of the 101st, was "not exactly easy."[28]

Miles to the west of An Ninh, in the heart of the rugged Central Highlands, Viet Cong forces fought in a battle of arguably greater historical import in the fall of 1965. Habitually touted as the debut of North Vietnamese Army regulars against American ground troops, the momentous battle in the Ia Drang Valley in November involved NVA *and* Viet Cong forces. The H-15 Battalion, a local VC unit from the Highlands, carried out "coordination" activities on behalf of the NVA units engrossed in the epic clash and later contributed troops to a ferocious early morning assault.

In the fall of 1965, the Communist B3 (Central Highlands) Front, the command to which the H-15 Battalion was ultimately subordinate, was expected to launch a major offensive. MACV worried, and with good reason, that a

Communist offensive from the Central Highlands region might drive down Route 19 to the coast and effectively split South Vietnam in half. As recently as July, and prior to various road-opening operations, links between the Highlands and the coast had to be preserved by air. Communist units, it was feared, might also launch attacks and establish an "autonomous district" in the Central Highlands, or simply engage and damage the ARVN as a means of facilitating the fall of the South Vietnamese government.[29]

North Vietnamese accounts of the campaign, however, insist that the attack plan was strictly an attempt to lure South Vietnamese and American forces into a fight on terms favorable to Communist forces. Rather than *liberate* an area in the Highlands, the Communist plan purportedly changed to launching the Plei Me campaign under the command of Major General Chu Huy Man.[30] North Vietnamese planners imagined each action as a distinct but interrelated phase of the upcoming campaign. In Phase I the 33rd NVA Regiment would attack and encircle the Plei Me Special Forces camp, setting the stage for the 320th NVA Regiment to ambush and destroy the expected ARVN relief force. Phase II sought to induce an American military response by prolonging the siege of the camp. Baited by an extended siege, the Americans would intervene, at which point a handful of American companies would be destroyed in the third and final phase. "First we attack Plei Me, then the ARVN reinforcements come into our ambush," General Man said after the war. "Then, I was confident, the Americans will use their helicopters to land in our rear, land in the Ia Drang area. It was our intention to draw the Americans out of An Khe. We did not have any plans to liberate the land; only to destroy troops."[31] Man remembered the events candidly inasmuch as the plan had changed, but neither the location nor the timing of the battle to destroy American troops would coincide with the new plan.

On the night of October 19, the North Vietnamese campaign commenced with Phase I. The 33rd NVA Regiment obligingly besieged Plei Me Special Forces Camp, and though it expected some enemy air activity, it endured extraordinarily punishing American air strikes in retaliation. Four days later, Major Ma Van Minh's 320th NVA Regiment ambushed a South Vietnamese relief column as planned. Minh, too, felt the sting of unremitting American airpower, however. Dismayed, and with the arrival of 1st Cavalry Division elements at Pleiku, Major General Chu Huy Man, the commander of the B3 Front, ordered a retreat on October 26.[32]

Over the next two weeks or so, Major General Harry O. Kinnard's 1st Cavalry Division harried the withdrawing NVA troops. Then, on the morning of November 14, choppers from the 229th Assault Helicopter Battalion unloaded Lieutenant Colonel Hal Moore and the lead elements of his 1st Battalion, 7th Cavalry Regiment into a small valley clearing east of Cambodia near a border-straddling mountainous outcropping called the Chu Pong Massif. "Here is your area of operations—north of Chu Pong in the Ia Drang Valley," 3rd Brigade commander, Colonel Thomas W. Brown, had told Moore the day before. "Your mission is the same one you have now: Find and kill the enemy."[33] Moore would not have far to look.

Presumably General Man's forces had been cognizant of, and primed for, the arrival of the 1st Cavalry Division in the Ia Drang Valley. Senior Lieutenant Colonel Nguyen Huu declared that Communist forces "were ready, had prepared for you [Americans] and expected you to come."[34] In reality Moore had achieved almost complete tactical surprise when he landed at LZ X-Ray, the official code name of the clearing Moore had selected for his assault landing. General Man had hoped to catch American troops out in the open in the flatlands of the valley, not below a ridge on which some of his own forces had gathered.[35] The timing of Moore's arrival was equally upsetting. Commanders from Man's nearest unit, the 9th Battalion/66th NVA Regiment, were not even at their posts when the first American helicopters landed.[36] If they had been, as Huu was, they would have been an eyewitness to the unit-crippling tube and aerial firepower being visited upon the 9th Battalion.

Spurred on by the personal initiative of lower level officers, the 9th Battalion regrouped and resisted tenaciously. Out among the gargantuan termite hills, tangled scrub brush, truncated hardwoods, and elephant grass near LZ X-Ray, North Vietnamese troops engaged the American air cavalrymen in furious firefights punctuated by an ever escalating crescendo of exploding American bombs and artillery shells. "All of a sudden the fire became heavier and heavier and the perimeter just seemed to erupt into a melee of constant fire," Sergeant George Nye exclaimed, drawing on memories of that fateful November day.[37] Landing Zone X-Ray and its immediate environs would see some of the most savage fighting of the entire war on the afternoon of November 14.

But for the raw gallantry and combat skill of Moore's men, not to mention the yeoman efforts of American supporting arms, the American position at LZ X-Ray might have become untenable. As it was North Vietnamese forces and the Viet Cong H-15 Battalion offered Moore's exhausted troopers little respite. Shortly before 7:00 AM on the following morning, November 15, two companies of North Vietnamese infantry from the 7th Battalion, 66th Regiment along with troops from the 9th Battalion slammed into the sector of the X-Ray perimeter defended by Company C. Twenty-five minutes after that, the H-15 Battalion assaulted elements of Company C's left flank neighbor, Lieutenant Larry Litton's dug-in Delta Company (Company D). NVA lieutenant colonel Hoang Phuong's postwar interviews help reconstruct the morning attack: "We had planned to launch our attack at two A.M., but because of air strikes and part of the battalion getting lost, it was delayed until 6:30 A.M. The attack was carried out by the 7th Battalion of the 66th Regiment. The H-15 Main Force Battalion, a local-force Viet Cong unit, was also in that attack."[38]

Staged by an estimated two companies of the H-15 Battalion and very likely groups of NVA, the 7:15 attempt to overrun Delta Company touched off a chaotic and ultimately uneven affair.[39] Specialist Will Parish, who had been attached to Delta, remembers well the scores of enemy soldiers materializing before him. "Have you ever seen those time lapse movies, you know, the ones from Disney or whatever where they show the flower coming out of the ground?" Parish asked. "Well, that's about the best way I can describe it. They [VC/NVA] were just growing out of the weeds out there in front of my hole. And they just kept on coming. At one point I said, 'Will they ever run out of men?'"

North Vietnamese troops and those of the H-15 Battalion, the latter clothed in black pajamas, were pressing home the attack when Delta's powerful M-60 machine guns began to bark. "Now, I didn't remember seeing those black pajama guys, what we called the VC," Parish confided, "but I remember when we were all watching the Mel Gibson movie, *We Were Soldiers*, the guy next to me said, 'Oh yeah, they were there.'"[40] And so were Parish and a few others, behind the barrels of M-60 machine guns. Arrayed across seventy five yards of defensive frontage, the American M-60s loosed a torrent of fire on the attackers while M-79 grenade launchers spewed deadly 40-mm projectiles. Before long VC and NVA dead littered the battlefield. The Communist attack collapsed by 10:00 AM.[41]

Regardless of the failed morning attack, Hanoi, perhaps with the ambush of other 1st Cavalry Division elements around LZ Albany on November 17 in mind, considered the fighting in the Ia Drang Valley to be a success overall. General Thanh concurred and he extolled the veterans of the Ia Drang battle in a message announcing, "The Army Achievement Medal, First Class is our Army's highest award. Therefore, to truly reflect the value of this battle, the Central Military Party Committee has awarded TWO Army Achievement Medals, First Class, to the Plei Me–Ia Drang Battle." COSVN thought highly of the VC/NVA performance as well.[42]

Additional fighting lay ahead for the Viet Cong H-15 Battalion. In January 1967 elements of the battalion assaulted Camp Holloway, a major American air and supply facility near Pleiku. Also that year, the battalion received the mission of interfering with road traffic while deployed south of Route 19 in the vicinity of the Song Ba River. Subsequently the H-15 participated in the 1968 Tet Offensive, launching an assault along with other Communist military units against the town of Pleiku.

7

The B2 Front

The molding of men into military leaders takes time, training, and hard-earned battlefield experience. General Tran Van Tra, commander of COSVN Military Headquarters, knew well the personnel and professional costs of reaching the pinnacle of man's most savage intellectual exercise: the management of a military command in war. Tra had cut his teeth in the war against the French and in 1954 had commanded Communist "regrouping forces during the move to North Vietnam."[1] He had served as the deputy commander of the NVA General Staff and had visited the Soviet Union for military study. Furthermore, he was an ardent and ambitious revolutionary.

Assigned as General Thanh had been to South Vietnam, Tra went on to command the all important B2 Front. Under the auspices of COSVN, the B2 Front managed Communist forces in the southern half of South Vietnam. Tra's front also contained a number of military regions. North of the B2 Front, in the northern half of South Vietnam, Hanoi established and administrated Region 5. In July 1965 Region 5 had three subordinate military commands, the B1 Front, the B3 Front (encompassing the Central Highlands area of South Vietnam), and the Southern Sector, carved out of the southernmost sections of the old B1 Front.[2]

Extending as it did over the eastern jutting southern half of South Vietnam, the B2 Front was rather expansive and thickly populated. It was, moreover, home to the Saigon area, the politico-military heart and burgeoning logistical hub of the enemy. General Tra addressed the location and significance of the B2 Front:

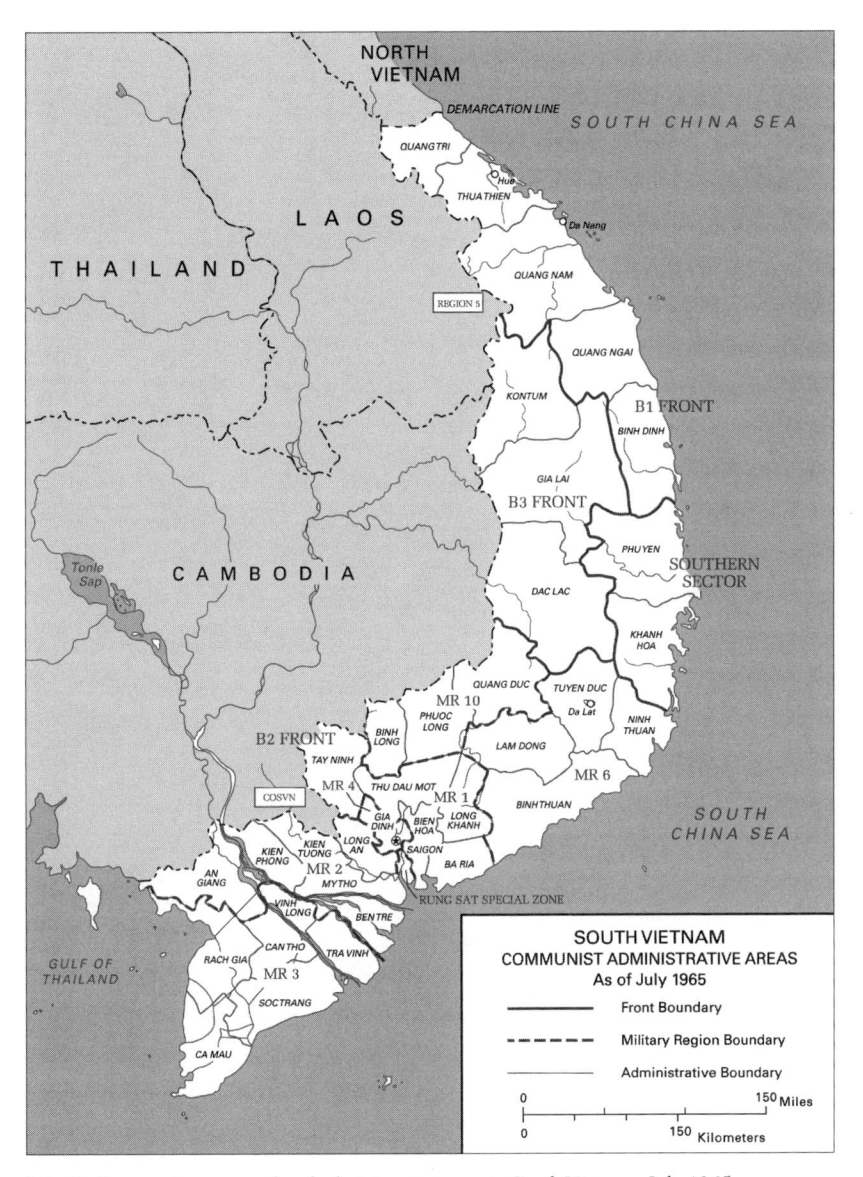

Map 3. Communist command and administrative areas in South Vietnam, July 1965
(From Carland, *United States Army in Vietnam*)

B2 was the code name of the land and people in the southernmost part of the homeland during the anti-U.S. war period. . . . Saigon, the capital of the lackey puppet administration, the largest city—at one time it had a population of 4 million—and the political, military, and economic center of South Vietnam, was situated in the center of the B2 theater and, along with many other large cities such as Da Lat, Phan Thiet, Bien Hoa, Tay Ninh, My Tho, Vinh Long, Can Tho, Ca Mau, and Rach Gia, formed a system of bases from which the U.S.-puppet operations were launched in all directions. It was also the center for the application of the neocolonial policy, a place where the debauched American lifestyle flourished, and a place which consumed American goods and served the large expeditionary armies and the lackey forces. The United States and its puppets organized South Vietnam into four tactical Zones. The area south of the Ben Hai River was Military Region I and the Mekong Delta corresponded to Military Region IV. Saigon, situated in the middle of Military Region III, was organized into the Capital Special Zone and was the command headquarters and the center of the U.S.-puppet war apparatus.[3]

In addition to its military and political importance, the B2 Front displayed a landscape that could scarcely have been more diverse. Rubber plantations and rich, verdant jungles occupied appreciable territory northeast and northwest of Saigon. In some of the suburbs of the South Vietnamese capital, fruit orchards and pineapple fields grew under the tropical sun. Venturing farther south, to the Mekong Delta area, rivers large and small crisscrossed rice paddies and flatlands. Mountains reached for the sky above dew-glistened pine forests far to the north and east in Tuyen Duc Province. Natural beauty, like the waterfalls near Da Lat, abounded throughout the B2 Front.

So did Communist strongholds. During the previous Indochina War, the French partitioned the area around Saigon into four quadrants. Using Saigon as a reference point, a line running north to south—Route 13, for all practical purposes on the ground—was traced through the city northward to the Cambodian border. The French called the territory that fell west of the line and north of Saigon War Zone C and called the area that lay east of the line and north of Saigon War Zone D. War Zones A and B covered the regions south of Saigon.[4] Heavily vegetated and sparsely inhabited, War Zone C, or what the Communist Vietnamese called the Duong Minh Chau War Zone, along with War Zone D, were centers of Viet Minh organization and resistance. Following in their predecessors' footsteps, the Viet Cong based and organized in both zones during the war against the Americans.

Over the period of American military involvement in Vietnam, War Zones C and D exhibited "flexible boundaries," although generally speaking, War Zone C was located in the northern region of Tay Ninh Province. War Zone D, meanwhile, was located to the north of the Bien Hoa Province capital.[5] Inhospitable terrain discouraged enemy penetration of these strongholds, and the Viet Cong made a point of fortifying them to accentuate the existing natural deterrents. Detailed descriptions of the history and locations of both zones can be found in Communist Vietnamese literature. One source, published in the mid-1990s, described War Zone C at length:

> Duong Minh Chau War Zone [Chien Khu Duong Minh Chau]: Used during the Vietnamese people's resistance wars against the French and against the Americans. It was located in the mountain jungles of northern Tay Ninh in Eastern Cochin China. The Duong Minh Chau War Zone covered an area of approximately 1500 square kilometers, bordered on the east by the Saigon River, on the west by the Vam Co Dong River, on the south by Route 13, and on the north by the Vietnamese-Cambodian border. The war zone was formed during the early days of the resistance war against the French, and it was the base area of the Cochin China Party Committee and the Eastern Cochin China Sub-Interzone [Phan Lien Khu Mien Dong]. During the resistance war against the Americans, it was developed into a base area organization of Tay Ninh province and was divided into many combat areas (which were called "districts," "villages," and "hamlets"). Many of the South Vietnamese revolution's most important headquarters agencies were located there, including COSVN, the Central Committee of the National Liberation Front, the COSVN Military Party Committee, the COSVN Military Headquarters, Liberation Radio, etc. It was a node on our strategic supply line from North

Vietnam into Cochin China and was the site where our first main force regiment was formed during the resistance war against the Americans.

As to the location, history, and role of War Zone D, the same resource read:

War Zone D [Chien Khu D]: A war zone in Eastern Cochin China during the Vietnamese people's wars against the French and against the Americans. It was formed in early 1946 and at that time was made up of five villages (Tan Hoa, My Loc, Tan Tich, Thuong Lang, and Lac An) in Tan Uyen District, Bien Hoa Province. Initially it was called the Dat Cuoc War Zone or the Lac An War Zone. Beginning in 1948 it began to expand and became the base area for many Party, government, mass organization, and armed forces headquarters of many districts of Bien Hoa and Thu Dau Mot provinces as well as of the headquarters of Region 7, the Eastern Sub-Inter-Zone, and of all of Cochin China. During the resistance war against the Americans, the center of the war zone gradually shifted to the northeast. . . . It was a node in the strategic transportation corridor from the Center [North Vietnam] to Cochin China. It was the base area for Party, government, NLF, and armed forces units and headquarters of Eastern Cochin China, from the district level up through province and Military Region, right up to the Central Office of South Vietnam. It was a location where Liberation Army and Eastern Cochin China main force units were formed and that they used as a springboard for their attacks and as their direct rear area. It was a local logistics base for Cochin China and for Region 6.[6]

War Zones C and D, despite their size and infrastructural importance, were not the only Viet Cong strongholds within the B2 Front. Located just 20–25 kilometers north of Saigon, under the very nose of the senior-most American command in Vietnam, U.S. Headquarters, MACV, the Iron Triangle consisted of a triangularly shaped, heavily fortified redoubt loosely framed by the Thi Tinh River to the east, the Saigon River on the southwest, and on the north by a line moving westward from "Ben Cat to the town of Ben Suc on the Saigon River."[7] The Iron Triangle, much like War Zones C and D, had been an area of Viet Minh resistance against French colonial rule. In the campaign against the Americans, the triangle was an important Communist logistical and organizational node, and reputedly the location of the B2 Front's Military Region 4 Headquarters.

Forests, wet rice lands, and VC-mined and -booby-trapped approach routes deterred enemy intrusion into the Iron Triangle. Inside the triangle, the terrain was honeycombed with tunnels. Some of these underground labyrinths stretched for several hundred meters or more and housed medical, supply, and other facilities. Approximately twenty-five kilometers north of the triangle, in an equally forbidding terrain of marshes and jungle, Communist forces maintained another stronghold, the Long Nguyen Secret Zone. The zone, which was located west of Route 13, sat astride a Communist "infiltration and supply corridor" between War Zone C and War Zone D.[8]

Accompanying the various strongholds north of Saigon were two Viet Cong divisions. Of the two the 9th Viet Cong Division was formed first. Code named Da Chien (Field) or Cong Truong 9 (Work Site 9) and formally established on September 2, 1965, the 9th fielded three infantry regiments: the 271st, 272nd, and 273rd. The division, dubbed a "mobile main-force division" at its announcement ceremony in a forest near the Nhung Stream, also contained a host of "combat arms," logistics, and service units in both company and battalion strength. Additionally each regiment possessed an "Assault Youth" company, whose duties entailed evacuating wounded soldiers and carrying rice and ammunition.[9]

The consolidation of the 271st, 272nd, and 273rd Viet Cong Regiments under a unified divisional command was regaled by the Communist Vietnamese as a "new turning point":

> Although they [the 9th Viet Cong Division's regiments] had achieved major successes in the Binh Gia and Dong Xoai Campaigns and had gained initial experience in applying mobile ambush and mobile raid tactics, their skill at attacking strongholds had remained poor. The founding of the Division was a new turning point. In the past, its units had been scattered, had operated in familiar localities, had been brought together periodically in specific campaigns, and had fought only when victory

was certain and conditions were favorable. But from now on the division would have to engage mainly in mobile warfare, in order to fight continually and attack enemy strongholds with both its tactical and organizational strengths, using a force composed of several combat-arms elements.[10]

To satisfy its manpower requirements, the 9th Viet Cong Division drew on locals, regrouped southerners, and native northerners. The definitive history of the division, Su Doan 9, took pains to recognize this diversity: "Serving in the ranks of the 9th Division were cadres and combatants from all parts of the country. Many cadres born in the South or familiar with the southern theater had been organized into main-force regiments in the North and then dispatched to the southern theater. There were young people who, driven by their hatred for the U.S.-puppet clique, had grown up in the concerted uprising movements in their localities and then joined the Liberation Army. There were also cadres who had set foot on the land of eastern Nam Bo for the first time."[11] And while only the men themselves can speak to the exact circumstances in which each one of them came to fight for the 9th, Communist historians can certainly point to this geographic mixture with some degree of pride.

A native of the North, Senior Colonel Hoang Cam commanded the 9th Viet Cong Division. After joining the "army" in 1945, Cam enjoyed a meteoric rise during the Viet Minh war against the French, vaulting from the lowly status of a private to that of a regimental commander. Cam's regiment, the 209th (312th Division), had fought with distinction at Dien Bien Phu and, allegedly, had captured the commander of the ill-fated French encampment, General Christian de Castries.[12] Following the Dien Bien Phu campaign, from September 1954 to 1963, the future general climbed the chain of command and assumed the posts of division chief of staff, deputy division commander, and division commander of the 312th Division. Cam was then reassigned to South Vietnam on the morning of January 10, 1965.[13]

In November 1965 the 5th Viet Cong Division officially joined the 9th in the B2 Front order of battle. "During this conference, in order to signal the division's initial formation and to commemorate the anniversary of the Cochin China Insurrection, 23 November," a history of the 5th said of a

November 23 meeting of the division's leadership, "the Division Party Committee unanimously agreed to make 23 November 1965 the Tradition Day [the official birthday] of the 5th Infantry Division."[14] Whereas the 9th operated primarily in Binh Duong, Binh Long, and Tay Ninh Provinces, the 5th Viet Cong Division operated in Phuoc Tuy, Bien Hoa, and Long Khanh Provinces. The primary mission of the 5th, as defined that November, was "to base itself in Ba Ria–Long Khanh for a long-term battle and to support the revolutionary movements at the local level."[15] This mission was deemed essential for the building up of a strategic base area that could then be used as a "springboard" for launching attacks against the enemy east of Saigon.

Nguyen Hoa was selected to command the 5th Viet Cong Division. A northerner like Cam, Hoa hailed from Hai Hung Province in the Red River Delta and his military career included stints as the chief of staff of the NVA 304th and 320th Divisions.[16] As commander of the 5th, Hoa had a number of units at his disposal, most notably the 274th and 275th Viet Cong Regiments. The 22nd Mountain Howitzer Battalion, the 12th Anti-Aircraft Company, the 23rd Mortar Company, the 95th Reconnaissance Company, the 25th Engineer Company, the 605th Signal Company, and the 96th Medical Company completed the long list of combat units under Hoa's command.[17] Cadres and soldiers from North Vietnam, the Mekong Delta area of South Vietnam, and personnel assigned to COSVN Headquarters staffs fleshed out the 5th Viet Cong Division.

Subordinate to what the Communists called Thu Dau Mot Province, the Phu Loi Battalion supplemented the forces of the 5th and 9th Viet Cong Divisions in the area north of Saigon.[18] Thu Dau Mot's Phu Loi Battalion—Phu Loi was a popular name for VC units, and several existed—was founded on May 6, 1965, with three infantry companies, one heavy-weapons company, a reconnaissance platoon, and a signal platoon. In honoring a Viet Cong unit with the title of Phu Loi, the Communist Vietnamese were exhorting the troops of that unit to avenge the alleged poisoning deaths of their imprisoned revolutionary comrades in 1958. A Communist history laid out the allegation for which vengeance was urged:

> To implement their "Denounce communists, Kill communists" policy, the U.S. and Diem turned all of South Vietnam into a gigantic prison

camp. Prisons sprouted up like mushrooms and were filled with hundreds of thousands of patriotic citizens and communist fighters. The enemy tried to use torture and repression to subdue the people of South Vietnam. Out of all the prisons and prison camps, Phu Loi was the largest prison in South Vietnam. There the enemy imprisoned thousands of cadres, Party members, and members of the revolutionary masses. At noon on 1 December 1958 they mixed poison in with the food, poisoning more than one thousand people, of which hundreds of people died.[19]

Additional formations such as the 69th Artillery Division, the U80 Viet Cong Artillery Regiment, and independent main-force regiments such as the Dong Thap II Regiment were available as well. The 69th and the U80, the latter composed of "artillery" and mortar battalions (code named Z35, Z37, Z39, and Z41) and a 12.7-mm antiaircraft machine-gun battalion, furnished a modicum of fire support for area forces.

In opposition to the B2 Front's clutch of bases and units in the Saigon area, General William Westmoreland counted the 173rd Airborne Brigade and the 1st Infantry Division to start. The 1st Infantry Division, the famed "Big Red One," based near Lai Khe (3rd Brigade), Phuoc Vinh (1st Brigade), Bien Hoa (2nd Brigade), Phu Loi (divisional air and artillery assets), and Di An (divisional headquarters and support assets). Basing in such a way accomplished two military objectives. First and foremost the bases defended Saigon against Communist forces to the north. Further, stationing elements of the 1st Infantry Division near Lai Khe and Phuoc Vinh challenged Communist transit routes between War Zones C and D. General Ellis W. Williamson's 173rd Airborne Brigade, meanwhile, fronted War Zone D from its encampment at Bien Hoa. By early November 1965, the 173rd and the 1st Infantry Division had put down operational roots.[20]

In November, and in the month that followed, Viet Cong forces of the B2 Front fought four major engagements against elements of the 1st Infantry Division and the 173rd Airborne Brigade. These battles heralded the dawn of a bloody and prolonged period of big-unit battle against American forces.

8

Cong Truong 9 Enters the Fray

Commanded by Deputy Regiment Commander Bui Thanh Van, the 3rd Battalion, 271st Viet Cong Regiment waited silently on the morning of November 8, 1965. Three days before two infantry battalions from the 173rd Airborne Brigade, the 1st Battalion/Royal Australian Regiment and the American 1st Battalion/503rd Infantry, had air assaulted into War Zone D near the Dong Nai–Song Be River junction. The Australians and Americans had come searching for the headquarters and composite battalions of the 272nd Viet Cong Regiment, and perhaps a battalion from the 274th Viet Cong Regiment. Operation Hump, the Americans called it. But on *this* morning it was the Viet Cong who would do the hunting. Indeed, when elements of the 1st/503rd decamped to scour the area around an elevation known as Hill 65, the 3rd Battalion planned to ambush the American Sky Soldiers (the nickname of the Americans of the 173rd Airborne Brigade).[1]

The 3rd Battalion belonged to a parent unit with a singular pedigree. Early in 1961 a group of cadre marched down the Ho Chi Minh Trail and into South Vietnam. These men represented the command framework of an emerging formation, the 271st Viet Cong Regiment. The Communist disclosure that "at that time, the first south-bound contingents were to be composed only of fully qualified cadres and combatants selected from among Southern Army units regrouped to the North" affirms that the men were regroupees.[2] Nor have they been forgotten. Culminating in the creation of the 271st, the very first of its kind in eastern Nam Bo, the odyssey south and the men who endured it have been immortalized in Communist Vietnamese history:

> The first infantry regiment to march to the eastern Nam Bo theater was the 1st Regiment [the 271st Regiment], made up of cadres ranging from regimental commander to squad leader. . . . On an early day of 1961, a special convoy carrying the cadre-frame group of the 1st Regiment (code named Group 562 during its southward march) left Xuan Mai (Ha Dong). . . . To ensure secrecy and security, during their march the group split up into several small teams, each comprising about 25 or 30 members. It was a long route dotted with many steep inclines, deep ravines, and perilous sheer mountain slopes. . . . On those days when they ran out of rice, they had to subsist on wild roots. At times some had to stay behind, downed by a sudden bout of malaria. . . . On 27 March 1961, after two months and 27 days of marching down more than 1000 kilometers of the Truong Son Trail, the group of 1st Regiment cadres arrived in War Zone D in southern Nam Bo.[3]

On February 9, 1962, a special ceremony in Tay Ninh Province officially introduced the 271st Viet Cong Regiment.[4] At that time the regiment was composed of supporting units and two infantry battalions, the 1st and 2nd Battalions. The 3rd Battalion formed up in June of the following year under the command of Sau Huan. North Vietnamese cadres and recruits from western Nam Bo filled its ranks.[5] Three infantry battalions strong and commanded by Nguyen The Truyen, the 271st fought against South Vietnamese forces in the pivotal Binh Gia campaign of late 1964–early 1965. For its military achievements in the campaign, the 271st was awarded the "Liberation Military Service Order Third Class and the glorious designation 'Binh Gia Regiment.'"[6] Hereafter the regiment carried that distinctive sobriquet into battle.

Now, in War Zone D northwest of the Dong Nai–Song Be River junction, on the eighth of November 1965, the 3rd Battalion had Captain Henry Tucker's Company C, 1st Battalion/503rd in sight and with it the chance to earn even more battlefield glory for the 271st Viet Cong Regiment. Van's men seized the opportunity, for when elements of Company C moved west

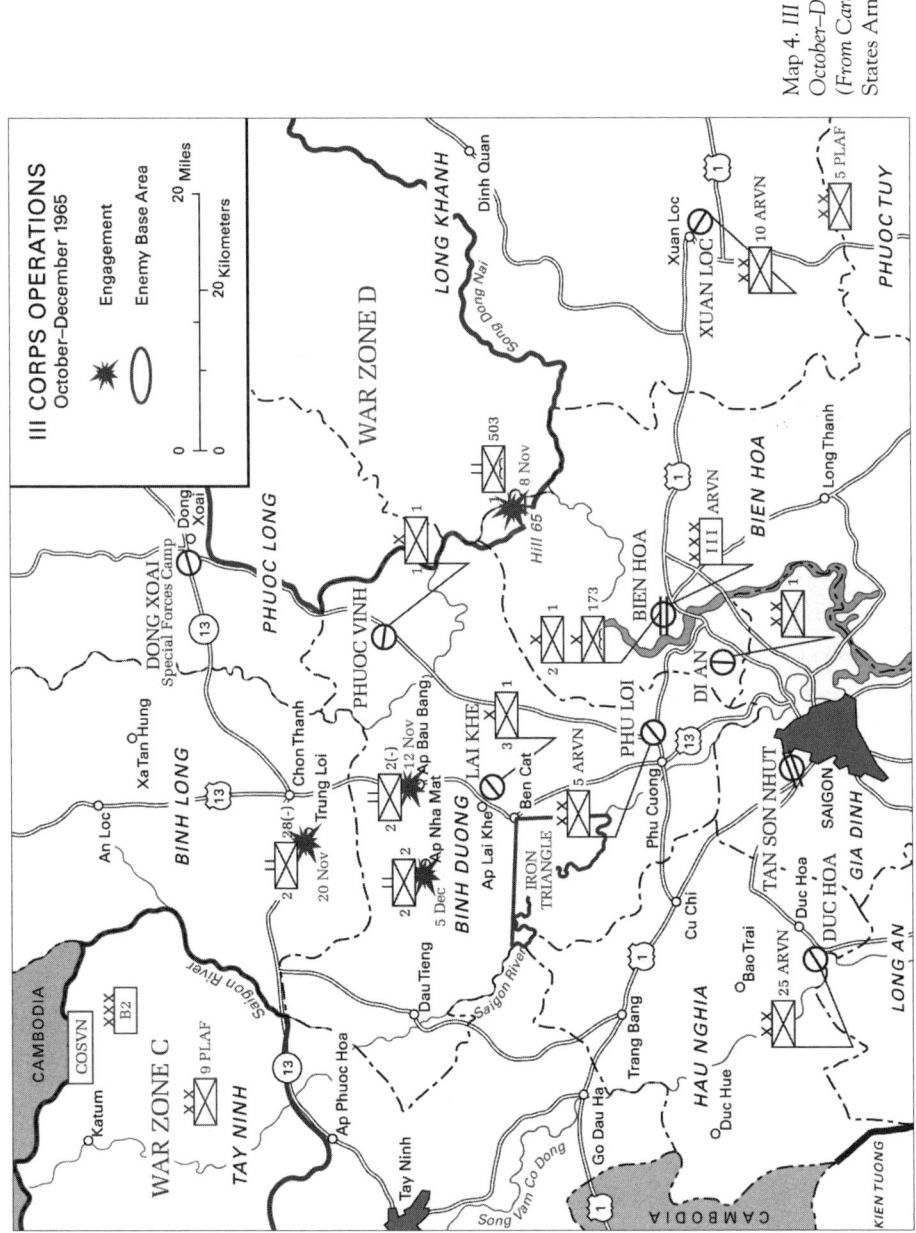

Map 4. *III Corps Operations, October–December 1965* (From Carland, United States Army in Vietnam)

in the general direction of Hill 65, seeking enemy forces thought to be in the area, the jungle erupted in gunfire and exploding mines. Unseen and well entrenched, Viet Cong machine gunners pumped .30- and .50-caliber fire at the dazed paratroopers. Small-arms fire from other hidden VC soldiers amplified the din of battle. Pinned down and isolated, Company C had only to be flanked and destroyed for the 3rd Battalion to record a resounding victory over the Americans.

Mindful of the potential for American air and artillery strikes, the Viet Cong hugged Company C to ensure that the subsequent engagement would force the paratroopers to fight for a time without close artillery support and in close quarters.[7] Tucker's men returned fire and hung tough. Commander Van then moved quickly to flank Tucker on the right (north) and encircle his company. The ongoing morning firefight had fixed the paratroopers, and a successful envelopment would finish them.

Tactically sound in its conception, the Viet Cong envelopment failed nonetheless. Cognizant of Company C's travails, Lieutenant Colonel John Tyler, commanding officer of the 1st/503rd, instructed Captain Lowell Bittrich's Company B to assist Tucker. Accordingly Company B advanced down from the northeast and, at approximately 9:30 AM, assaulted across a creek located near Hill 65 and right into the flank and rear of the attacking Viet Cong. Blessed with the element of surprise, Bittrich's men shot down a number of VC and secured Company C's endangered right flank. Undeterred, the Viet Cong attempted yet another encirclement maneuver, although it too ended unsuccessfully after heated fighting.

The Viet Cong attempted a final envelopment later that morning. Ambitious in scope, the VC attack aimed to encircle both Companies B and C. This time Company A foiled the VC maneuver. Determined to aid their comrades, Captain Walter Daniels' troops negotiated a stretch of rough country to fire into the left flank of the VC and stop the Communist attack. The Viet Cong, though doubtlessly surprised at this unexpected appearance of American troops, adjusted to the new threat and counterattacked Company A. The VC also launched repeated assaults against Company B and Company C as the day wore on. About midafternoon, however, after a good bit of hard fighting, the troops from the 3rd Battalion, 271st Viet Cong Regiment were beginning to disengage.[8]

In the battle at Dat Cuoc, or Hill 65 as the Americans referred to it, the 3rd Battalion, 271st Viet Cong Regiment had been defeated.[9] Despite some undeniably tense moments, Lieutenant Colonel Tyler's companies staved off encirclement and killed dozens of VC in the process. The exact casualty figures inflicted on the Viet Cong will never be known for certain, but they were indisputably higher than the 49 killed and 83 wounded suffered by the 173rd Airborne Brigade. Nor could the Viet Cong ascribe the defeat solely to American supporting arms. American artillery and TAC (tactical) air had concentrated to a significant extent on Viet Cong escape routes and rear areas while American boots on the ground grappled, sometimes literally, with enemy infantry. And it was in these highly personal infantry exchanges that American machine-gun, 40-mm grenade, and rifle fire inflicted the majority of the Viet Cong casualties.[10]

In 1967 the U.S. 25th Infantry Division recovered a VC document referencing the combat achievements of the 9th Viet Cong Division. "The document," said the official American military accounting of it, "states that Cong Truong 9 has never been defeated."[11] Word of the 9th Viet Cong Division's untarnished combat ledger would have undoubtedly amused the American veterans of Hill 65. Major General Pham Quoc Thuan, on the other hand, was not amused. As a matter of fact, he faced a dilemma. Thuan, the commanding officer of the 5th ARVN Division, wanted to advance his 7th Regiment north up Highway 13 for operations in the Michelin Rubber Plantation. Unfortunately the threat of a Viet Cong ambush or attack along the way made him rather uneasy about the prospect of "going it alone." Thuan's trepidation was not unfounded. South Vietnamese forces, once in the throes of an ambush, usually lacked the mobility and firepower to fend off Communist forces.

Reluctant therefore to act unilaterally, Thuan petitioned to have the American 1st Infantry Division secure a roughly thirteen-kilometer stretch of Route 13 from Lai Khe to Bau Long Pond. On November 10 and 11, 1965, a task force built around Lieutenant Colonel George Shuffer's 2nd Battalion, 2nd Infantry (3rd Brigade, 1st Infantry Division) performed the requested road security mission, and just before 4:00 PM on the afternoon of the eleventh, the last of the South Vietnamese forces passed through uneventfully.

Shuffer's operation, while successful in its objective, alerted Colonel Cam's 9th Viet Cong Division to the presence of a substantial American military force in the area. The American operation and the corresponding effect it had on the 9th's adoption of a contingency plan to deal with encroaching American forces are recalled in the divisional history:

> At that time, the 9th Division was continuing to carry out its plan by preparing to attack Dau Tieng. In its combat plan, the Division Command had provided for the contingency of U.S. troops encroaching on Route 13 and Route 16 and for the possibility of opening the campaign with a raid on or an ambush of U.S. troops, and not necessarily with an attack on the district town of Dau Tieng. On the morning of 11 November, upon receiving a report from the division's and 2nd Regiment's reconnaissance teams on the enemy operation, the Division Party Committee and Command decided to use the 2nd Regiment (minus one company), the 1st Battalion (1st Regiment) augmented by two infantry companies of the 8th Battalion (3rd Regiment), and most of the division's artillery pieces and mortars to raid and destroy the concentration of enemy troops north of Bau Bang during the night. . . . The 9th Battalion (3rd Regiment) was given the task of intercepting the enemy force moving up from Dong So, while the 7th Battalion (3rd Regiment) would serve as a reserve force.[12]

Shuffer's task force, elements of which the 9th Viet Cong Division intended to attack, combined infantry (2/2), armored cavalry (Troop A, 1st Squadron, 4th Cavalry Regiment), and artillery (Battery C, 2nd Battalion, 33rd Artillery Regiment).[13] During the Route 13 security detail, Shuffer split his task force into "company size units" with each assuming responsibility for a different segment along the road. Company A (2/2), Battery C, and Troop A along with the command group and the battalion recon platoon occupied the middle segment. Road segments to the north and south were assigned to the other two infantry companies of the 2/2.

As soon as the South Vietnamese regiment had passed through on November 11, Shuffer directed his three groups to move into night defensive positions. In the middle grouping, Troop A and Battery C were situated north of Bau Bang (Binh Duong Province) until Shuffer redeployed both units to positions south of the village. There the guns and the armored cavalry merged into a single defensive perimeter with the infantry of Company A.[14]

Shuffer's decision to consolidate his forces did not go undetected. Ever watchful, Viet Cong reconnaissance teams noticed the redeployment and relayed word of the American force realignment to the leadership of the 9th Viet Cong Division. After some deliberation, Colonel Cam decided to attack and destroy "both concentrations" of American troops.[15] Rather audacious, the proposed Viet Cong attack aimed to annihilate the American units positioned south of Bau Bang: Company A, Troop A, and Battery C. Colonel Cam later articulated some of the reasons he opted to strike:

> A few units requested permission from division headquarters to withdraw, because they said they could find no indication that the enemy was still there. The Division Party Current Affairs Committee and the Division Command Group immediately met and concluded that it had not been easy to send forces to this location and that we still held the element of surprise. That was a precious advantage that we must exploit to the maximum. The enemy force was still in this area, we concluded. It might have shifted location, but it had not gone far. . . . Although the enemy force was large and had many modern weapons, the enemy troops had halted in a temporary field position, their fortifications would be minimal, and there would be many weaknesses and gaps in their defenses. Not only was there no reason for our forces to withdraw, if we withdrew at this time our forces would become exposed, and that would ruin our overall plan.[16]

Cam confirmed that the combat-hardened 272nd Viet Cong Regiment "would still be the primary assault force to attack and destroy" the Americans at Bau Bang.[17] In ticketing the 272nd for glory, Cam could hardly have chosen a more able, experienced, or decorated unit. The second main-force regiment in eastern Nam Bo, the 272nd, was formed on December 22, 1961, at Xuan Mai in North Vietnam. Two days later, on Christmas Eve, the regimental command along with the 6th Battalion departed for South Vietnam. Arriving in War Zone D in March 1962, the group was joined thereafter by the 4th and 5th Battalions. That June a ceremony was held in War Zone D to formally recognize the founding of the 272nd.

Once in battle, the 272nd earned an honorary title, Dong Xoai Regiment, for decimating South Vietnamese forces at Dong Xoai in June 1965 while under the command of Ta Minh Kham. Additionally the regiment accepted the "Determined To Fight and Vanquish the U.S. aggressors" traveling banner at the conclusion of the campaign. Suitably accomplished, the 272nd could be trusted to embody that banner, and the slogan "Use the Americans' blood to dye our bayonets," at Bau Bang.[18]

Colonel Cam rounded out his task force with troops from the 271st Viet Cong Regiment and Chin Hien's 273rd Viet Cong Regiment, and conceivably some troops from the Phu Loi Battalion.[19] For employment in the main assault, the 1st Battalion of the 271st Viet Cong Regiment was attached to the 272nd Viet Cong Regiment. Cam and his staff also borrowed two infantry companies from the 8th Battalion, 273rd Viet Cong Regiment to further reinforce the main assault element. Established in eastern Nam Bo in 1964 largely out of "concentrated armed units transferred from central and western Nam Bo" and northern cadres, the 273rd Viet Cong Regiment released its 9th Battalion to block American forces at Dong So from moving up and interceding in the battle.[20] The 7th Battalion of the 273rd, meanwhile, was to act as a reserve force.

Obliged to move swiftly because of their distance from the battle area, Cam's assault forces had to run, some for hours, to reach their staging areas. Final missions and assignments for some units had to be hashed out on the move and in the moonlight. Gradually and only after extraordinary individual exertion, the assault troops converged around the American position. Easing into Bau Bang after dark, they quickly set up mortar positions for the morning assault. In the berm south of Bau Bang, not far from the American defensive perimeter, they embedded machine guns and recoilless rifles. East of the American position, near Route 13, and in the rubber tree forest to the south-southwest of the laagering Americans, Cam's troops assembled in quiet anticipation.[21]

Meanwhile, when Shuffer authorized his forces to prepare defensive positions for the night, Company A, Troop A, Battery C, and the command group circled the wagons south of Bau Bang. Here, as well as at the other NDPs, the infantry strung concertina wire and dug foxholes. Troop A pitched in and towed a wrecked APC around the perimeter, bringing down immature rubber trees and other forms of vegetation to clear out and improve fields of fire. In front of the guns of Battery C the artillerymen constructed earthen walls. Ambush patrols slipped out after sundown. Come what may on November 12, the Americans had clearly taken all reasonable defensive precautions.

Cam attacked in any case. At 6:05 AM on the morning of November 12, the Viet Cong assault began with a mortar barrage. Crashing to earth in a flurry, some fifty to sixty 60-mm mortar rounds exploded within the American perimeter. Shortly after that the Viet Cong opened fire with automatic weapons. Since Cam could only communicate with one of his battalions, the 1st Battalion of 271st Viet Cong Regiment, he relied on the sounds of battle to spur the remainder of his forces to action. Euphemistically dubbed "coordinating actions in accordance with the sound of gunfire," this bygone method of command and control nevertheless succeeded in signaling the assault against the American perimeter.

Moving to the "sound of the guns," hordes of VC troops huddling in the rubber tree forest to the south-southwest began crawling through bushes and high grass toward the American task force. After reaching a point less than 50 meters from the American perimeter, they stormed the wire.[22] Shuffer's men were not caught off guard, however. Troop A's armored cavalrymen, tasked at the time with defending the southern half of the American perimeter, frantically engaged the oncoming VC with heavy defensive fire. M-113 APCs from Troop A's 3rd Platoon then raced out of the perimeter and counterattacked the Viet Cong, throwing them back with significant losses.[23]

Battered but not beaten the Viet Cong struck again, this time from staging areas to the east of the initial attack. As in the first assault, the attack force crept through concealing vegetation before storming the American wire. Coming forward, the VC collided with a wall of fire from dug-in American infantry and the mounted machine guns from American APCs. The attackers retreated, leaving a number of bullet-torn bodies behind. Southeast of the American position, the Viet Cong launched a third attack with a westward assault across Route 13. Deadly fire from American infantry and APCs chewed up the assaulting VC, however. Withdrawing behind a railroad embankment to the east, the survivors of this failed assault were then clobbered by shellfire from American gun batteries firing out of the Lai Khe area.

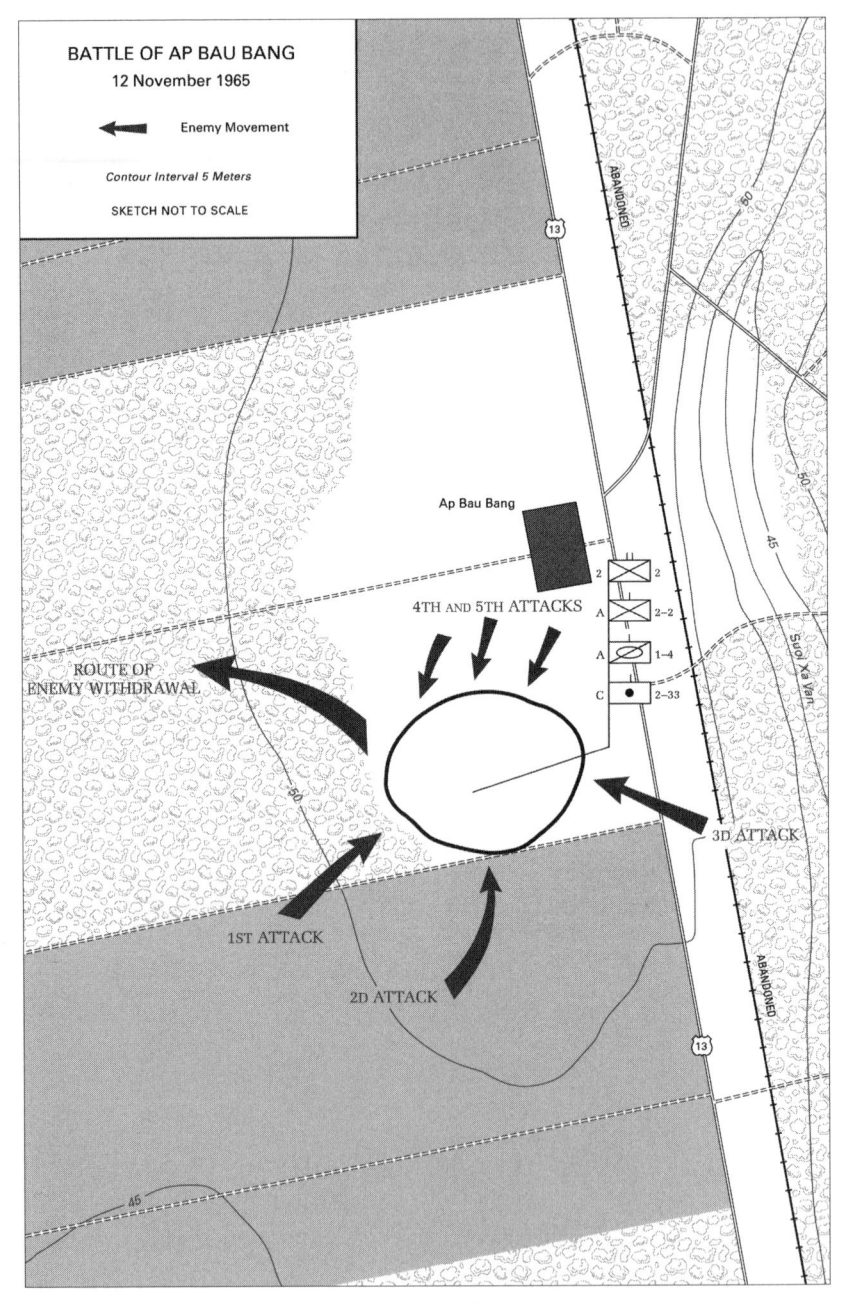

Map 5. Battle of Ap Bau Bang, November 12, 1965 (From Carland, United States Army in Vietnam)

Despite nearly an hour of frenetic fighting, Cam had yet to launch his main attack against the "stubborn and wily" Americans.[24] Finally, at 7:00 AM, over the east-west berm south of Bau Bang and under the cover of mortar, recoilless rifle, and machine-gun fire, Cam's troops streamed southward against the American lines. Coordinated American "all-arms" fire ultimately derailed the VC attack. First, a flight of U.S. Air Force A-1H Skyraiders bombed and strafed the wooded area north-northwest of the American position. The bombing run took place around 6:45 AM, and it may very well have disturbed a likely VC assembly area. Fifteen minutes later Cam's infantry surged across the berm and from the nearby woodlands all the way to the American wire, where they were turned back by the infantry of Company A and the devastating effects of delayed-fuse rounds fired at point blank range by Battery C.[25] Remarkably, considering the volume of American defensive fire, one squad of VC managed to penetrate the American perimeter and hurl a grenade at the No. 1 howitzer position. The blast killed two Americans and wounded four more.

At 9:00 AM the Viet Cong attacked from the north once more. In the interim, however, American supporting arms had received permission to strike Bau Bang. Acting on that authority, a flight of A-4 Skyhawks followed by Air Force A-1E Skyraiders dumped bombs and napalm on Viet Cong recoilless rifle positions emplaced in the berm south of the village. Battery C, moreover, fired rounds directly into Bau Bang. VC troops involved in the assault fared no better. Swooping down without mercy, a flight of F-100s dropped napalm on the assaulting VC and the guns of Battery C fired 65 rounds into their ranks.[26] Devastated by the effects of American firepower, the Viet Cong retreated once again. By 1:30 that afternoon, Cam's forces had effectively withdrawn from the battlefield.[27]

On paper the battle at Bau Bang was a one-sided beating. The Viet Cong had lost, at a minimum, between 146 and 198 killed and an untold number of wounded. Captured documents indicated that the mostly supporting 273rd Viet Cong Regiment alone had sustained 30 killed and 58 wounded.[28] American casualties were much lighter: 20 men killed in action (KIA) and 103 wounded in action (WIA). Major material losses for the Americans amounted to two M-113 APCs and three M-106 mortar carriers. Three M-113s suffered damage.[29]

Astoundingly Colonel Cam was heartened by the results of the fighting. In his memoir Cam relayed a conversation he says he had with General Tran Van Tra about the battle:

> Because he had been forced to both anxiously monitor the developing situation at this turning point in the war as well as to hold planning discussions with all our units about how to deal with the increasing level of B-52 attacks, when he saw me walk up, Tra immediately asked, "Have you fought yet?"
> "We've fought, and its over," I replied.
> "Why was the battle over so quickly? They were Americans, after all! What were the results?" Tra asked.
> "Very good."
> Tra laughed out loud, grabbed my hand and shook it again, and said, "Then we must go back and brief [General Nguyen Chi] Thanh."[30]

Long a proponent of big-unit battle, General Thanh was overjoyed. "I received radio reports of your victory over the Americans at Bau Bang," he is said to have remarked to Colonel Cam and General Tra after the fighting. "I was so happy that I could not sleep. . . . This means that we were able to fight and beat the Americans from the very first round of the match! I want to congratulate all of you."[31] Thanh also informed Cam of a decision by the COSVN Military Headquarters to award a commendation—Thanh had suggested the Army Achievement Medal, First Class—for the battle.

Bau Bang, in addition to some of the other early battles of the big-unit war, had convinced Thanh that, in battles fought at close quarters, the U.S. Army was not as formidable an opponent as some might have suspected. Thanh believed that the American infantryman eschewed close-quarters combat with the VC/NVA out of fear. "Grab the enemy by the belt to fight him," he declared. "The Americans are terrified of close-quarters fighting against our soldiers."[32] Thanh's emasculating attitude was certainly shared by a proportion of Viet Cong soldiers, and it is probably fair to say that most Communist Vietnamese military thinkers of the era shared his advocacy of the "grab the enemy by the belt" dictum.

Cong Truong 9 Enters the Fray | 117

■ ■ ■

At dusk on November 20, 1965, a motor convoy from the 1st Infantry Division, the renowned Big Red One, rumbled down muddy Route 239 toward the village of Trung Loi. Aware of the convoy's movements, the 4th Battalion of the 272nd Viet Cong Regiment scampered through the jungle to intercept it. A history of the 272nd described the VC regiment's subsequent ambush, if through decidedly Communist lenses:

> The combat achievements in the Cam Xe Battle on 20 November demonstrated the high determination among cadre and soldiers of d4 (4th Bn) and d6 (6th Bn). While cadre were reconnoitering their way, the troops followed so that they could instantly engage in combat if necessary. These units cut off an enemy formation consisting of 500 armored vehicles and an infantry unit. After two hours of fighting we destroyed 47 armored vehicles and killed more than 500 Americans. With a strong determination, the C2/d4 (2nd Co, 4th Bn) and Ta Quang Ty, a brave company commander, were successful in holding and blocking the enemy's rear element. Because of this, the d (bn) effectively fulfilled its mission. In addition the 75-mm RR Unit of C17 (17th Co), along with Ha Minh Quang, an excellent gunner, scored glaring combat achievements. Before his gun, all the US's modern armored vehicles were smashed into pieces. If one man fell, another advanced and fought to the end.[33]

Historians for the 9th Viet Cong Division, much like the chroniclers of the 272nd Viet Cong Regiment, lauded the ambush of the 4th Battalion and its 2nd Company commander, Ta Quang Ty, as well. According to the history of the 9th:

> Ten days after the Bau Bang battle (on 21 November 1965), the 4th Battalion (2d Regiment) discovered the movement of a U.S. armored column comprising more than 300 vehicles on the road between Cam Xe and Dau Tieng. The battalion blazed a passage in the jungle and pushed through several sites of B-52 bombing to cut off a section of the long enemy convoy. . . . After knocking out more than 20 vehicles and putting

out of action nearly 100 Americans, the 4th Battalion safely withdrew from the battlefield. Company commander Ta Quang Ty had once again won the affection and admiration of his men, who gave him a third title: Rear-blocking company commander.³⁴

The writing of military history, it has been suggested, is an exercise reserved for the victors. In the Second Indochina War, the Communist Vietnamese were unquestionably victorious. Yet renowned Soviet military scholar Colonel David M. Glantz astutely observed a critical oversight in the historical practices of the Soviet Union in the wake of World War II, and it applies to the Communist Vietnamese as well. "History, however, has a long memory and a terrible vengeance," Glantz wrote of an attempt by the victorious Soviets to expunge a largely unsuccessful, and hence unflattering, military operation from the historical record. "Soviet authorities could not eradicate the thousands of German accounts and the treasure trove of archival documents that chronicled the operation."³⁵ The long arm of historical truth to which Glantz refers and military history as documented by the Communist Vietnamese intersect at Trung Loi in that, while the latter have certainly earned the right to pen the history of the battle as they saw it, they could not, like the Soviets before them, eradicate the wealth of enemy accounts and archival material that also recorded the action on November 20, 1965.

An unidentified concentration of troops and vehicles in the Communist histories, the ambushed American convoy was actually made up of Company C (2nd Battalion, 28th Infantry), Battery B (2nd Battalion, 33rd Artillery), and the command groups of the 2/28 and 2/33. Company C and the artillery battery were destined for Lai Khe, home of the 1st Infantry Division's 3rd Brigade. Rainy weather and a muddy track, however, slowed the pace considerably. Disregarding the inclement conditions, the convoy proceeded on until, finally, at about 6:20 PM on November 20, its lead elements advanced on the village of Trung Loi. Two platoons from Company C headed up the strung out column, trailed by the company command post, an 81-mm mortar platoon, the company's third platoon, and the battalion command group. Battery B pulled up the rear.³⁶

Were it not for an observant American NCO, the Viet Cong ambush at Trung Loi might have unfolded much like the accounts found in the aforementioned Communist histories.[37] Instead, as the vanguard of Company C approached the village, an American sergeant with the lead platoon noticed an armed Viet Cong soldier fleeing from the road. Instinctively the sergeant shot the man dead. The shooting must have spurred the Viet Cong into springing the ambush, possibly precipitately, because within moments of the incident they began firing at the 1st and 2nd Platoons of Company C from the village and from both sides of the road. The two American platoons dismounted, arranged a perimeter, and fired back. Tactical surprise, with which the Viet Cong had expected to initiate the ambush, had been squandered.

Expanding over time, the VC ambush eventually stretched down each side of the road to engulf the rest of Company C and the 2/28 command group.[38] At 6:37 PM a Viet Cong recoilless rifle positioned off to the east fired on Company C's command group and the 81-mm mortar platoon. A particularly daring VC weapons crew made it out to the road with a recoilless rifle, but the Americans shot down the crew and a replacement team before either could fire a round. In spite of the fate of the two previous crews, a third VC crew was said to have come forward to man the weapon.[39] At approximately the same time, the Viet Cong showered Company C's command group, the battalion command group, and the 81-mm mortar platoon with grenades and mortar fire.

American aviation broke the developing stalemate. Appearing over the battlefield at 6:40 PM, helicopter gunships flew "firing passes" from west to east along the southeastern side of the road. Succeeding passes engaged targets on both sides of the road. Unloading on ground targets with each pass, the marauding gunships induced groups of Viet Cong to leave their ambush positions and close on the road at about 7:00 PM. Given that the American convoy retained control of the road, thanks in no small part to the work of the mortar platoon in dropping 81-mm rounds on either side of it, the Viet Cong move proved unwise. Bunched in groups, some of the VC were then shot down in the road by American ground forces. To compound the VC's difficulties, the American air attacks were not over. When the gunships that had driven the VC onto the roadway finally quit the skies, the Americans marshaled Air Force fighters to drop napalm along the east-southeastern side of the road. The Viet Cong attackers, unwilling or perhaps unable to endure any more punishment, finally retreated after this napalm strike.[40] Casualties for the battle, which lasted two hours and fifty-five minutes, were relatively moderate. Trung Loi had cost the Americans 6 dead, 38 wounded, and 6 damaged vehicles. On the Communist side of the ledger, the human toll was higher, with an estimated 40–142 Viet Cong KIA.[41]

Following the engagement at Trung Loi, the big-unit war resumed in the volatile area northwest of Saigon when the 271st Viet Cong Regiment and perhaps elements of the 273rd attacked and nearly overran the 7th ARVN Regiment (5th ARVN Division) in the Michelin Plantation on November 27, 1965. General Jonathan O. Seaman, commander of the U.S. 1st Infantry Division, responded by ordering the airlift of a task force from his 3rd Brigade to the scene. From shielding the shaken 7th ARVN Regiment, the objective of the task force quickly morphed into a hunt for Viet Cong units. Military agents and information garnered from South Vietnamese civilians hinted that the Phu Loi Battalion might be in the vicinity of the plantation. It was also conceivable that the attacking units of the 271st and 273rd Viet Cong Regiments were still lurking in the area. Apprised of this intelligence and the possibility of tangling with major Viet Cong units, General Seaman redirected his forces for a more significant action.

On December 1 Colonel William Brodbeck's 3rd Brigade task force launched a "search-and-destroy" operation to comb the dense jungle southeast of the Michelin Plantation.[42] Absent during the first few days of the American operation in the Long Nguyen Secret Zone, the 272nd Viet Cong Regiment appeared abruptly on December 5 in a camp north of the village of Nha Mat. The night before Lieutenant Colonel Shuffer's 2nd Battalion, 2nd Infantry, one of two infantry battalions earmarked for the search, had established an overnight defensive perimeter about a mile north of the Communist encampment. On the morning of the 5th, Shuffer's troops started south along a jungle road only to collide that afternoon with the camp and elements of the 272nd Viet Cong Regiment. Now whether the 272nd had been regrouping at the camp after earlier battles, as Shuffer surmised, or whether the regiment had raced some five kilometers through the jungle on December 5 to head off and attack the American battalion, as one prominent Communist history asserts, remains unclear.[43] Colonel Cam, the commander of the 9th Viet Cong Division, claims that the appearance of the 272nd in the path of the Suffer's 2nd

Battalion was not an accident: "On 5 December, after discovering that two battalions of the U.S. 2nd Brigade/1st Infantry Division were conducting a search and destroy operation in the area from Thi Tinh–Nha Mat to Bau Da Dot (in Long Nguyen Village, Ben Cat district), 2nd Regiment (following its victory at Cam Se) was ordered by the division to move quickly to this area to lay in wait. The regiment quickly cut through the jungle and deployed into position to surround the enemy force."[44]

In any case the camp was certainly swarming with 272nd soldiers by the time Shuffer's lead elements, bushwhacking south along both sides of the jungle road, approached around noontime. The game of hide and seek had come to an end. Without so much as a whisper of forewarning, VC in camouflaged bunkers, tree-mounted firing platforms, and other defensive positions blazed away at the lead elements of Companies B and C with mortar, machine-gun, and recoilless rifle fire. Bugle blasts, which the VC evidently used as a crude command and control mechanism during the battle, preceded volleys of concentrated automatic weapons fire that sliced trees in half.[45] Company B, operating at the time on the east side of the north-south road, and Company C, then on the west side, were pinned down. Shuffer answered with a request for artillery fire on the camp.

Believing that the Viet Cong's western flank was the weaker and therefore the more exploitable, Shuffer directed Company A, which had been trailing behind Company C, to sweep around it.[46] Superior in number, the Viet Cong halted Company A's flanking move shortly after it had deployed to the left of Company C. Company A, for the moment, could advance no farther. At the same time, the Viet Cong attempted to outflank Shuffer with a massive assault against Company B, then east of the road. Violent but not decisive, the VC flanking maneuver nevertheless pushed Company B in a westward direction across the road.

A definable American perimeter began to take shape around Company B to the east, the battalion command group to the north, Company C to the south, and Company A arrayed to the west and south-west.[47] With American infantry consolidating into a perimeter and American artillery shells impacting in their camp area, the Viet Cong knew they had to close the distance and hug the American companies. Bau Bang had taught the officers of the 9th Viet

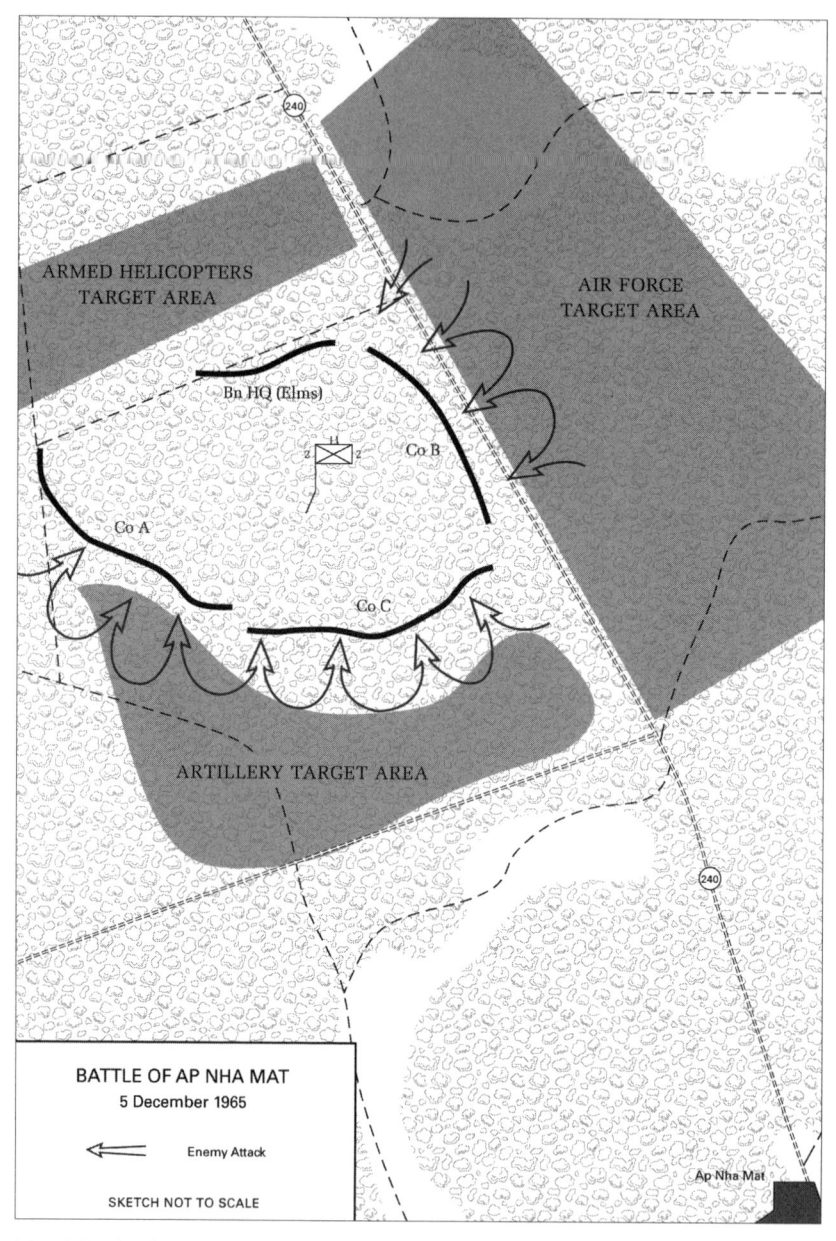

Map 6. *Battle of Ap Nha Mat, December 5, 1965 (From Carland, United States Army in Vietnam)*

Cong Division as much. Accordingly, and assisted by the fire of Chinese-made 12.7-mm machine guns in tree-mounted platforms, the Viet Cong abandoned their defensive dispositions and charged the Americans.

Try as they might, however, the VC could not get close enough. Shuffer's men, some sheltered behind three-foot-tall laterite anthills, maintained a steady stream of accurate small-arms fire, preserving the separation required for American supporting arms to safely intervene.[48] These arms were soon operating simultaneously and with impunity. Batteries of American artillery, including 175-mm self-propelled guns, fired round after round on the Communist camp and defensive positions south of Shuffer's infantry companies. Opposite Company B, on the east side of the American perimeter, Air Force fighters buried the Viet Cong in bombs, napalm, and cluster bomb units. And when several groups of VC shifted around to harry the American battalion CP and interdict American reinforcements moving down from the north, roving helicopters pounced on them with rockets and machine-gun fire.

Suppressed at the point of contact by American artillery and airpower, the outgunned 272nd now faced a rejuvenated American infantry assault. Companies A and C, under the cover of heavy artillery fire, assaulted the Communist defensive positions. Viet Cong snipers and machine gunners were caught up in the maelstrom and blown out of trees. Although other VC troops surrendered ground reluctantly, by 2:30 PM that afternoon, the two American companies had driven deep into the Communist camp's well-bunkered defensive system.[49] Dispirited and suffering heavy casualties, the Dong Xoai Regiment finally cracked. Panicked troops fled in disorder to the rear, discarding their weapons and leaving behind wounded comrades. The battle had devolved into a rout.

The battle north of the village of Nha Mat on December 5, 1965, had gravely injured the 272nd Viet Cong Regiment. Over 300 of its soldiers had been killed and an untold amount of equipment had been lost. Regimental prestige had also been bruised. That the Americans suffered a fraction of those losses (39 killed and 119 wounded) made for even more bitter pill to swallow.[50] The 272nd's prestige could obviously be restored in time. But it, as well as finding replacements for the dead and irretrievably wounded at Nha Mat, required time. Indeed, it would be some time before the 272nd returned to the battlefield.

FIGHTING THE AMERICANS

> Your combat formulas are out there on the battlefield!
> —General Thanh, in Military History Institute of Vietnam,
> *Dai Tuong Nguyen Chi Thanh*

As soon as it became abundantly clear that the United States had embarked on a policy of "limited war" in defense of South Vietnam, Communist Vietnamese military leaders and soldiers wondered: How should we fight the Americans? Communist field commanders pondered the same question during the opening period of big-unit battle, and some even broached the subject at COSVN. While attending military meetings, for example, these commanders requested that "the COSVN Military Party Committee" provide them "with combat formulas." The commanders in the field, quite frankly, were appealing for help in figuring out how to fight the Americans and their state-of-the-art technology.

General Thanh heard these appeals and offered a terse reply. "Your combat formulas are out there on the battlefield," he said. "You have to go out there and find them."[51] Thanh's ambiguous counsel more or less summarized the Viet Cong's empirical approach to the question of how to fight the Americans. The Viet Cong and the NVA would learn *how* to fight Americans by *fighting* Americans. Hence the closing months of 1965, and the battles fought therein, were a period of tactical trial and error for the Viet Cong and NVA. Battles would be fought, outcomes would be reviewed, and tactics and techniques would be revised and refined.

Colonel Cam's 9th Viet Cong Division, in fact, received instructions to review its first month of combat against American forces. As one might expect, the findings were generally laudatory of division forces and disdainful of American forces. It was also, however, refreshingly frank in some areas:

> [On American firepower and its tactical application.] The enemy's air and artillery firepower was very strong and used to great effect when we were unable to get close to the enemy. . . . Under normal conditions, when their command and communications were stable, and when we had not got close to them, U.S. troops could put to good account their command skills and their material and technical strengths.

[On the use of the "hugging" tactic.] . . . The 9th Division had actively held on to the enemy. . . . As U.S. troops depended on air and artillery support and tried to keep their distance from us in order to use their firepower to kill us, the 9th Division kept moving when engaged in operations or camping. It constantly stayed close to the enemy to limit their strength in terms of firepower, bringing into full play our superiority in terms of morale and available equipment.

[On tactics that were considered effective against American ground forces.] The tactics used to good effect by the 9th Division in fighting against U.S. troops were surprise attack, ambush, and mobile attack. . . .

[On tactics/techniques to master or improve.] In particular, in fighting against U.S. troops, we must be able to destroy their armored vehicles. Once their armor was annihilated, the enemy infantry would quickly disintegrate. . . . We should secretly get close to the enemy and open fire simultaneously in several directions but concentrate on the main direction and make deep thrusts into vital positions such as command posts, artillery emplacements . . . and should stand ready to fight enemy troops dropped by helicopters on our flanks or behind us, etc.[52]

Colonel Cam agreed that his troops had indeed grabbed the enemy by their belts. "We aggressively pressed in close to the enemy, creating a situation in which our troops were intermingled amongst the enemy troops, thereby implementing our slogan of 'grabbing the enemy's belt to fight him,'" he wrote. "We carried out our troop movements, constantly shifted our troop positions, and always stuck close to the enemy in order to limit the effectiveness of the American strength, since they would always try to create a line separating their forces from ours so that they could use their heavy firepower to kill and wound our troops."[53] Cam likewise agreed that "surprise attacks, ambushes, and mobile ambushes" were effective tactics against American troops.

Cam, to his credit, also admitted in his memoirs that his forces had entered into a dramatically different kind of conflict. "First of all, the fighting was clearly more ferocious than was the case during the period when we were only fighting the puppet army," opined the commander of the 9th Viet Cong

Division. "The percentage of casualties the division suffered was higher. . . . The number of casualties we suffered during the attack against puppet troops holding solid fortified positions at the Dong Xoai district military headquarters, fighting that lasted for one full day and one night, were approximately equal to the number of casualties the division suffered when it attacked the U.S. troops occupying a rough, unfortified field position at Bau Bang, fighting that lasted for only around three hours."[54] Left unspoken of course was the realization that, in order to win, Communist forces would have to remain relatively impervious to casualties.

COSVN Military Headquarters and the COSVN Military Party Committee digested the lessons Cam and the 9th Viet Cong Division had garnered from its experiences and in early 1966 generated a document titled "A Number of Lessons about U.S. Tactics and How Our Main Force Troops Can Fight the Americans."[55] This guideline was then widely distributed in South Vietnam.

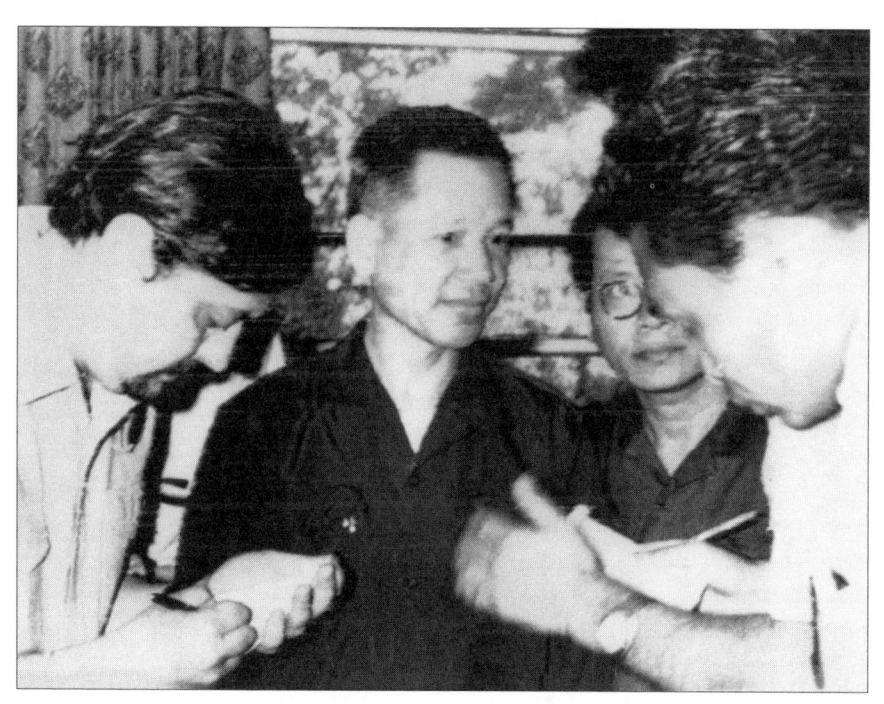

General Tran Van Tra speaks to foreign correspondents. (VA002316, 08 February 1973, Douglas Pike Photograph Collection, The Vietnam Archive, Texas Tech University)

Le Duan (*white shirt on right*), General Vo Nguyen Giap (*second from left, shirtsleeves*), General Van Tien Dung (*third from left*), and senior NVA officers converse and laugh. (VA001458, 21 July 1971, Douglas Pike Photograph Collection, The Vietnam Archive, Texas Tech University)

Ap Bau Bang burns in the background after being hit by American air and artillery strikes during the Battle of Bau Bang, November 1965. (Photo by Frank Alva; 1/4th Cav. Assn. Archives)

Smoke drifts over the American perimeter from the remains of Ap Bau Bang. (Photo by Frank Alva; 1/4th Cav. Assn. Archives)

Viet Cong RPG or recoilless rifle fire destroys an American mortar carrier during the Bau Bang battle. (Photo by Frank Alva; 1/4th Cav. Assn. Archives)

An American jet delivers a napalm strike against VC forces assaulting the American perimeter near Bau Bang. (Photo by Gerald Forker; 1/4th Cav. Assn. Archives)

Uniformed Viet Cong soldiers mount an infantry assault. (VA002444, 21 August 1971, Douglas Pike Photograph Collection, The Vietnam Archive, Texas Tech University)

An unidentified Viet Cong unit marches along a dirt track. (VA030903, Donald Jellema Collection, The Vietnam Archive, Texas Tech University)

Two Viet Cong soldiers take aim in the bush under the watchful eye of a comrade. (VA030905, Donald Jellema Collection, The Vietnam Archive, Texas Tech University)

In an apparently staged photograph, VC soldiers swarm over a destroyed armored vehicle. (VA030913, Donald Jellema Collection, The Vietnam Archive, Texas Tech University)

9

The Die Is Cast

Time magazine's decision to anoint General William Westmoreland "Man of the Year" for 1965 in a sense commemorated the success of Westmoreland's Phase I goal of halting "'the losing trend' by the end of 1965."[1] It also highlighted the failure of the VC/NVA to shatter ARVN and bring about a decisive "General Offensive–General Uprising" in South Vietnam. Hanoi had no choice but to concede that its attempt to resolve the matter of reunification before the United States transitioned from "special war" to "limited war" had been unsuccessful.[2]

Seduced by the allure of big-unit war—"We started fighting the United States troops when we were winning," said a subordinate of General Thanh, "[and] this gave us an advantageous combat position"—Communist military forces had but a series of costly big-unit setbacks to show for their year-end exertions.[3] And strategic momentum had been lost as a result. Westmoreland, conversely, had known nothing but big-unit victory and the gradual realization of his other major objective for Phase I, the creation of a base and logistical infrastructure to sustain future operations and the expected American troop buildup.

With Washington's decision to escalate American military involvement in South Vietnam now crystal clear and with the prospect of Westmoreland's Phase II on the horizon, a phase that would ask American forces to "gain the initiative, penetrate, and whenever possible eliminate the enemy's base camps and sanctuaries," the question of how Hanoi would respond militarily assumed critical importance.[4] Two strategic options immediately availed themselves: attempt to match the American buildup in men and materiel or ratchet down the military effort (likely to a lower stage of "revolutionary war") and reemphasize political *dau tranh*.

Toward the close of December 1965, on the occasion of the Twelfth Plenum, the future course of the Communist military campaign against South Vietnam was decided in North Vietnam. Hanoi's decision makers, in the end, elected to prepare for the possibility of protracted war while proposing to "concentrate the forces of both North and South Vietnam and seek an opportunity to secure a decisive victory within a relatively short period of time."[5] At this critical juncture, the North Vietnamese Politburo had recommended, and the Central Committee had approved, a strategy of investing North Vietnam more heavily in the war down South.[6]

North Vietnam would henceforth match the American buildup and, strategically speaking, escalate in kind. Domestic programs and initiatives were put on hold. Although American advantages in mass and movement, not to mention the defeats of November and December, had lobbied persuasively for retrenchment and a return to reduced intensity warfare, Hanoi's hardliners could not give up the conviction that a decisive military blow might yet be struck by the Viet Cong and the North Vietnamese Army. Recalibrating the intensity of the Communist war effort was apparently out of the question, even if the number of American troops in South Vietnam swelled from 200,000 to 400,000. The VC and NVA would simply kill 60,000 American troops and 20,000 ARVN troops.[7] Indeed, no matter how many troops or how much modern war materiel the United States dispatched to the battlefield, Hanoi crowed, the Viet Cong would triumph in South Vietnam.[8]

Though ultimately outmaneuvered by the hardliners, the opponents of intensified armed struggle and its big-unit battles raised spirited objections at the end of 1965 and the beginning of 1966. Within the Viet Cong leadership down South, some objected to the strategy on the grounds that military methods "do not bring victory" but rather misery and economic weakness.[9] In the North the "North-first" contingent of the party echoed those concerns. Initially they had lamented the decision to appropriate significant resources to the southern revolution, resources that in their opinion should have been invested in the economic and social development of the North. Now, however, they worried that American bombing runs over North Vietnam might disrupt socialist development in the North far more severely than the mere misallocation of precious resources. Understandably alarmed, these "North-firsters" argued, along with other moderates in the party who had perhaps grown disillusioned with the human costs of the big-unit war, for an adjustment of the current military strategy and for negotiations with the United States on ending the war.[10]

Negotiations with the United States were not ruled out entirely by the hardliners per se, but as a practical matter and prelude to any such talks, a degree of consensus within the "fraternal socialist nations . . . about the concept of fighting and talking" would have to be reached, according to Le Duan.[11] Moreover, favorable circumstances would first have to be "created on the battlefield" by shattering the South Vietnamese forces and bloodying the nose of the Americans.[12] These circumstances could be created, it was thought, through a continuation of medium-sized and large-scale campaigns by VC/NVA main-force units, heightened guerrilla warfare activity, and attacks against enemy rear installations and lines of communications. Here again, though, a significant victory on the battlefield was the key prerequisite to any "talk-fight" strategy. "As long as we have not won such a victory," warned Nguyen Duy Trinh, then North Vietnamese foreign minister, during discussions on yet another resolution in early 1967, "we cannot achieve success at the conference table."[13] Trinh's words were no less valid in the winter–spring of 1965–66.

Dat Cuoc–Hill 65, Bau Bang, Trung Loi, Nha Mat, and the Ia Drang Valley, therefore, would not be anomalous historical footnotes to an otherwise asymmetrical guerrilla war. There would be additional big-unit battles against American ground units backed by a potent and responsive fire-support system. Le Duan, General Thanh, and their hardliner cronies had once again won the great strategic debate. The big-unit war would continue.

Interestingly, Professor Pike termed the Communist military strategy going forward "Regular Force Strategy" and contextualized it through the prism of North Vietnam's defense minister, General Vo Nguyen Giap. Essentially Regular Force Strategy prescribed a quick military decision through the employment of regular military forces. The strategy stipulated that the American buildup in manpower and arms should be matched and, controversially, it did not proscribe slugging it out with American forces on occasion.[14] Giap, according to Pike, digested a rather unpalatable lesson from the fighting in the Ia Drang Valley, namely, that technology had changed warfare. The battle there with the 1st Cavalry Division allegedly convinced Giap to advocate matching American advantages in mass and movement (a key tenet of Regular Force Strategy) whenever possible and "shunting" the pair to the side when not.[15]

Whether Giap embraced military escalation willingly and as an outgrowth of personnel introspection or whether he was swept along by the seemingly irrepressible tide of the hardliners in Hanoi is, of course, open to debate. Indeed, while reflecting back on the war against the Americans, one officer who served in the NVA General Staff admitted that disputes surfaced in the North Vietnamese Politburo over strategy and tactics and that Giap was evidently not on the winning side of some of these debates. However, according to the officer, Giap sided with the majority when he couldn't get his way "in order to maintain unity."[16]

At any rate, and consonant with Pike's aptly named Regular Force Strategy and its preference for *military* victories over American units, Hanoi sent fresh forces south for the coming winter–spring campaign of 1966. No fewer than nine infantry regiments, three field artillery regiments, and an assortment of artillery, antiaircraft, engineer, and signal units were ordered south to join the existing "mobile main-force" units already in South Vietnam.[17]

Communist firepower in particular received a boost from the 68th Artillery Regiment (outfitted with 105-mm howitzers), 19th Artillery Battalion (outfitted with A-12 Rockets), and the Artillery Regiment 84A (outfitted with DKB rockets). In a strategic sense, the battlefield impact of the Viet Cong was inversely related to this North Vietnamese buildup; the greater the endowment of men and material from North Vietnam, the less militarily influential the Viet Cong would become in the long run.

Regardless of the future strategic ramifications for the Viet Cong, the course had been set for military escalation and big-unit battle. "We will fight,"

Le Duan had bragged, "whatever way the United States wants."[18] Given that the Viet Cong and NVA had already been exposed to a sobering tutorial on the U.S. military's multiarm battlefield riposte, what compelled the hardliners in Hanoi to opt for such an aggressive policy? To begin with, those predisposed to escalation were reasonably confident that the policy would not invoke any disastrous repercussions. The United States, Le Duan confided in a November letter to General Thanh, was unlikely to expand the war precipitately by attacking North Vietnam, because such an attack might provoke the North's fraternal allies.[19] Furthermore, as a global power with worldwide military obligations and yet only finite resources, the United States surely could not have considered *South Vietnam* a vital strategic interest. If it could therefore be made to face a failing proposition in what *had* to be considered a strategic backwater in Washington, the United States would invariably cut its losses and withdraw from the country.

Supporters of this strategy fashioned other arguments as well for emphasizing military intensification and big-unit victories over American forces. General Thanh, for one, theorized that the United States should fail much like the French because it, too, lacked the manpower to advance pacification *and* mount major offensive sweep operations to upset the insurgency. Thanh felt that this strategic conundrum could be exacerbated, in part, by striking with big units when and where it was deemed militarily advisable.[20]

And while idealism factored into American grand strategy, safeguarding Southeast Asia from the tentacles of Marxist-Leninism among them, the notion of waging a *just* war against a morally impoverished enemy permeated the outlook of many Communist Vietnamese leaders and even some in the rank and file. "We are just while the enemy is unjust," decreed the captured notebook of a high-ranking Communist political cadre. "The righteousness of our cause as well as the lack of righteousness of the enemy cause was clearly exhibited."[21] Similar remarks were found in the contents of a Viet Cong notebook. "The US Diem clique doesn't have right on its side since it acts against the will of the people," the notebook read. "Our revolution, on the other hand, is the right course. Those on the side of the right cause win support and friends. Those who embrace the wrong cause will be isolated and destroyed.

This is the advantage of we who uphold the revolution and the disadvantage of those who counter the revolution."[22]

Faith in a certain *providence* born of a supposedly just cause may also have encouraged the hardliners in Hanoi to advocate such a high-intensity, big-unit military campaign. Brian Michael Jenkins authored a paper for the RAND Corporation that expounded on this mindset: "Terms such as 'just cause,' and 'legitimate government,' dominate the speech of their leaders. Vietnamese Communists firmly believed that they possess the 'Mandate of Heaven' to rule all of Vietnam and therefore must emerge victorious eventually."[23]

General Van Tien Dung, chief of the North Vietnamese Army General Staff, touched on that theme as well as others expressed by the advocates of military escalation and big-unit battle in a monograph published in 1966. Discussing the perceived constraints on America's commitment to the war and the *unjustness* of the American cause, Dung lectured:

> Generally speaking, in the whole process of the war, the U.S. imperialists cannot throw all the economic and military potential of the United States for the sole purpose of invading the South of our country. This is because their unjust war of conquest is opposed by the American people and the world people, because they have to cope with the situation in many places and in various fields, including the military field, in order to rule over and repress other people, in the role of an international gendarme, and guard against other imperialist powers. Furthermore, they have to a wage a war thousands of miles far from the U.S.A., which places them in a disadvantageous position as regards climate, terrain and support of the population. That is why they can only deploy a limited military strength in South Vietnam; they cannot put in as many troops as they like, and pour in as much money as they please; they cannot prolong the war indefinitely. We thus have not to cope with all their military might.[24]

Deeper into the text, General Dung addressed another familiar theme. This time, rather than elaborate on the reasons why the United States could not commit the full weight of its economic and military might to the conflict,

Dung repeated Thanh's argument of why the forces the United States *had* committed were insufficient for the multiple objectives assigned to them: "The enemy himself deplores that his mobile forces have often to carry out occupation and pacification duties while 'Vietcong regiments are entirely mobile units.' He has been vainly trying to muster a bigger mobile force but his troops remain scattered around his bases and posts. If he withdraws from his posts and watch towers to have more mobile forces he will not be able to control the population and the areas under his control will shrink. If he tries to expand these areas, he will thin out his force and reduce his mobile effectives."[25]

These convictions may very well have led the hardliners to believe VC and NVA main-force units could retain the initiative and win big battles against American forces. After all, if one already believed that the reunification of Vietnam was destined to happen irrespective of the odds, was it any more of a leap of faith to believe that a strategy of big-unit war represented the most appropriate and efficacious use of what was essentially a light infantry force? It certainly did not require as much willing suspension of disbelief as General Thanh's contention that the "militant spirit" of the Viet Cong and North Vietnamese Army could counteract American advantages in firepower.[26]

Faulty postbattle appreciations did not exactly encourage strategic lucidity in military affairs, either. The August battle at Van Tuong, for example, was deemed a "Stalingrad" for American forces according to one Communist after-action report.[27] In terms of battle deaths, Van Tuong cost the Communists about six hundred KIA. The Marines lost a fraction of that number. The Ba Gia Regiment had been manhandled at Van Tuong by American combined arms warfare, and yet the battle was likened to a Stalingrad for the Americans. Who then, when fed reports of such dubious accuracy, could not have imagined a few more VC/NVA big-unit victories, and maybe even a decisive one, in the year ahead?

The North Vietnamese eventually acknowledged the decoupling of battlefield reporting and battlefield reality, and its consequential effects, as the war dragged on. An especially incriminating critique of activity in the Saigon area stated, "We can see that reporting from subordinate commanders to their superiors did not accurately reflect the real situation. Successes were usually exaggerated and mistakes and failures were not reported. This had a not insignificant impact on our operations. It caused senior commanders to misjudge and misevaluate the situation, which in turn led them to make incorrect policy decisions and to set goals and objectives which were unattainable."[28] Several years of battle and many thousands of combat deaths were necessary to arouse such candor. Why it should have taken so long speaks to either a widespread institutional failure to report accurately or a widespread case of cognitive dissonance.

In the final analysis, the resolution reached at the Twelfth Plenum established Communist military strategy for 1966 and beyond. High-intensity warfare would continue through a mixture of guerrilla and big-unit activity. Above all, in the words of North Vietnamese Army general Nguyen Van Vinh, head of the Central Committee's "Unification Committee" (the group responsible for managing support for the ongoing revolution in the South), Communist forces "must fight to win great victories with which to compel the enemy to accept our conditions."[29]

Hereafter, until later revisions altered the course of Communist military strategy, Viet Cong and NVA regiments and battalions fought to smash the armed forces of South Vietnam and hand Hanoi and COSVN "great victories" over American forces. The forthcoming year would either produce a war-changing breakthrough or a painful reminder of the difficult battles of 1965.

PLANNING AHEAD

In January 1966 the COSVN Military Party Committee convened a conference to examine the previous year and to strategize for the year ahead. To begin the conference analyzed the situation during 1965. The attention of those in attendance then turned to deducing the strategic military intentions and plans of the enemy. After careful contemplation the conference posited that the Americans and South Vietnamese would persist in 1966 with the basic strategic plan of 1965. That is to say, American and South Vietnamese units would aim to improve population security, attack and destroy Communist forces in South Vietnam, and magnify efforts against the recalcitrant North. Further, the conference surmised that this strategy was calculated to accomplish two goals: (1) counterattack and eliminate a significant chunk of the Communist main-force army, which would alter the balance of forces in favor of the allies and "on that basis regain the offensive initiative," and (2) stress pacification to "gain control of our civilian population and our territory in the lowlands, in the areas around strategic military strong-points" and in Communist base areas.[30]

After forecasting the enemy's likely strategy, the COSVN Military Party Committee focused on developing the "strategic military plans and missions" for implementing the resolution passed down by the Twelfth Plenum of the Central Committee. Not surprisingly the basic "strategic military plan" laid out for 1966, an intensification of both guerrilla warfare and of maneuver attacks by "massed large units," merely regurgitated the essential guidelines worked out at the Twelfth Plenum. Nor was there any real variance in the basic military goals proposed by the conference. Communist forces were to engage and destroy an "important portion of U.S. forces," which would prevent the U.S. military from arresting the collapse of the ARVN and the South Vietnamese government. Concurrent with that undertaking, every effort would also be made to eradicate the U.S. military's "main base of support for continuing the war" by shattering or causing the "disintegration" of the greater part of the ARVN.[31]

With the "strategic military guidelines" for 1966 in place, the COSVN Military Party Committee conference proposed three "primary missions" to fulfill those guidelines. Collectively these missions reflected the broad agenda approved by Hanoi in December 1965:

1. *Military:* The goal set for all of South Vietnam was to strive to annihilate between 30,000 and 40,000 U.S. troops and 200,000 puppet and satellite [allied] troops and to destroy 1,000 enemy aircraft of all types.
    - Intensify broad-based, wide-ranging guerrilla warfare.
    - Make powerful and continuous attacks against the enemy's land and water lines of communications.
    - Conduct powerful attacks against the enemy's rear bases.
    - Firmly hold and expand our base areas and liberate more people and more territory.
2. *Force-Building:* We must pay attention to all three types of troops [main force, local force, guerrilla] and strive to achieve the follow-

ing goals: approximately 250,000–300,000 civilian militia members, approximately 220,00–230,000 guerrillas, more than 200,000 district local force troops . . . while continuing to make quality our primary goal.
3. *Building Up Our Logistics Reserve Stockpiles:* Not only provide sufficient supplies for 1966, but ensure that we have sufficient supplies on hand for 1967 as well.[32]

The military missions and goals put forth for 1966 were not a means unto themselves in that they were designed to advance a "strategic formula." Here, too, the COSVN Military Party Committee conference hewed to the Twelfth Plenum: "In the actual, concrete conditions we face today, on the basis of continuing to digest and employ our formula of fighting a protracted struggle, we must make a maximum effort and concentrate the forces of both North and South Vietnam to strive to create an opportunity to win a decisive victory on the South Vietnamese battlefield within a relatively short period of time."[33] Under the circumstances it would have been illogical to expect a command creation of Hanoi to do anything but repackage and reissue the strategy the Communist Party Central Committee had already approved of.

COSVN was not the only command body planning and strategizing for 1966, however. In December 1965 the Region 5 Party Current Affairs Committee and the Military Region 5 Headquarters Party Committee released a resolution petitioning the soldiers and civilians of Region 5 to "strive to attack and counterattack the enemy and resolutely annihilate U.S. and satellite troops in order to defeat the enemy's strategic counteroffensive plan."[34] Communist main-force units were instructed to draft plans for combat cooperation with local forces in their areas. In the meantime "local areas" were to construct combat villages and other defenses.

Then, on January 16, 1966, the armed forces of Region 5 received a sweeping order. Communist forces were to launch counterattacks wherever the enemy had attacked first and to "continue preparations and take the initiative to launch attacks in accordance with the spring 1966 combat plan" wherever the enemy had yet to attack.[35]

Conceived on something of a *crash* basis, this spring battle plan shaped the upcoming missions of Nguyen Nang's 2nd NVA Division, to which the

1st Viet Cong Regiment belonged, and Giap Van Cuong's 3rd NVA Division ("Yellow Star" Division), to which the 2nd Viet Cong Regiment belonged. A divisional history summarized the mission handed down to the 2nd NVA Division and the corresponding formation of a new Communist command:

> According to this [spring battle] plan, 2nd Division was given the mission of coordinating with Quang Ngai local forces in conducting an offensive campaign in the area north of the Tra Khuc River, primarily in western Son Tinh district. The division's mission was to conduct massed combat operations designed to annihilate large numbers of both American and puppet soldiers (with the primary focus on killing American troops) and to support local areas in continuing to shatter the enemy's apparatus of repression and expand our liberated zone in order to thereby make a positive contribution to the effort by the soldiers and civilians of the entire region to defeat the enemy's strategic counteroffensive. . . .
>
> In mid-January 1966, the Quang Ngai Front Headquarters and Front Party Committee were formed, consisting of the members of the Province Party Current Affairs Committee and the members of the Division Current Affairs Committee. Comrade Pham Thanh Bien, Secretary of the Province Party Committee, was named as Secretary of the Front Party Committee and Front Political Commissar, and Comrade Nguyen Nang, the Division Commander, was named as Front Commander.[36]

South of the Quang Ngai Front, in Binh Dinh Province, the 3rd NVA Division had its own mission to execute and Communist command organization to help staff. According to a history of the Yellow Star Division:

> In the southern portion of the military region, the Yellow Star Division and the 10th Regiment, in cooperation with local armed forces, would operate in northern Binh Dinh and Phu Yen, liberate the remaining district capitals and district military headquarters, and stand ready to mount counterattacks to defeat the enemy's "search and destroy" operations. This meant that Military Region 5's 1966 Spring Campaign was targeted primarily against U.S. forces and that American troops were

to be our principal battlefield opponents. . . . In January 1966, the Binh Dinh Front Headquarters was formed. The headquarters was made up of the senior officers of the Yellow Star Division and the members of the Binh Dinh Province Party Current Affairs Committee. Comrade Giap Van Cuong, the Division Commander, was designated as the Front Commander, and Comrade Tran Quang Khanh, the Province Party Secretary, was the Front Political Commissar.[37]

Hanoi and its war managing bodies in the South, in anticipating and preparing for a major American offensive action, seemed rather prescient about American military intentions for 1966. "The military tasks facing the United States," declared a history of the U.S. Joint Chiefs of Staff, "had to be accomplished therefore both in NVN and RVN. The United States . . . must selectively destroy the NVN military capabilities, reducing its capability to import and distribute war materials. In addition, the United States must destroy other 'high value' targets in NVN in order to punish that nation increasingly for its part in the war. In RVN the task was to find, harass, pursue, and defeat VC/NVA units, destroying their bases and disrupting their LOCs in the country and outside it."

American strategy acknowledged, in a nod to pacification, that the South Vietnamese people had to be secured from "communist 'subversion and oppression'" and that certain areas in South Vietnam had to be freed from Viet Cong control.[38] In all fairness, however, piecing together the disparate challenges confronting the American military in Vietnam into a coherent intelligence picture on the probable path forward for American military strategy should not have proven unduly difficult for Hanoi and its intelligence organs—not with the print coverage devoted to MACV's general strategy.

Much maligned for his supposed *predilection* for big-unit war to the near exclusion of counterinsurgency and population security, General Westmoreland at MACV actually had a better grasp of the military-security situation in South Vietnam and a better strategy for how to proceed than some are willing to admit. "Many of the actions that have drawn criticism, such as the use of large operations and heavy firepower," wrote Andrew J. Birtle, a historian at the U.S. Army Center of Military History and the author of two books dealing with the U.S. Army and counterinsurgency doctrine, "stemmed less from a lack of understanding of counterinsurgency theory than from the fact that the realities on the ground and the enemy's sheer military strength often demanded a 'conventional' response."[39] A 1970 report supported Birtle's argument. Issued by a study group commissioned by the National Security Council, the report recognized that major advancements in pacification had not taken place until after such time as the "allies were able clearly to gain the upper hand in the main-force war, destroying, dispersing, or pushing back the enemy main force units."[40] If Westmoreland's strategy was guilty of putting the cart (big-unit war) before the horse (pacification/population security), the actual situation on the ground in South Vietnam cast some doubt as to which was in fact the cart and which was the horse.

Critics of Westmoreland's approach have argued that since Communist main-force units relied on the support of local guerrillas and the civilian populace of South Vietnam, denial of that support through successful counterinsurgency/population security measures would have brought about their ultimate defeat. Plausible and persuasive, the argument advanced by these critics is only partially correct. In the late 1950s and early 1960s, Communist military units in South Vietnam may very well have withered and died on the vine if deprived of local civilian support. Yet from the fall of 1965 onward, the logistical situation changed and many Communist main-force units were simply not beholden to that support. NVA regiments operating in the Central Highlands and in Quang Tri Province depended on *Hanoi*, not the South Vietnamese civilian population, for their logistical survival. Correspondingly Colonel Cam's 9th Viet Cong Division, the foremost Communist main-force unit menacing Saigon in the years 1965–68, relied on external support. No measure of population security or pacification, consequently, would have denied those units of the means to continue the big-unit war.

Oft forgotten, Westmoreland was also encouraged in early 1966 to "attrite, by year's end, VC/NVA forces at a rate as high as their capability to put men into the field."[41] Quite naturally Westmoreland chided his subordinates to seek out and destroy the VC and NVA in South Vietnam, and he wanted to begin Phase II of his roadmap to victory at some point in 1966. But the transition to Phase II would not be instantaneous, mainly because he did not possess at the beginning of 1966 the additional American forces required to prosecute it full stop. Time was needed to amass and deploy those forces. In the interim Westmoreland had to keep the enemy at bay. Thus he had to prioritize where and when to strike in order to keep the Communists from regaining the initiative.[42]

The "Combined Plan for Military Operations in the Republic of Vietnam, 1966" provided an initial inkling as to where Westmoreland might commit to offensive action. Authored in December 1965 by MACV and the South Vietnamese Joint General Staff, the plan singled out the populous regions around Saigon, in the Mekong Delta, and sections of the coastal flats in I and II Corps for clearing out and securing. Westmoreland ultimately conferred top "operational priority" to the areas around Saigon followed by the thickly populated coastal plains of I and II Corps, and it was in these regions where he would begin offensive operations in early 1966.[43]

PART III

THE BIG-UNIT WAR: 1966

10

An Inauspicious Beginning

General Westmoreland began 1966 probing uncharted territory for American combat troops—the western marshlands of Communist-infested Hau Nghia Province northwest of Saigon. On January 1 elements of the 173rd Airborne Brigade penetrated the marshy, inhospitable Plain of Reeds in the Mekong Delta. No previous American combat unit had ever ventured out onto the plain. Although technically a "coordinated Search and Destroy" operation with ARVN forces, Westmoreland handed the primary mission of Operation Marauder I to the 173rd Airborne Brigade under the command of General Ellis W. Williamson. Williamson's brigade was to find and destroy the 506th Viet Cong Local Force Battalion and exert control over the Vam Co Dong River.

Fulfilling the operational mandate of Marauder I would not be easy. Relatively unchallenged for months in its area of operations to the east and west of the Vam Co Dong River, the 506th had an estimated strength of five hundred men divided into three infantry companies and a combat support company.[1] Nor was the 506th alone. The 267th Battalion of the Dong Thap II Regiment also operated east of the river. Guerrilla elements and several local-force companies roamed the area as well. Including the 506th, these units were reportedly endowed with .50-caliber machine guns, 57-mm and 75-mm recoilless rifles, heavy mortars, and possibly 75-mm pack howitzers.[2] Moreover, despite the open marsh and paddy terrain, the vegetation on paddy dikes and next to the many canals in the area enabled the Viet Cong to construct numerous neatly concealed fortifications.[3]

A little after noon on January 1, Lieutenant Colonel John Tyler's 1/503rd (173rd Airborne Brigade) landed west of the Vam Co Dong River, effectively kicking off Operation Marauder I. Other than a minor skirmish in which his Company B, after air and artillery strikes, attacked and displaced a group of sixty to seventy VC deployed in bunkers close to the river, Tyler encountered light resistance on the 1st. East of the Vam Co Dong, Lieutenant Colonel Alec Preece's 1st Battalion, Royal Australian Regiment disembarked at LZ Scotch. Preece's men unearthed a number of vacant enemy bunkers but encountered virtually no enemy units to speak of.

Uninspired at the start of Marauder I, Viet Cong resistance stiffened almost immediately on the morning of January 2. When Lieutenant Colonel George Dexter's 2/503 attempted a heliborne assault onto LZ Wine southeast of Preece's Australians on the east side of the Vam Co Dong River, the VC were lying in wait. Viet Cong troops arrayed to the south and west, in between the landing zone and the Vam Co Dong, opened up on the helicopters attempting to land Dexter's men around 8:00 AM. Shooting back from inside the choppers, the Skytroopers struggled to match the volume of incoming fire. Meanwhile those already on the ground returned fire furiously. Eventually the paratroopers had enough boots on the ground to mount an infantry assault and secure the landing zone. Falling back, the Viet Cong disengaged and retreated toward the river, conceding LZ Wine to the Americans.[4]

With the harrowing helilift over and the landing zone now secure, Dexter's airborne assault force swept outward in the direction of the Vam Co Dong River. Unlike the previous day, however, the Viet Cong would not melt away after their initial engagement with American troops. Nestled in bunkers one hundred to three hundred meters to the southwest, the dug-in 267th Viet Cong Battalion halted Companies and A and B with heavy fire. One particular concrete bunker housed a machine gun, which the Viet Cong trained on Company B and with noticeable effect. The heavy volume of VC fire also denied Company A the opportunity, pinned down as it was in the soggy expanse, to close up with Company B.[5]

High above the battlefield, American aerial reconnaissance observed the extent of the VC defenses blocking Dexter's airborne spearhead. The Viet

Cong, it appeared, were hunkered down in a succession of rice paddy dikes that extended to a depth of approximately several thousand meters.[6] Evicting the VC from their entrenchments would necessitate a massive investment in American combat power. Reluctant to surrender as a general rule anyhow, the troops of the 267th now had an added inducement to stand and fight—with the Americans all but assured of calling on supporting arms, a withdrawal now during daylight hours would only invite crippling losses from American firepower.[7] The question of whether to cut and run or hold out and weather the inevitable storm was almost a rhetorical one. The 267th would stand and fight.

Until well into the afternoon of January 2, the 267th Viet Cong Battalion, along with any ancillary forces that may have been present, endured a battering at the hands of American supporting fires. "For eight hours," began a vivid *New York Times* description of the battle, "the Americans crouched in the muck behind paddy dikes and watched bombs, napalm, artillery, and mortar shells hit the enemy."[8] In addition to the ordnance mentioned by the *Times*, American helicopters dropped two E-158 CS (tear gas) clusters from an altitude of five hundred feet on "known VC locations" at 9:15 AM. Although the impact on the Viet Cong below could not be gleaned through visual observation, VC fire from the targeted area apparently decreased considerably.

To its credit the 267th held out as the shellacking from American supporting arms continued without abatement. Then, late that afternoon, the 2/503rd staged a ground assault to oust the VC once and for all from their defensive positions and "pin" the survivors up against the Vam Co Dong River. All three of Dexter's companies, each with an artillery battery in support, assaulted the Viet Cong defensive front. Company B managed to flank the Viet Cong force but could not roll it up or compel it to quit. Unsuccessful but not obdurate, the Americans softened the VC up with additional air and artillery strikes. Finally, about 5:00 PM or so, the Americans achieved a breakthrough. Five soldiers from Company A's 2nd Platoon overran a Viet Cong position near the concrete bunker. The men then traveled along the dike and eliminated VC positions one by one, allowing Company A to fully breach the 267th's defenses.[9]

Hammered mercilessly by American supporting arms, and with its defensive front collapsing under the weight of a determined American infantry assault, the 267th Viet Cong Battalion withdrew in haste. Soldiers scattered in multiple directions and that, along with the watery, soft soiled topography, hindered the American pursuit. Behind them, on the battlefield, lay the bodies of 111 dead comrades.[10] The 267th had paid a steep price for its stoicism.

Four days after the January 2 battle, elements of Lieutenant Colonel Dexter's battalion happened upon the deserted headquarters of the 506th Viet Cong Local Force Battalion. Reams of administrative records and documents pertaining to the makeup, strength, and weaponry of the 506th were recovered, so much so in fact that one American military interrogator marveled at how the intelligence *haul* "would provide a historical background for the 506th Battalion as nothing else could."[11] Operation Marauder I had chewed up one VC battalion and had raided and destroyed the headquarters of another. For the Viet Cong, the 1966 big-unit war was off to an inauspicious start.

Immediately after Marauder I, Viet Cong forces north of Saigon were subjected to yet another American "search-and-destroy" initiative. West of the infamous Iron Triangle, on the west bank of the Saigon River, the Viet Cong maintained the Mat Khu Ho Bo, the "Ho Bo Secret Zone," or what the Americans simply called the Ho Bo Woods.[12] Heavily fortified, this Communist base area contained subterranean tunnel complexes and, reputedly, the headquarters of Military Region 4, the Communist command element overseeing military affairs in the Saigon region of South Vietnam.[13] General Westmoreland again tapped the 173rd Airborne Brigade along with elements of General Seaman's 1st Infantry Division for a sweep into the area, with the 173rd specifically charged with locating and destroying the headquarters of Military Region 4.

Dubbed Operation Crimp, Westmoreland's foray into the Ho Bo Woods commenced on January 8. Tran Bang was confined to a tunnel when the Americans attacked. "Have spent four days in tunnel. About 8 to 9 thousand American soldiers were in for a sweep-operation," Bang wrote in his diary. "The attack was fierce, in the last few days. A number of underground tunnels collapsed. Some (of our men) were caught in them and have not been able to get out yet."[14] Dozens of Bang's comrades were indeed killed by American air strikes, artillery, and small-arms fire during the operation; the 173rd Airborne Brigade concluded Crimp on January 14 and listed a brigade tally of

128 confirmed enemy KIA.[15] Meanwhile, on January 10, Lieutenant Colonel Preece's Australians investigated a tunnel complex and discovered an abandoned Communist headquarters, almost certainly that of Military Region 4. Whatever it was, the headquarters yielded a wealth of vital documents, compelling the Communists to, in the words of one analysis, "adjust their planning for some time to come."[16]

Notwithstanding the *crimp* Crimp had put in Communist planning, the most salient aspect of the operation from a Communist perspective may have been the countersweep conduct of the Viet Cong. Nguyen Thanh Linh, a lieutenant in the Viet Cong's 7th Cu Chi Battalion, explained how his unit reacted to the American offensive:

> I had divided my men into small cell-like units. I told them under no circumstances to concentrate. I spread my men into each hamlet where we had well-hidden firing positions to hold back the Americans.... I ordered my men to fire, one GI fell down, the others just stood around looking at him. They were so bewildered, they did not hide or take defensive positions. They did not even know where the bullets had come from. We kept on shooting.... Although their fellows kept falling down, they kept on advancing. They should have retreated. Then they called for artillery. When the first shells landed we simply went into the communication tunnels and went on to another place. The Americans continued advancing, but we'd gone.... Those tunnels were everything to us in Crimp.[17]

Obviously not every Viet Cong unit had the luxury of vanishing into such an intricate, and in some places commodious, tunnel network like Lieutenant Linh. Still, Linh's actions and those of his men testified to a larger point. Stalked by an American sweep operation, the VC dispersed, engaged American forces when it was expedient, and retreated when it was not or when they had no inclination to fight. Much like Linh, the Viet Cong as a military adversary could dictate the battle tempo of the big-unit war against the Americans. Unless trapped—and as Lieutenant General Bernard W. Rogers decried after a 1967 offensive, "It was a sheer physical impossibility to keep him [Viet Cong] from slipping away whenever he wished to, if he were in terrain with which he was familiar"—the Viet Cong could on balance accept or decline battle at their own discretion.[18] In contrast, American units, dragooned as they were to "find Charlie," more or less accepted battle whenever Charlie saw fit to give it.

To the extent that the Viet Cong *could* dictate battle tempo, Communist proficiency in the information war played a vital role. Dreadfully permeable, South Vietnam's civilian and military command establishment, with whom the U.S. military had to coordinate and cooperate, suffered from extensive Communist penetration. These security breaches, in turn, leaked sensitive information to the Viet Cong, some of it forewarning them about forthcoming allied military operations. Intercepted American radio transmissions and information picked up from Vietnamese civilians employed at American bases supplied additional intelligence and sharpened the focus of the intelligence outline.

Noisy American field craft and a debatable operating doctrine also provided the Viet Cong with advance notice, and hence the choice beforehand of whether to fight or take flight. Weighted down with burdensome equipment and frequently exhausted, the average American infantryman "humping the boonies" could not ape the hushed movements of many of his Viet Cong counterparts. Sizable American infantry units, in the opinion of one decorated American veteran, sounded like "a herd of elephants coming" when on the move.[19] Conspicuously loud American war machines only added to the racket generated by infantry units with dubious noise discipline. Doctrinally the practice of "prepping" landing zones with air and artillery strikes before an American airmobile assault broadcast American intentions as well. A CINCPAC (commander in chief, Pacific Command) study openly questioned the advisability of a doctrine that sacrificed the element of surprise when fighting the VC/NVA: "This doctrine may be unsuitable against an enemy that withdraws in the presence of force, ambushes and interdicts in situations of its own choosing, and then melts into the jungle where it is indistinguishable from the native population. To provide this kind of enemy with tip offs is to ensure that we will plunge full force into a vacuum. Subsequent contacts with the enemy will be at best fortuitous, at worst the result of enemy counterattack and ambush."[20]

Tactical familiarity with the Americans, moreover, assisted the Viet Cong in controlling battle tempo. "Their [Americans] idea was to surround us with ground forces, then destroy us with artillery and rockets, rather than by attacking directly with infantry," one Viet Cong officer said. "Usually we could get away from that, even when they used helicopters to try and surround us, because we knew the countryside so well and could get out fast."[21] Knowing in effect what to look for, the Viet Cong were frequently able to recognize developing American offensives and disperse accordingly, leaving American units lunging into dry holes.

REGION 5

Coordinated American-allied offensive operations in Quang Ngai and Binh Dinh Provinces in late January validated Communist concerns about the possibility of a major enemy action in Region 5. On the morning of January 28, 1966, and after a preliminary reconnaissance phase to locate Communist forces inland, elements of a Marine task force splashed ashore at Red Beach northeast of Duc Pho to begin the "amphibious landing phase" of Operation Double Eagle. Initiated at the behest of General Westmoreland, the Marines, assisted by the 2nd ARVN Division, launched the operation to destroy Communist forces in southern Quang Ngai Province. Also on the morning of the twenty-eighth, and part of an ongoing offensive effort orchestrated to coincide with Double Eagle to the north, the 1st Cavalry Division continued Operation Masher/White Wing in Binh Dinh Province with a "hammer and anvil" operation on the Bong Son Plain.

Disregarding a stipulation in the Viet Cong Oath of Honor to "go forward in combat without fear" and "never retreat regardless of suffering involved," the Viet Cong essentially abstained from big-unit battle during Double Eagle and its successor, Double Eagle II.[22] The Marines had hoped the amphibious landing at Red Beach would deceive VC/NVA troops, and the B-52 bombing strikes inland would kill scores of them. Marine heliborne assaults would then cut off and destroy those fleeing the air raids. But the VC/NVA, abetted by inclement weather and the rugged terrain on the western edge of the Marine operating area, slipped the hangman's noose. The Viet Cong, protested one Marine company commander, "would hit us—pull out. Hit us and pull out.

They wouldn't stick around for firefights."[23] Much of that hitting and pulling out, furthermore, was perpetrated by VC guerrilla bands.

Double Eagle finally concluded on February 17. Regarding enemy main-force contact, the after-action report of Task Force Delta noted, disappointingly, "In analysis of DOUBLE EAGLE operations, the single factor of most significance was the complete lack of contact with main force VC elements." Advance knowledge of the time and location of the attack, something Communist prisoners confessed to possessing when interrogated, may explain the dearth of noteworthy contacts with Communist main-force elements.[24] Double Eagle II, which had targeted but failed to find the 1st Viet Cong Regiment to the north in the Que Son Valley area, ended just as frustratingly on March 1.[25]

Juxtaposed between the Central Highlands region and the South China Sea, and the site of Operation Masher/White Wing, Binh Dinh Province to the south held great importance for both sides. If General Westmoreland wished to prosecute the war with a reasonable expectation of success, he had to pacify the southern extremities of I Corps as well as the northern and central sections of II Corps. In order to do that, he would have to gain the upper hand in restive Binh Dinh Province.[26] For Hanoi and the Viet Cong, a serious military setback in Binh Dinh could reduce Communist influence in the province's heavily populated coastal plain and help resuscitate enemy pacification efforts. Farther inland, secluded and splendidly fertile valleys such as the An Lao and Kim Son afforded the VC/NVA refuge and a place to base, train, and cache supplies. Successful American and allied operations in these sanctuaries would have a disruptive effect on the Communist infiltration-logistical system in Binh Dinh Province. Northern Binh Dinh, in fact, functioned as the rear base for the 3rd NVA Division.

Giap Van Cuong's 3rd NVA Division was actually dispersed throughout northern Binh Dinh at the time of Operation Masher/White Wing. The 22nd NVA Regiment was in Hoai Nhon District, and the 12th NVA Regiment was in northern Phu My District. The 2nd Viet Cong Regiment, in the interim, was situated in Hoai An District. Albeit spread out, the Yellow Star Division had prepared for battle. Each of its regiments had coordinated with local military forces, and each had been alerted to the possibility of American airmobile operations. Sufficient quantities of food had also been furnished to provide for the division in the event of a protracted action. Preparations of a political nature, such as "political activities" for lower level units and political training for "command-level cadres" at the battalion level and higher, had accompanied this logistical planning. Consistent with the premium the Communist Vietnamese placed on the political aspects of battle preparation, the commander of Military Region 5, Comrade Nguyen Don, paid a visit to "personally inspect the preparations of the Northern Binh Dinh Front." Don also arrived to direct the political training of divisional cadre.

While elements of the 22nd NVA Regiment, the Binh Dinh Province local-force unit, a local-force unit from Hoai Nhon District, and village guerrillas contested Operation Masher/White Wing north of Bong Son on January 28, the 2nd Viet Cong Regiment was relegated to a supporting role. "To support 22nd Regiment," a history of the Yellow Star Division explained, "the division headquarters ordered 2nd and 12th Regiments to launch a wave of attacks in southern Bong Son district, behind the enemy combat formations."[27] These attacks, to the extent that they occurred, do not appear to have affected the outcome of the fighting on the Bong Son Plain or the subsequent conduct of Masher/White Wing.

Assuming that some Communist units had vacated the coastal plain area for the An Lao Valley and the hills in between, the 1st Cavalry Division pursued westward into the valley in early February. The pursuit into the An Lao, though appearing purely reactionary and predicated on Communist movements, actually conformed entirely to plan. After maneuvering about the Bong Son Plain, General Kinnard, the commander of the 1st Cavalry Division, had intended to mount similar "hammer and anvil" operations to flush, block, and destroy VC/NVA forces in the adjoining valleys.[28] Other than local guerrilla units and an "engineer" company from the 3rd NVA Division, however, the An Lao Valley was virtually empty. The 22nd NVA Regiment, contrary to expectation, had remained behind in the northern Bong Son area. Consequently, despite closing the northern and southern exits of the valley with U.S. Marine and South Vietnamese forces, the 1st Cavalry Division (2nd and 3rd Brigades) search for Communist main-force units in the An Lao Valley turned up vast quantities of rice but few substantial contacts.

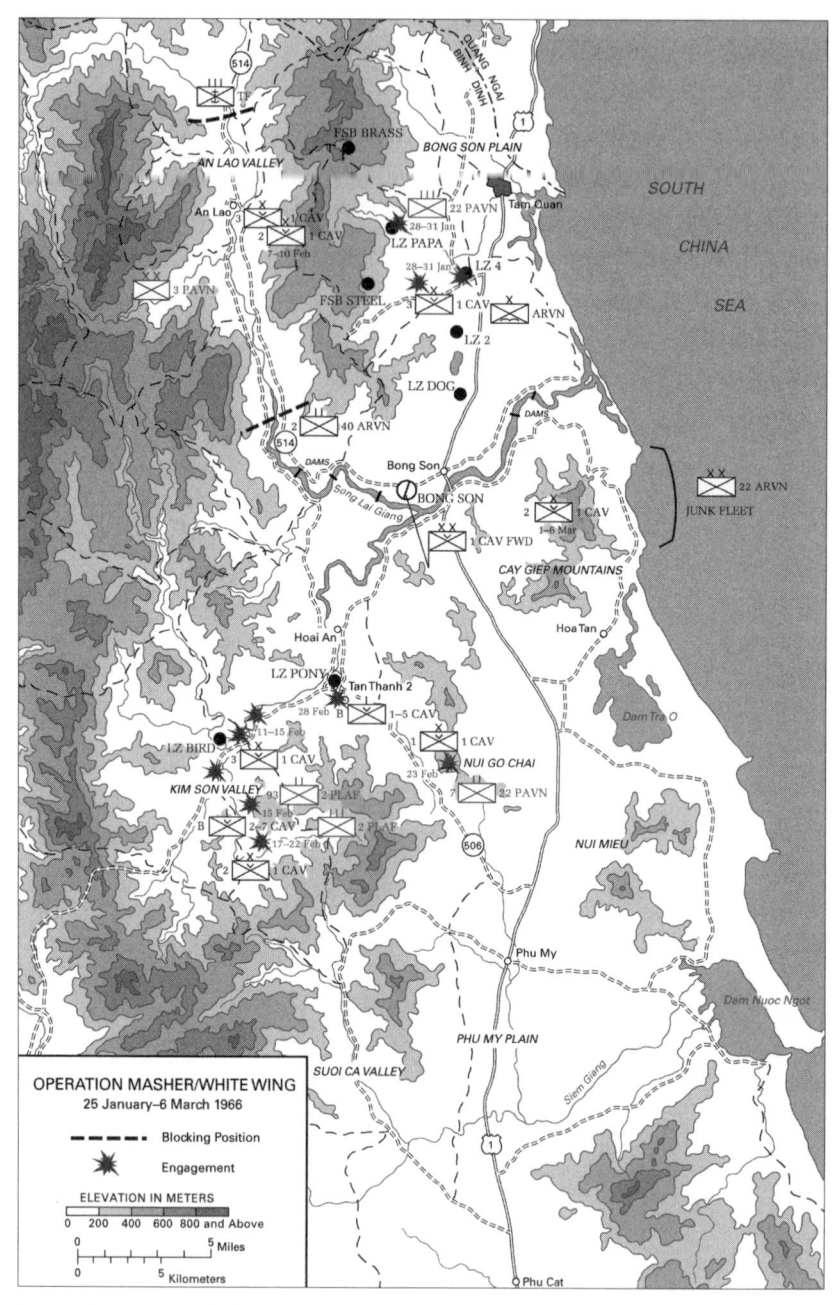

Map 7. *Operation Masher/White Wing, January 25–March 6, 1966 (From Carland, United States Army in Vietnam)*

In the meantime, the 2nd Viet Cong Regiment was asked to bide its time to the south rather than travel north to reinforce the 22nd NVA Regiment. Divisional headquarters, it seems, had decided to hold the 2nd back:

> When the American operation began in the An Lao Valley, and based on our knowledge of the enemy's reconnaissance activities, the Yellow Star Division Headquarters concluded that the enemy would certainly 'jump into' the Hoai An area to redeem their loss of face for their missed blow into the An Lao Valley. For this reason, the division decided not to send 2nd Regiment from Hoai An out to Hoai Nhon to work with the 22nd Regiment as had originally been intended. Instead the regiment was ordered to quickly prepare for battle in southeastern Hoai An, where it would cooperate with 12th Regiment in engaging the American troops when they arrived.[29]

A cigarette-smoking, newspaper-reading southerner and a member of the Lao Dong Party, Regimental Commander Khanh would lead the 2nd in the upcoming battles against the American air cavalrymen. Khanh, though he had only the equivalent of a ninth-grade education and was thus not especially well educated by traditional American standards, was experienced in combat and as a commander. Subordinate to Khanh, Nguyen Tai Nhue and Dang Doan commanded the 95th and 93rd Viet Cong Battalions, respectively.

As Khanh and his battalion commanders prepared for combat, Huynh Huu Anh, the deputy division commander for the 3rd NVA Division, and Dang Hoa, the division's political commissar, arrived to "personally inspect" the regiment and to supervise the battle. Gambling that the 1st Cavalry Division would come to them, the division had withheld the 2nd Viet Cong Regiment and had posted two of its top military and political leaders to oversee the action. The rest was up to the Americans.

General Kinnard kindly obliged. In mid-February Colonel Hal Moore's 3rd Brigade swooped into the Kim Son Valley south of the An Lao Valley. Encompassing seven smaller valleys interrupted by various streams and the Kim Son River, the Kim Son Valley was identified as a staging area for Communist military units and a component of the Viet Cong "infiltration route system" into Binh Dinh Province. American intelligence also theorized that Communist units may have left the An Lao Valley and infiltrated into the Kim Son. Motivated by those reasons, as well as the stated desire from the outset to operate on the Bong Son Plain and in the contiguous valleys, Moore commenced a sophisticated block and sweep maneuver in the Kim Son area on February 11.[30]

The Viet Cong skirmished with Moore's air cavalry troopers over the next few days, but on February 15 a more substantial clash developed. Entrenched along a stream bank covered in vegetation, elements of the 93rd Viet Cong Battalion hit two platoons from Company B, 2nd Battalion (7th Cavalry Regiment) with small-arms and mortar fire. Company B, commanded by Captain Myron Diduryk, was out on patrol when the shooting started. After air strikes and artillery worked over the estimated two companies of dug-in VC, one of Diduryk's platoons "fixed bayonets" and charged toward the VC located across the stream.[31]

Abandoning their lines abruptly, the Viet Cong fled the bellowing Americans in disarray. Some floundered out into the open and were gunned down. Some retreated northward and unwittingly into the gun sights of another of Diduryk's platoons. Others, included the commander of the 93rd Viet Cong Battalion, Lieutenant Colonel Dang Doan, were captured. Fifty-nine of Doan's soldiers, and maybe many more, were killed in the encounter along with two Americans from Company B.[32]

Formerly a middle-class farmer with the equivalent of an American junior high school education, Lieutenant Colonel Doan was born on October 15, 1929, in Thua Thien Province. A southerner by birth, Doan volunteered in 1949 to fight with the Viet Minh. He left for North Vietnam in February 1954 and remained in the North until March 1957, traveling thereafter to China for artillery training. He then returned to North Vietnam and prepared for his infiltration into South Vietnam with political and military "refresher training" from August 1961 to January 1962. On January 13, 1962, Doan reentered South Vietnam, where he spent time as a "security assistant" for the 2nd Viet Cong Regiment.

Considering his membership in the Lao Dong Party and his extensive military service, Doan did not figure to be a particularly garrulous or helpful prisoner. Yet, in time, he proved to be a cooperative detainee. Indeed, when queried about South Vietnamese–American propaganda leaflets, Doan recommended certain messages and themes that he felt would resonate with Viet Cong soldiers.[33] Wounded and found hiding in a cave at the time of his capture, however, Doan was combative and insolent. But his ego apparently got the better of him during a subsequent interrogation, and he unintentionally disclosed the locations of other elements of the 2nd Viet Cong Regiment:

> "Tell me how you could have been so stupid," asked the interrogator, his tactical map in front of him, "to have deployed your battalion so badly that our division was able to inflict such heavy casualties on them so easily?" Senior Captain Dang Doan was an experienced field commander who wasn't about to let his command ability be challenged by the young American facing him. "You're wrong!" he replied. "I deployed my battalion well against your sweeping forces. There is no way you could have caused my unit to suffer the kinds of causalities you've described." To illustrate his point, he showed the interrogator how the American forces had been moving against his battalion and how he had redeployed it to guarantee that they would survive, also locating the remainder of his regiment. The interrogator looked at Senior Captain Doan silently, stood up, and took the map with the regiment's position to the G-2 for immediate follow up.[34]

The 1st Cavalry Division moved quickly. Colonel William Lynch, commander of the 2nd Brigade, settled on a block and sweep operation in the area where the 2nd Viet Cong Regiment was believed to be located. On February 16, the day after the intelligence windfall on the whereabouts of additional enemy forces, the 2nd Battalion/5th Cavalry Regiment established one blocking position at Recoil, located less than ten kilometers east of the Kim Son Valley, and another to the southwest of Recoil. A third blocking position was installed north of Recoil. Northeast of Recoil, the 1st Battalion (5th Cavalry Regiment) landed at LZ Coil for a sweep west toward the aforementioned blocking positions.[35] Wrapped in dense forests, the Ho Son Mountains and a river valley covered in five- to six-foot-high elephant grass highlighted the terrain features in the projected area of operations.

Over the next five days, elements of the 2nd Viet Cong Regiment—including troops from Nguyen Tai Nhue's 95th Viet Cong Battalion—fought to avert annihilation. Booming away on the morning of February 17, American artillery announced the coming fury by firing some 431 rounds into the area between Recoil and Coil.[36] Companies A and B of Lieutenant Colonel Frederic Ackerson's 1/5, advancing in the wake of the artillery "time on target," headed westward toward the blocks established by Lieutenant Colonel Edward Meyer's 2/5. But Meyer had troubles of his own. Setting out to seize another blocking position, Company B of the 2/5 crashed into a very well-equipped Communist force deployed "upslope" shortly after 9:00 AM. Armed with mortars, recoilless rifles, and automatic weapons and deployed in an area honeycombed with bunkers and defensive positions, the dug-in VC/NVA laced Company B with heavy fire.

The 2nd Brigade's AAR surmised that Meyer's troops had more than likely encountered a heavy-weapons battalion, presumably from the 2nd Viet Cong Regiment. Communist sources, on the other hand, mention a "battle area defended by 2nd Regiment and the anti-aircraft battalion."[37] The latter unit, considering the manner in which it is discussed, seems to have been organic to the 3rd NVA Division, not necessarily the 2nd Viet Cong Regiment. In any event Company B was unable to uproot the Communist force alone. Meyer, accordingly, asked for air and artillery strikes before committing his two remaining companies. Company B of the 2nd Battalion, 12th Cavalry Regiment was also attached to the 2/5 to further reinforce the effort. Hours into the fight, and after losing at least 127 of its men, the VC/NVA force withdrew from the battlefield early in the evening.[38]

The next day, February 18, the Viet Cong engaged Ackerson. Occupying bunkers and other defensive emplacements, a company-sized VC force opened up on 3rd Platoon/Company B with a welter of automatic weapons fire early in the afternoon. Just before 2:00 PM, a second platoon (2nd Platoon/Company A) from the 1/5 entered the scrum, followed by American air and artillery. Ackerson reinforced the two pinned down platoons with Companies A and

B, but the Viet Cong refused to budge. "Artillery and TAC air strikes, in the objective area, supported the attack by friendly forces," the 1st Cavalry Division's AAR admitted, "but the enemy defenses were not penetrated."[39] The first to break contact and retreat on the previous day, the VC watched the American air cavalrymen fight stubbornly during the day on the eighteenth, only to then disengage at night to recover fallen comrades.

In hindsight the decision to dig the 2nd Viet Cong Regiment in and await General Kinnard, rather than redeploying it north to assist the 22nd NVA Regiment, appears to have been a wise decision. Colonel Lynch's 2nd Brigade had certainly fought well, attacking and defeating enemy counterattacks for the next two days, but it could not deliver a knockout blow. Choked with dense tropical fauna, the setting of the fighting contributed significantly to the American difficulties, as did the multiplicity and craftsmanship of the Communist fighting positions. American troops, perhaps in a bit of gallows humor, went so far as to nickname the location of the severest fighting the Iron Triangle out of respect for the "disposition and elaborateness" of the Communist defensive positions.[40] Had the 2nd moved north as planned, it may have been discovered and forced to fight on a less advantageous battleground.

Inasmuch as they were able to grab American troops "by the belt" during the fighting, the Viet Cong were unable to hang on. Twice, once on February 19 and then again on the twentieth, American troops broke off heated contacts and summoned punishing air and artillery strikes, sometimes as a prelude to renewed ground attacks. "After every surprise attack by our troops and after every time that we repelled one of their attacks," a Communist source complained, "the American soldiers hastily pulled back and rained bombs and artillery shells on the entire area around them."[41] On the twenty-first Colonel Lynch performed the maneuver on a grand scale and withdrew all of his units from the Iron Triangle in advance of two B-52 bombing runs over the area. The big bombers, along with a massive CS strike from the air, finally quelled the Viet Cong.

After February 21 Viet Cong resistance essentially ceased and those that could exfiltrate the area did so. The 2nd Viet Cong Regiment had survived the air cavalry blitz but not without significant losses. Confirmed by body count,

Communist forces suffered 313 killed in the action. American combat deaths were, as usual, much less: 23 KIA and 106 WIA. The 2nd Brigade, 1st Cavalry Division calculated that its operations had seriously damaged Doan's 93rd Viet Cong Battalion, Nhue's 95th Viet Cong Battalion, and perhaps the regimental headquarters.[42]

11

Winter–Spring Battles: Region 5

A Communist since the 1930s, Le Duc Tho served in the South during the war against colonial France and later "presided" (along with Le Duan) over the conference in the U Minh Forest that established the Cochin China Party Committee in October 1954. Now a Politburo member in Hanoi and the director of the Communist Party's Organization Department, Tho naturally expressed a keen interest in the ongoing Viet Cong and NVA military campaign against South Vietnam and its American patron. Tho's views coincided more or less with the decision of the Twelfth Plenum to match the American buildup and strive for military successes and perhaps a negotiated settlement to the situation in the South.[1] In a March 1966 missive, Tho articulated a policy for carrying on the war not unlike that of Le Duan and General Thanh. Writing under the guise of a pseudonym, he pointed out that the United States was constrained strategically and could not expand the war without risking trouble with North Vietnam's allies. Tho, furthermore, reiterated one of General Thanh's principal arguments when he suggested that the United States military would not be able to accomplish simultaneously the multiple missions—pacification, defeating VC/NVA main forces, revamping South Vietnamese forces, and so forth—it was poised to attempt. This was partly so because, according to Tho, the South Vietnamese government and armed forces were nearing a complete collapse. As a result the U.S. military would have to concede the initiative and disperse its forces to defend areas of South Vietnam.[2]

Believing as he did that the South Vietnamese government and armed forces were the weak links in the enemy chain, Tho centered his own proposed strategy around those two institutions. Tho posited that the basic goal of revolutionary strategy should be to "annihilate the puppet army."[3] If the Viet Cong and North Vietnamese Army could smash the South Vietnamese armed forces, the regime in Saigon would implode all the more quickly. And if the Saigon regime ceased to exist, the entire rationale behind the American armed intervention in South Vietnam would unravel. The United States would then have little recourse but to retire from the country on Communist terms.

Though undoubtedly sound, Tho's logic was hardly novel. Communist leaders had long discussed the practicality of destroying the weakest link in the allied military chain—the South Vietnamese forces—and of depriving the Americans of a basis for remaining in the war. In 1963, for example, Hanoi's Central Committee Resolution 9 said the strategic objective of Communist military units in South Vietnam should be to "shatter the puppet army, the primary tool of the enemy regime, in order to create conditions that will allow us to carry out the general offensive–general uprising to overthrow the reactionary government in South Vietnam."[4] Likewise, the COSVN Military Party Committee conference two months earlier in January had called for, as a basic military goal for 1966, destroying the bulk of the ARVN.

Throughout February and March 1966, and on into the spring, Viet Cong units in Region 5 repeatedly locked horns with allied forces as they toiled to implement spring and "winter–spring" battle plans. Frequently, as Tho and others had counseled, the VC battled South Vietnamese forces. Unfortunately for the VC, the Americans became embroiled in some of these battles in what could then be regarded as a microcosm of the war in South Vietnam writ large. On other occasions the Viet Cong squared off with American forces first, but in either case, the big-unit war showed no signs of relenting in the late winter and spring of 1966.

In Quang Tri and Thua Thien, South Vietnam's two most northerly provinces, February was very much an active month for the Viet Cong. According to a Communist history of the region: "In February 1966, in coordination with our forces throughout the country, the [Tri-Thien] Sub-Region conducted an offensive campaign down into the lowlands using a large number of troops operating over a wide area in four districts: Trieu Phong and Hai Lang districts in Quang Tri Province and Phong Dien and Quang Dien districts in Thua Thien Province."[5] By late February the campaign in Thua Thien certainly seemed well under way as the 810th Viet Cong Battalion mixed it up with the 1st Battalion, 3rd ARVN Regiment and a "small group" of Regional Force and Popular Force troops on Phu Thu Peninsula, southeast of Quang Dien and to the east of the U.S. Marine enclave at Phu Bai.

Engaged by the ARVN battalion and the "Ruff-puffs," the 810th resisted tenaciously, prompting General Nguyen Van Chuan, commander of the 1st ARVN Division, to seek assistance on the evening of February 27. Chuan, naturally, called on the Marines stationed at Phu Bai. The day before the Marines had activated a battalion-sized outfit, Task Unit Hotel, precisely for "the purpose of providing a reserve for CG [commanding general] 1st ARVN Division."[6] Led by Lieutenant Colonel Robert Hanifin Jr., the Marine task force had just returned to Phu Bai from a search of the Pho Lai village complex when it received Chuan's plea for help. Hanifin's Marines, despite their exhaustion, clambered aboard helicopters and landed north of Phu Thu Peninsula in the early morning hours of February 28. The South Vietnamese needed help and Hanifin was dispatched to provide it.

Approximately two football fields in length, the defensive arrangements of the 810th Viet Cong Battalion on sandy, pine forested Phu Thu Peninsula consisted of masterfully camouflaged bunkers that provided tactical concealment and substantial protection from small-arms fire. The three Marine companies of Task Unit Hotel had been advancing abreast when troops of the 810th opened fire from these bunkered redoubts with machine guns and rocket-propelled grenades. Exhibiting excellent fire discipline, some of the VC withheld their fire until the Marine squads had practically maneuvered on top of them.[7]

Jarred by the initial enemy outburst, the Marines hugged the ground and returned fire. A furious firefight quickly ensued. As the Marines wriggled forward to assault individual enemy bunkers, air strikes and artillery buffeted the entrenched VC. Eventually the grinding forward impetus of the Marines' frontal assault and the presence of South Vietnamese blocking forces on its flanks unnerved the 810th and its defenses fell apart. Breaking contact, the Viet

Cong withdrew in "small disorganized groups."[8] Meaningful Viet Cong resistance lessened considerably during the remainder of the Marine operation, which lasted until March 3.

New York, the official name of the multiphased Marine offensive that included the operation on Phu Thu Peninsula, dealt a damaging blow to the 810th Viet Cong Battalion. Generally a reliable source, the Marines reported that 120 of the enemy were killed in the operation. That number probably stems primarily from the actions involving the 810th. Therefore, if one accepts the figure of 360 men (as of January 1966) or something near to it as the nominal prebattle strength of the 810th, then the Marines killed no less than one-third of the formation on the peninsula. Whatever the final figure of enemy dead, the Marines judged the "effective combat potential" of the 810th to have been destroyed in the fighting.[9] Marine losses totaled 17 killed and 37 wounded.[10]

Well to the north of Phu Bai and the Phu Thu Peninsula, near the Thua Thien–Quang Tri provincial border, the 802nd Viet Cong Battalion was the next to tangle with the Marines. Along with the 804th Viet Cong Battalion, the 802nd belonged to the 1st Viet Cong Provisional Regiment, not to be confused with the 1st Viet Cong Regiment of Van Tuong fame. At the time the 802nd was deployed east of Route 1 between Routes 597 and 555 in the Ap Chinh An area. Ap Chinh An was situated eight hundred meters to the east of Robin, the landing zone where two Marine companies from Lieutenant Colonel Ralph Sullivan's 1st Battalion, 4th Regiment had debarked on the afternoon of March 20 for a drive down Route 597. Coded Oregon, the Marine operation was launched to clear the hamlets of Ap Phu An and Ap Tay Hoang to the south of Ap Chinh An.

The Marines based the effort on allied intelligence that had placed, erroneously in hindsight, elements of the 802nd in the hamlets of Ap Phu An and Ap Tay Hoang. Consequently, when Company B of the 1/4 Marines blundered into a minefield around Ap Chinh An, wounding one Marine, Lieutenant Colonel Sullivan committed Companies B and A to an assault against the hamlet, unaware that it is was well fortified and defended by two infantry companies and a heavy weapons company from the 802nd.[11] Ensconced in bunkers camouflaged as straw houses, the Viet Cong repulsed the Marine attack with 60-mm mortar and machine-gun fire.

The 802nd Viet Cong Battalion had rebuffed the first Marine attack on Ap Chinh An, yet as always, more would follow. But before the ground assault on the hamlet resumed, the Marines pounded the Viet Cong with artillery and air strikes. Naval gunfire from the USS *Richard B. Anderson* chipped in to bombard the VC as well. Bloodied but unbowed, the 802nd clung to its defensive strongholds and in tough fighting turned back repeated Marine ground assaults. Sullivan, doubtlessly influenced by Marine casualties (nine killed, forty-one wounded), decided to suspend further ground attacks on Ap Chinh An until the following morning, March 21.[12] Fourteen Viet Cong were thought to have been killed before dark.[13]

On the morning of the twenty-first, a thick fog blanketed the battle area, frustrating Marine air strikes. With American aircraft grounded and fog permeating the area, the 802nd Viet Cong Battalion, save for a small rear-guard detachment, deserted Ap Chinh An. Marine and South Vietnamese forces searched for the Viet Cong on March 22 and 23, but the dragnet failed to rustle up much in the way of VC contacts. Having fought with enough skill and determination to delay the Marines, the main body of the 802nd had quietly exfiltrated the battle area and deftly avoided complete destruction. "The tactics they utilized," said Lieutenant Colonel Sullivan of the 802nd, "were not uncommon to good soldiering."[14] The tactics to which Sullivan referred limited the Viet Cong body count to a very manageable forty-eight KIA (eight VC were captured). Eleven Marines were also killed.[15]

South of Da Nang a laagering Marine company presented the R-20 or Doc Lap Viet Cong Battalion with an opportunity to display some "good soldiering" of its own. After menacing ARVN outposts along Route 4 for some time, the Doc Lap Battalion set its sights on Company E (2nd Battalion, 9th Marine Regiment) at the end of March. Company E had been committed along with other Marine forces in an operation (Operation Kings) to help clear the area south of Da Nang and perhaps alleviate some of the pressure on the ARVN outposts. As Company E camped in the early morning hours of March 25 between the La Tho River and Route 4, a small element from the Doc Lap Battalion tried to penetrate the Marine defensive perimeter. Failing, the Viet Cong shelled the Marines with a seventy-five-round mortar volley before launching a two-company attack sometime around 1:00 AM. The Marines, bolstered by the fire of 105-mm howitzers, resisted stubbornly. A little after 2:00 AM, the attacking Viet Cong infantry broke off the assault. The Doc Lap lost forty soldiers—eight times the number of Marines—in the aborted attempt to overrun Company E.[16]

While defeated, the Doc Lap Battalion nonetheless impressed the Marines with its professionalism. Reviewing the attack on Company E, the 9th Marine Regiment would write approvingly, "The preliminary contacts, sequence of attacks, scheme of maneuver, large-scale employment of mortars, use of a diverting force, speed and ferocity of attack once the battle was joined and the very evident seeking out of the specific key targets and objectives during the attack, all indicate that was a well planned, deliberately executed, and hard fought action conducted by seasoned well-trained Main Force Viet Cong troops."[17]

Nothing if not resilient, the Doc Lap Battalion scuffled with the 1st Battalion, 9th Marine Regiment in May. Approximately one month earlier, on April 16, the VC battalion had attacked Company H, 2nd Battalion/9th Marine Regiment after the Marines had set up defensive positions north of Route 4. In the attack a force of about 150 VC assaulted across Route 4 without success, while another company-sized force came to grief in a Marine ambush. On May 21, however, it was the Doc Lap Battalion that laid in wait.

East of Route 540, on the west bank of the Yen River across from An Trach (1), elements of the Viet Cong battalion engaged a squad of Marines from Company C (1/9 Marines) at approximately 11:15 AM. The fighting escalated and soon the Viet Cong were enmeshed with elements of Company A (1/9 Marines) on the eastern bank of the Yen River. Hiding in well-concealed tree-line positions, the VC used mortars, machine guns, and small arms on a group of Marines exiting a helicopter near a cemetery. Most of the twelve Marines killed during the seven-hour battle on the twenty-first were killed in this encounter.[18]

Gradually the momentum shifted. Employing the tried and true tactic of fire and maneuver, Company A assaulted the fortified tree line and displaced the defending Viet Cong. Driven from their tree line hideouts, many

Viet Cong panicked. Some fled westward toward the Yen River. The Marines, sensing victory, pursued the fleeing VC with infantry and artillery. In a rather dramatic turn of events, the situation on either side of the Yen River had deteriorated rapidly for the two engaged companies of the Doc Lop Battalion. A 3rd Marine Division summary reads: "In the initial stages of the contact, the Viet Cong fought from trenches until they were overrun by Marines. Later, Viet Cong were seen attempting to run from the Marines, even digging frantically, to evade contact with Marine units. During the later stages . . . the Viet Cong became very confused and appeared to be without leadership."[19]

To be fair, Marine artillery and airpower, not to mention infantry reinforcement and the addition of M-48 tanks, played a significant role in the final defeat of the Doc Lap Battalion on May 21, 1966. Marine infantry acting alone probably could not have accounted for the startling turn of events, nor were they entirely responsible for the Viet Cong casualty count of 53 dead (and perhaps substantially more).[20] But the seminal event of the engagement, the rout of Viet Cong forces manning the tree line on the eastern bank of the Yen River, was the result of a Marine infantry action. By routing the enemy in the tree line, Company A eased pressure on Company C on the opposite side of the river. That development, more than any other, sowed the seeds of defeat for the Viet Cong.[21]

Prior to either of these attacks by the Doc Lap Battalion, however, an old acquaintance of the Marines, the 1st Viet Cong Regiment, resurfaced in Quang Ngai Province to take part in the "spring battle plan" for the 2nd NVA Division. Comrade Nguyen Nang's division began the campaign, in tandem with "provincial unit local force troops and the armed forces of Binh Son and Son Tinh districts," on February 20.[22] The second phase of the campaign opened on March 17, when a company from the 21st NVA Regiment (2nd NVA Division) paired up with Son Tinh District local-force troops and guerrillas to attack two Civilian Irregular Defense Group (CIDG) platoons. On the very next night, March 18–19, elements of the 1st Viet Cong Regiment raided and overran a South Vietnamese outpost near the village of An Hoa, to the west-southwest of the Binh Son District capital.

The attack by the 1st Viet Cong Regiment devastated the defending 936th Regional Force Company and provoked an allied response. Working in concert, the Marines and the South Vietnamese developed Operation Texas, a joint ARVN-Marine initiative to recapture the An Hoa outpost. The two units selected for the allied operation, Lieutenant Colonel Charles Bodley's 3rd Battalion, 7th Marine Regiment and the 5th ARVN Airborne Battalion (2nd ARVN Division), were to land via helicopter west of An Hoa and sweep eastward, and with any luck find the Communist forces responsible for the attack. As was so often the case, the Viet Cong had absconded from the area by the time Marine helicopters carrying Company I (3/7) alighted atop Hill 141, site of the Regional Force outpost, on March 20. At first Marine intelligence speculated that the VC/NVA would track west after raiding the outpost, toward the mountains and jungle in the area of Nui Hon Doat.[23] Lieutenant Colonel P. X. Kelley, commanding officer of the 2nd Battalion, 4th Marine Regiment, thought differently:

> I then talked with Colonel Bruce Jones, the Senior Advisor to the 2nd ARVN Division, and suggested that the VC might have moved towards the Vin Tuy Valley, an area which had had considerable activity in the past. My original suggestion at the time was to have the 2/4 land there. After considerable discussion, I mentioned the fact that possibly the VC may have done the reverse of the obvious—that they may have moved in an easterly direction from Hill 141, towards the coastal plains. I then suggested the possibility of 3/7 changing its axis of advance to the Vin Tuy Valley, and once it had passed through the Valley it could join with 2/4 for a two battalion sweep eastward to National Route 1.[24]

Kelley's proposal moved through the proper channels and was approved after consultation with General Lam, commander of the 2nd ARVN Division. Lieutenant Colonel Bodley's 3rd Battalion, 7th Marines would push southeast through the Vin Tuy Valley and meet up with Kelley's 2nd Battalion, 4th Marines at Phoung Dinh (2). Bodley's ARVN partner, the 5th ARVN Airborne Battalion, was reinforced and ordered to proceed down to and then along Route 527 until it rendezvoused with an ARVN battalion occupying blocking positions west of Route 1. Kelley's 2nd Battalion, 4th Marine Regiment, meanwhile, received instructions to land west of Phuong Dinh (2), consolidate, and await Bodley's 3/7. United, the two Marine battalions would then sweep eastward to Route 1.[25]

Holed up in the village of Phuong Dinh (2), to the east of Kelly's projected landing zone, was an estimated battalion of VC troops along with two "engineer companies" and the regimental headquarters of the 1st Viet Cong Regiment. Since the village was quite likely one of the campsites in which the regiment and other Communist units bivouacked from time to time, VC forces in the village occupied an amply fortified stronghold. Multiple defensive perimeters, three bands of wire entanglements, spider holes, supporting bunkers, and a fighting trench covering the western approaches to the village had transformed Phoung Dinh (2) into what General Westmoreland would later call the most heavily fortified village he had seen in Vietnam to date.[26] Additionally, though the adjoining terrain was mostly flat and featureless, an abundance of trees and heavy vegetation shrouded the village itself.

At a quarter to nine in the morning on March 21, the day after approval had been granted for the new operational concept, Marines from the 2nd Battalion, 4th Regiment landed west of Phoung Dinh (2). Mobilizing quickly the Viet Cong raked Company F (2/4) with machine-gun and small-arms fire. Already a point of emphasis, VC/NVA antiairmobile activity was stressed even more during Operation Texas to counteract the adverse effect American air mobility was having on "favored" VC/NVA schemes of maneuver. A volume on the 2nd NVA Division acknowledged: "When they had to shift locations, they called in helicopters to move them, thereby neutralizing, at least to a certain extent, our favored tactics of maneuver attacks and mobile ambushes. Faced with this situation, the Ba Gia Regiment [1st Regiment] and the 21st Regiment quickly drew lessons from experience. They launched sudden assault attacks as soon as enemy troops debarked from their helicopters, or they placed forces in ambush positions in locations where we thought enemy troops might land."[27]

Elements of the 1st Viet Cong Regiment and 21st NVA Regiment, the two 2nd NVA Division regiments in the crosshairs of Operation Texas, certainly attempted to kill the debarking Marines "as soon as their boots hit the ground." Carbine, rifle, and machine-gun fire from the north, south, and east assailed the Marine landing zone and hampered Company F's attempts to consolidate it. Marine A-4 Skyhawks retaliated with air strikes against Phoung Dinh (2), and following the arrival of Companies D and E (2/4), Marine artillery batteries to the south slammed the village with 155-mm rounds. The barrage lasted for an hour and fifteen minutes. When the big guns finally fell silent around 12:30 PM, Company E marched off toward Phoung Dinh (2) with Company F in tow. Company D headed off as well but was later maneuvered toward the high ground north of the village. Inside Phoung Dinh (2), the combined effects of Marine A-4 Skyhawks, Huey gunships, and extensive artillery fire had apparently driven the Viet Cong defenders to ground. Ground and aerial observation reported no movement in the village as the Marine companies staged their assault.

At 12:35 PM, however, an airborne forward air controller radioed Lieutenant Colonel Kelley and announced frantically, "My God, I can't believe it! They're erupting from the ground. There are hundreds of them."[28] Down below, Company E had closed with a tree line and was preparing to traverse the trench along the western approaches to the village when the front line exploded in a hail of fire. Commencing the fight for Phoung Dinh (2) in dramatic fashion, the Viet Cong had cut loose with mortars, small arms, 57-mm recoilless rifles, and a .50-caliber machine gun.

Out on the western edge of the village, the VC engaged Company E in a gruesome battle of attrition. Grenades and bullets flew back and forth across the trench in frantic fashion. The closeness and sheer intensity of the fighting hastened the appearance of casualties on both sides. Included in the mounting casualty count were fourteen killed and wounded from Lieutenant Colonel Kelley's command group some fifty meters to the rear (west).[29] By 1:15 PM the depth of the Marine penetration into the VC's defenses—a platoon from Company E had fought its way through the outer barbed wire and underbrush only to stall before yet another defensive perimeter—was much too shallow for exploitation.

With ammunition also running low, Lieutenant Colonel Kelley ordered Company E to physically disengage and maintain contact by fire. Company D, which had become pinned down on the front slope of the rise north of the village, provided a base of fire to assist Company E's withdrawal. Despite heavy aerial and artillery bombardment, and aggressive probing on the part of Marine

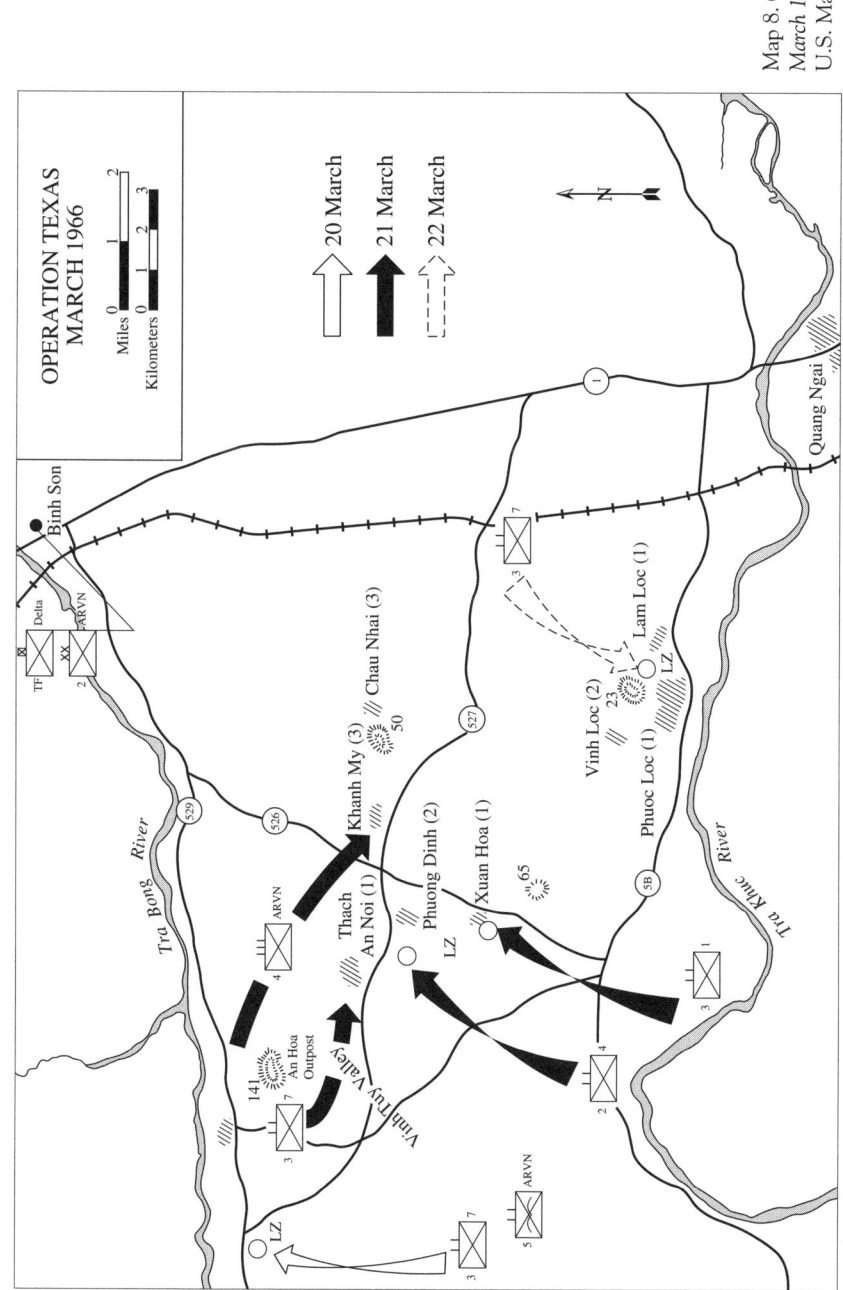

Map 8. Operation Texas, March 1966 (From Shulimson, U.S. Marines in Vietnam)

infantry, the deeply entrenched soldiers of the 1st Viet Cong Regiment had defeated the 2nd Battalion's effort to capture and clear Phoung Dinh (2) on March 21.

Momentarily triumphant, the Viet Cong in and around the village had one final incentive to fight on: Company E was still out there, entangled in the outlying defensive system. However fleeting, the VC would have a chance to finish off the Marine unit before it could extricate itself. And for awhile they were successful. Company E seemed unable to break free and disengage without the intervention of supporting arms.

In some quarters the Vietnam War is viewed wholly through the prism of American firepower omnipotence. More often than not, this view overestimates the influence of firepower on the battlefield, but at Phuong Dinh (2) Marine artillery provided a sanguinary demonstration of American firepower at its best. Four artillery batteries consisting of 155-mm and 105-mm howitzers battered the village and its environs, with some 1,346 rounds fired as part of a continuous two-battery fire mission that began at 1:30 PM and did not end until 3:00 PM.[30] Delayed-fuse rounds were specifically fired to give incoming rounds an opportunity to crash through the dense overlay of trees in the village before detonating. At the same time, the Marine artillery liaison team requested white phosphorus rounds to obscure Company E's withdrawal with smoke.[31] The combined effects of this diverse fire, along with numerous air strikes, pummeled the Viet Cong and allowed Company E to fall back in good order.

During the evening, the surviving elements of the 1st Viet Cong Regiment departed Phoung Dinh (2). The following morning, March 22, the Marines entered the village and discovered dozens of dead bodies. Most had been mortally wounded by shrapnel.[32] In total the Marines counted 168 Viet Cong dead. The evacuating Viet Cong had also abandoned large caches of ammunition and an extremely well-fortified redoubt. Within Phoung Dinh (2), the Viet Cong had carved out extensive communications trenches, tunnel networks, and even caves. Many if not all of these defensive fortifications and arrangements were then destroyed by the Marines. Some time afterward the NLF asserted that over 250 Viet Cong soldiers were never located after Operation Texas.[33] It is plausible that some of these missing soldiers perished in the tunnel complexes razed by the 2nd Battalion, 4th Marines.

Phoung Dinh (2) was one of four notable contacts between the VC/NVA and the Marines during Operation Texas. Aside from the engagement at Phuong Dinh (2), however, it is exceedingly difficult to ascertain where elements of the 1st Viet Cong Regiment were located and when, or for that matter where elements of the 21st NVA Regiment were located and when. The Marine Corps official history states, laconically: "From captured enemy documents, the allies determined that they had encountered elements of three battalions, the *60th* and *90th* from the *1st VC Regiment* and the *11th* from the *21st NVA Regiment*."[34] Volume 1 of the 2nd NVA Division history, *Su Doan 2*, confirms the participation of the 1st Viet Cong Regiment and the 21st NVA Regiment in opposing the Marine operation. It does not, unfortunately, afford posterity a great deal in the way of specifics regarding their movements and locations during each of the engagements. Nor does the Communist history, *Quang Ngai: A History of 30 Years of People's War (1945–1975)*.[35]

Calculating the exact tally of VC/NVA killed in Operation Texas demands a degree of guesswork as well. The Marines put the figure at 283. How many of those, other than the figure derived from the fighting at Phoung Ding (2), could be ascribed to 1st Viet Cong Regiment? Only history knows for sure. Marine losses were an infinitely more quantifiable 99 killed and 212 wounded. Irrespective of the precise figures, neither side left the battlefield unscathed.[36] Whether the battle signified a victory and the degree of American bloodletting Hanoi had hoped for probably depended on the perspective of the individual in question. An unapologetic proponent of big-unit war would probably have been overjoyed with the news of more than 300 Marine casualties. An advocate of a more measured or less confrontational military campaign, on the other hand, might have wondered how many more "victories" like Phoung Dinh (2) the war effort could stand and whether the victory could be parlayed into a strategic bargaining chip at a future negotiating table.

In April a VC deserter rekindled the big-unit war with word that the 1st Viet Cong Regiment was east of Phoung Dinh (2) in the west-central region of Son Tinh District. On April 20 the deserter had surrendered to the South Vietnamese at an ARVN outpost and he later identified the location of the headquarters and several battalions of the 1st Viet Cong Regiment on a map and from the air in a helicopter. Agent reports generated by the 2nd ARVN Division backed the Marines' inclination to act on the deserter's intelligence.[37] Sacrificing little time, the Marines and South Vietnamese swiftly organized a multibattalion offensive—Operation Hot Springs—to locate and destroy any and all elements of the 1st Viet Cong Regiment in the objective area.

Hot Springs opened with a pair of heliborne assaults on April 21. West of the objective area, the 2nd Battalion, 7th Marines alighted first, landing at "LZ 1."[38] Lieutenant Colonel Leon Utter's Companies G and H were on the ground and advancing eastward by 11:45 AM. The 3rd Battalion, 7th Marines disembarked at LZ 2 northwest of the objective area early in the afternoon. Extensive air and artillery preparation prior to the insertions permitted the Marine heliborne assaults to land unopposed or against, in the case of the 2/7, only token Viet Cong opposition.

Bruised by Marine forces in Operation Texas, the 1st Viet Cong regiment fought a delaying action during Hot Springs, with one company-sized element, likely from the regimental "combat support" or heavy-weapons battalion, engaging Lieutenant Colonel Utter's 2/7.[39] Save for a smattering of hill masses, the terrain in this area of the Marine operation was generally flat and unremarkable, but as Company H advanced across it, a nearby hamlet crackled with automatic weapons fire. At first the Viet Cong fired only short bursts from a single .50-caliber machine gun, leaving the impression that they had deployed only one such weapon. But there were more, and each one was cleverly camouflaged and hidden from view. One particular Viet Cong machine gun, "position number 3" in Marine postbattle diagrams, was so well concealed that it was not found until the following morning when a Marine inadvertently fell through the camouflage covering where the gun was sited.[40]

Halted temporarily by the VC fire, the Marines replied with rifle fire, air strikes, and personal initiative. Company H dropped 81-mm mortar rounds and lashed the Viet Cong with small-arms fire while air strikes, the great equalizer against a dug-in enemy, arrived next. Soaring across the sky from the south, two F-8 Crusaders tore into the VC positions with 20-mm cannon fire around 1:45 PM. Elements of Company G (2/7), meanwhile, occupied Hill 97. At 2:30 PM American aviation delivered another air strike, after which Company H attacked for the second time. Rising to the occasion, the Viet Cong pinned the Marines down again and the attack stalled.

Stalwart against the first two Marine ground assaults, VC defenses buckled on the third. Following yet another air strike, and with supporting fire from 3rd Platoon/Company G, Company H attacked at 3:15 PM and "successfully carried the enemy position."[41] Viet Cong forces seeking to escape through the southern end of the village area were then shot up by a platoon from Company H. An additional ten to fifteen VC out of a group of about forty were observed in the open by Company G and wiped out in A-4 bombing runs.[42] The VC delaying action in this sector had run its course.

Elsewhere, a second company-sized delaying force from the 1st Viet Cong Regiment tackled elements of the 3rd Battalion, 7th Marines. Sweeping to the east after touching down in LZ 2, Company M of the 3/7 ran into entrenched VC around Chau Nhai. When the Marines first approached the area, the VC resorted to sniper fire from multiple directions. Sniper fire did not always presage a major combat action, however. Commensurate with guerrilla war, the Viet Cong frequently sniped at American combat units solely for its harassing effect on the psyche of American infantry. The sniper fire could also have been a ruse to encourage the Marines to deploy prematurely. More than likely, though, it was a prelude to the delaying action the Viet Cong planned to wage.

By 3:00 PM the Viet Cong had made firm contact with Company M and for several hours or so the fighting flared. Well armed, the VC maintained a steady volume of automatic weapons fire; the Marines answered with artillery and maneuvered one platoon into an assault position. A second Marine platoon deployed as a covering force. Bombarding the covering platoon with 60-mm mortar rounds, the Viet Cong trained their automatic weapons on the assault platoon. Five Viet Cong soldiers and one Marine fell in the exchange.[43] Pulling back to evacuate their casualties, the Marines requested more air and artillery and regrouped for another attack.

Gritting their teeth, the Viet Cong endured the bombing and the shelling yet refused to surrender. Unfortunately for the Viet Cong, the Marines were equally intractable. About 6:00 PM Company M attacked Chau Nhai (5) for a second time with an assault platoon supported by a covering platoon. The battle on that sweltering afternoon then devolved into a highly personal affair with the attacking Marines and the defending VC trading intense small-arms and automatic weapons fire at close range. Hand grenades were tossed short distances, and incidents of hand-to-hand combat broke out between the combatants. Mixing skill with raw courage, the Marines eventually bested the entrenched Viet Cong and expelled them from the hamlet, killing twenty-six VC soldiers in the process. Three Marines also died in the vicious, close quarters combat.[44]

Drawing the curtain on their delaying efforts, the Viet Cong offered little opposition over the final two days (April 22 and 23) of Operation Hot Springs. All that could be done to forestall the Marines had apparently been done, and the bulk of the 1st Viet Cong Regiment, including its regimental headquarters, had escaped the battle area without being captured or destroyed. Success in exfiltrating the regiment from the battle area did not come cheaply, however. The Viet Cong had lost at least thirty-two KIA opposing elements of the 3/7 Marines and another sixty-four KIA, excluding the estimated ten to fifteen killed by American airpower, opposing the 2/7 Marines. South Vietnamese forces killed a number of VC during Hot Springs as well. Immediately on the heels of Operation Texas, and less than a year after the heavy losses at Van Tuong in August 1965, these losses must have further exacerbated the turnover rate in the 1st Viet Cong Regiment. The Marines also netted a small VC arsenal of U.S.-made Browning automatic rifles, .30-caliber machine guns, .50-caliber machine guns, and 106-mm recoilless rifles.

More troubling, Viet Cong losses fairly dwarfed those sustained by the Marines (five KIA, twenty-nine WIA).[45] Sooner or later, if the Viet Cong big-unit war was to pay strategic dividends, units like the 1st Viet Cong Regiment would have to begin winning some battles outright and/or eliciting a far greater "pound of flesh" from their American adversaries.

12

Winter–Spring Battles: The B2 Front

Colonel Hoang Cam rejoined his division around twilight, then little more than a small crimson colored band of vanishing light on the western horizon. Tomorrow would dawn hot and sunny, he thought briefly, but he had other more pressing concerns to think about because he had just returned from a meeting attended by members of the COSVN Military Headquarters Command Group. The atmosphere at the meeting was cordial and upbeat, and he had briefed and had been briefed by the likes of General Nguyen Chi Thanh, speaking on behalf of the COSVN Military Party Committee, and General Tran Van Tra.

Retiring now to his headquarters back at division, Cam arranged for a staff meeting to talk over matters with his division command group. They had been, as one might expect, eagerly awaiting his return from the meeting. Very much versed in the violent and expansive nature of the ongoing American limited war and now thoroughly briefed by higher headquarters, Cam shared what he knew about the plans for the B2 Front and the mission of the 9th Viet Cong Division. The agenda for the B2 Front had, in fact, been relayed to him by the front commander, General Tra:

> Based on our understanding of the guidance concepts laid out in Central Committee Resolutions 11 and 12 as well as in Politburo resolutions, Central Military Party Committee resolutions, and the battle plans sent

down from the General Staff, the COSVN Military headquarters had approved its Phase 2 Plan of military operations for the entire B2 Front. This plan had been reviewed and approved by COSVN and the COSVN Military Party Committee. Eastern Cochin China [eastern Nam Bo] was the focal point of this plan, and the goal was to exploit our aggressive, offensive posture by continuing to attack the different counter-offensives being mounted by U.S. forces aimed at achieving General Westmoreland's stated goal of "breaking the back of the Viet Cong" during the current dry season.[1]

In the "main battlefield" of eastern Nam Bo, the 9th Viet Cong Division would assume responsibility for the north and northeast sectors, covering War Zone D as well as Tay Ninh, Binh Long, and Binh Duong Provinces. General Thanh had no qualms about assigning the 9th to areas where American forces might wage big-unit battle, but he reminded Cam that his "operations plan" should not be "too ambitious" but "based on your actual strength."[2] Cam, in a nutshell, was being asked to attack *while* remaining mindful of the very real possibility of having to defend against American attacks.

Operations in the northern and northwestern sectors were assigned to the main-force, local-force, and guerrilla units in those areas. Guerrilla warfare against American base areas was encouraged. Finally, as a means of enhancing Communist chances for success in eastern Nam Bo, COSVN Military Headquarters mandated a supporting plan of action in central and western Nam Bo. Communist main-force regiments from "Military Regions 8 and 9" were to withdraw to basing areas in the Plain of Reeds and in the U Minh Forest, work with local forces to defeat enemy pacification operations, and launch attacks to disperse enemy forces.[3] These measures, Communist planners hoped, would help defeat the expected enemy counteroffensive in the "main battlefield" of eastern Nam Bo.

Neither Colonel Cam nor COSVN Military Headquarters would have long to wait for an opportunity to attack an American counteroffensive. In February the U.S. 1st Infantry Division embarked on Operation Rolling Stone in Binh Duong Province, a region within the designated purview of the 9th

Viet Cong Division. The American operation, which began on February 11 in an area dominated by rice fields, rubber plantations, and jungle, assigned the construction of a new "all weather" road between Routes 13 and 16 to the 1st Engineer Battalion. If properly constructed and maintained, the road would upgrade the links between the two northernmost bases of General Seaman's 1st Infantry Division. And as an ancillary benefit, the road would run astride—and perhaps negatively impact—an important Communist supply and infiltration route between War Zone D, C, and the Delta. Colonel Edgar Glotzbach's 1st Brigade was to provide security for the road construction mission and search for Communist forces in the area.[4]

Colonel Cam may not have been overjoyed about the prospects of better communications links between the bases of the 1st Infantry Division, but he was understandably troubled by the potentially adverse effects of a new road astride a key supply and infiltration route. Cam feared, quite reasonably, that Rolling Stone sought to cut off and isolate War Zone D. Of all the Communist bases and base areas in General Tran Van Tra's B2 Front, War Zone D ranked among the most indispensable: "War Zone D was the last back-up position for all of the war zones in Eastern Cochin China, and it was the B2 Front's link with the Ho Chi Minh Trail. It was in a very advantageous position for our strategic infiltration corridor, for us to establish supply warehouses and supply caches, and for us to mass and maneuver our forces. It was a place where we could establish a solid natural foothold and at the same time use it to attack the enemy's vital nerve-center. 'If War Zone D survives, Saigon will fall!'"[5]

Deferring to the general orders of COSVN Military Headquarters to attack American counteroffensives and, perhaps more importantly, his own intuition about the likely threat posed to War Zone D, Cam resolved to strike back against Rolling Stone. Where, he wondered, should his forces strike? Each night, after a long of day of sweep operations, American forces curled up into defensive perimeters. Cam desperately wanted to mount a mobile raid against the Americans, but he could not do so responsibly until he had solid information as to the locations of the American field positions. Lengthy reconnaissance and careful study of American operating procedures were needed to obtain the necessary intelligence. Remarkably Cam himself even sneaked out to reconnoiter the American positions.

By the evening of February 23, twelve days after the start of Rolling Stone, an American encampment west of Route 16 near Tan Binh had been selected as the target of Cam's prospective raid. Serving as the "primary attack element," the 271st Viet Cong Regiment would strike from the northeast, according to the attack plan, in conjunction with an assault by the 273rd Viet Cong Regiment from the southwest. Cam withheld his third frontline infantry regiment, the 272nd, for use as a reserve force. Factoring in all of the possible participating elements, the estimated troop strength of the raid force numbered between 1,500 and 1,800 men.

No soft target, Colonel Glotzbach's 1st Brigade base in the Tan Binh area contained a strong, multiarm force of infantry, artillery, and armored cavalry. Glotzbach's infantry contingent consisted of elements of Lieutenant Colonel Erskine Smith's 1st Battalion, 26th Infantry and Company B, 1st Battalion/28th Infantry. For firepower and mobility, the commander of the 1st Brigade could turn to Batteries B and D of the 1st Battalion, 5th Artillery and Troop B, 1st Squadron/4th Cavalry. These forces ensured that the American camp was quite capable of defending itself. Additionally the big guns of the 6th Battalion, 27th Artillery stationed at Phuoc Vinh were available for general support and reinforcing fires.

Well before dawn on the morning of February 24, a group of about ten to fifteen VC were "observed and engaged" by American troops manning a listening post (LP) beyond the camp perimeter. This encounter tipped off Glotzbach's forces inside the camp to the possibility of an enemy assault.[6] Relative quiet returned thereafter, but at 1:45 AM the Viet Cong assailed Company B (1/28), Battery D, and Troop B with mortar and small-arms fire. Building on these earlier fires, the VC opened up with rockets, recoilless rifles, and heavy automatic weapons at 2:15 AM in a perimeter-wide assault by fire on the 1st Brigade camp. The firestorm did not taper off until about 2:45 AM.

Colonel Cam's troops were also making life miserable for American forces outside the perimeter. An American AAR read:

> During this period the LP's established by B 1/28 attempted to withdraw to the Bde perimeter but were cut off by the VC. Co B 1/28 requested assistance to retrieve his patrols at approx 240300H and B 1/4 Cav dis-

patched two armored patrols to assist in the withdrawal of the LP's. The first patrol departed at 240310H and moved south attempting to link up with the patrol located at XT 852362. At 240320H, the patrol leader, Lt. Burke, B 1/4 Cav, reported his M113 knocked out by a 57-mm Recoilless Rifle (the M113 was evacuated) and Lt. Burke joined the tank crew and continued on to the rendezvous point. Burke's M48A3 tank was then knocked out by a 75-mm Recoilless Rifle and remained in that position throughout the battle with eight men inside the tank. At 240320H, the second motorized patrol departed the perimeter but returned after failing to link up with the LP located XT862367.[7]

Up to this point neither of the two units Cam had designated for the main effort, the 271st and the 273rd Viet Cong Regiments, had sallied forth to decisively assault the American camp. If there *was* a holdup in launching the main assault, it may very well have stemmed from the effects of American firepower on the attacking VC formations. Colonel Cam's memoirs reference American firepower and the need to "reorganize" the attack formations of the 271st and 273rd Viet Cong Regiments during the battle: "The opening blows were volleys of mortar and 75-mm recoilless rifle rounds hitting the enemy's troop concentrations, and next our infantry spearheads launched their assaults. The enemy, relying on the firepower of his armored vehicles, fought back ferociously. Our 1st Regiment struck the first blow and the enemy pulled back into the clumps of bamboo. We continued the attack using nighttime assault and daylight pursuit tactics. Our 1st and 3rd Regiments had to reorganize their attack formations, after which they resumed the attack."[8]

Similarly the history of the 9th Viet Cong Division makes mention of American troops falling back and relying on their "armor and firepower" and of elements of the 271st and 273rd having to "rearrange their formations" and commit reserves to continue the attack.[9] Notwithstanding the more propagandistic aspects, these Communist accounts of the action may shed light on the time period between 3:00 and 4:30 AM. During that time the Viet Cong were observed in assault formation some seventy-five meters from American positions. Whenever a VC attack developed, however, American small-arms, 81-mm mortar, and artillery fire repelled it. Sporadic VC fire around the perimeter of the American camp persisted despite these setbacks, as did periodic ground attacks in the southern, northwest, and eastern sections of the perimeter. Yet the attacks produced negligible results, and women and children in the area were seen evacuating Viet Cong dead and wounded shortly before 5:00 AM.

Forty-five minutes after American forces reported the use of civilians in the removal of VC dead and wounded, what passed for the main Viet Cong assault began. Attacking in assault groups of thirty to forty, the VC absorbed heavy fire forward of the camp wire from American infantry and the two 105-mm batteries on site. The latter, in fact, delivered 166 "high explosive" rounds of direct fire on VC positions and assault troops over the course of the battle. Off to the northeast, the 6th Battalion, 27th Artillery complemented the batteries of the 1/5 Artillery with supporting fires on suspected VC troop locations and on identified and suspected VC mortar positions.[10] Badly beaten, the VC withdrew around 6:45 AM.

On March 2 the curtain closed on Operation Rolling Stone. In arguably its first major action of 1966, the 9th Viet Cong Division had failed to destroy Glotzbach's encamped forces. The losses, moreover, were reasonably heavy: 142 confirmed KIA (though 90 more KIA estimated). Eleven crew-served weapons were lost as well. Alternatively the VC killed 11 Americans and wounded 74. The Viet Cong also destroyed one American tank and two three-quarter-ton trucks.[11]

■ ■ ■

In March 1966 COSVN called to order its fourth plenary conference. The COSVN conference began by analyzing the military events of 1965 and the beginning of 1966. It was then determined that Communist forces were capable of "defeating the enemy in 'limited war.'" Informed by this conclusion and by the need to implement the resolution passed by the Twelfth Plenum on "intensifying the struggle" to "advance toward our goal of defeating the enemy's 'limited war' strategy," the 4th COSVN Plenary Conference proposed a series of missions:

> Strive to powerfully intensify our three high-tide movements (armed struggle, political struggle, and military proselytizing efforts); build up our forces so that they are large and powerful in every respect; incite

wide-ranging and all-out people's guerrilla warfare, while at the same time working quickly to build up our main forces so that they are strong enough to inflict truly large numbers of enemy casualties (both American and puppet army); defeat the enemy's military plans, political and economic plots, rural pacification efforts . . . make the enemy continue to be on the defensive and to become mired down even further; crush the will to commit aggression of the American imperialists; gain a decisive victory within a relatively short period of time while at the same time creating solid opportunities to defeat the enemy in the event that the war become protracted and is expanded so that it encompasses our entire nation.[12]

Colonel William Brodbeck, commander of the 3rd Brigade, 1st Infantry Division, would probably have endorsed COSVN's appeal to intensify the armed struggle, if only because it enhanced his own prospects of bringing Communist main-force units to battle. In February Brodbeck's brigade along with the 2nd Brigade deployed north of Saigon for Operation Mastiff, but the expected enemy contacts and the succeeding battles of annihilation never materialized. Mastiff wrapped up without bringing any major Communist units to battle. Afterward Brodbeck theorized that smaller, battalion-sized search-and-destroy operations within his brigade "tactical area of responsibility" (TAOR) stood a better chance of generating contact with large enemy units than brigade- and division-sized operations. The Viet Cong, the theory held, would likely avoid larger American units but would be more inclined to engage smaller American units. Governed by the guiding principle of rotating subordinate battalions into and through their appointed areas, the 3rd Brigade "concept of operation" for the month of March envisioned a series of battalion-sized operations within the brigade TAOR.[13]

Certainly innovative, the 3rd Brigade plan went into effect on the morning of March 3 with the initiation of Operation Boston/Cocoa Beach. Traveling without the benefit of motorized vehicles, Lieutenant Colonel Kyle Bowie's 2nd Battalion, 28th Infantry marched north out of Lai Khe and into the Lo Ke Rubber Plantation. Bowie's troops dug in and established a battalion perimeter about 1,500 meters west of Bau Bang. Bordered by rubber trees to the south

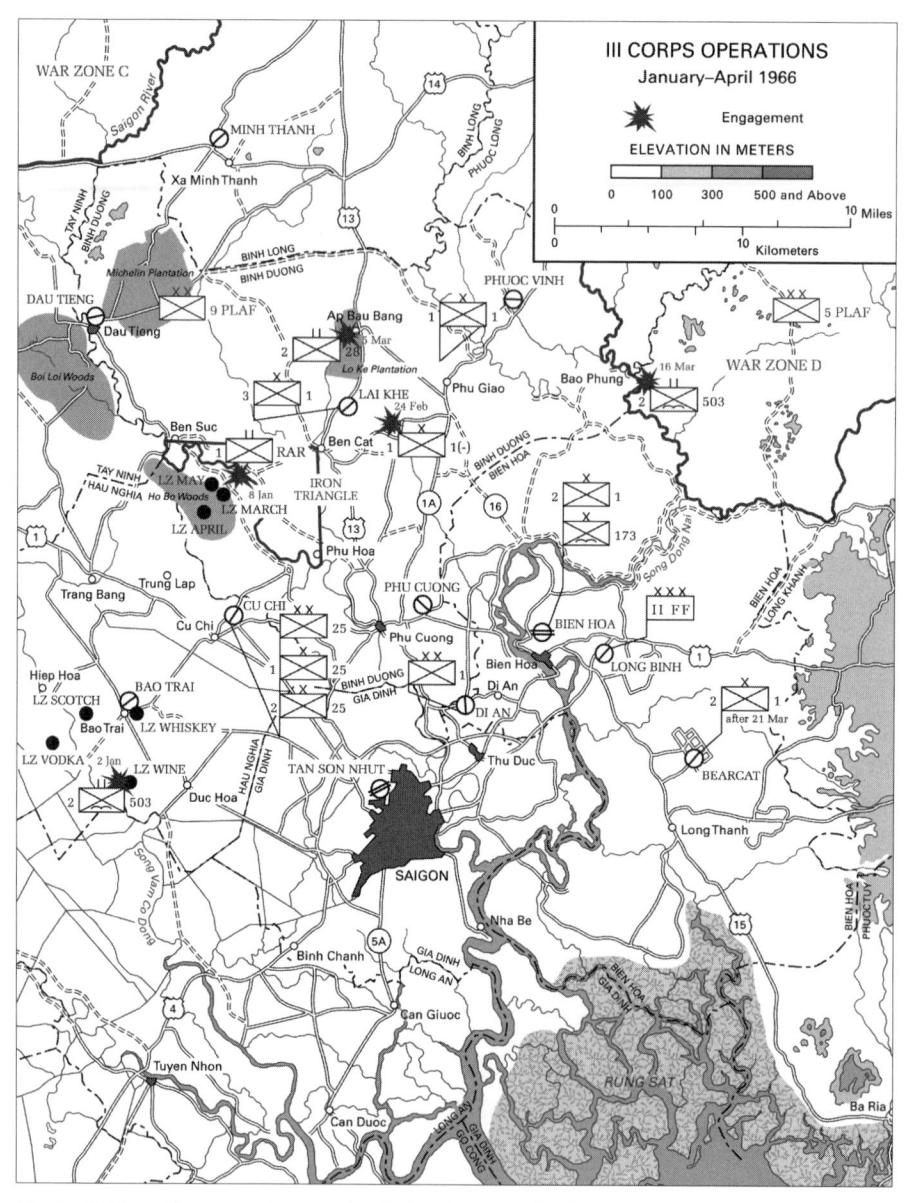

Map 9. III Corps Operations, January–April 1966 (From Carland, *United States Army in Vietnam*)

and east and jungle to the west, the area chosen for the 2/28 perimeter was virtually wide open and thus blessed with outstanding fields of fire. After dark Bowie covered the most likely avenues of approach with ambush patrols. The night elapsed without incident.

The next day, March 4, Bowie's patrols produced two interesting finds. Probing to the north of the 2/28 perimeter, Company B investigated a group of plantation buildings but uncovered nothing of significance until it happened upon a trench ("trench 1") on its return trip to the battalion. Approximately nine feet deep and with dug-out compartments in its sides for cooking facilities and protective cover, the trench ran westward from Bau Bang for about two kilometers. More ominously the trench appeared to have accommodated a large force as recently as two days before. Notified of this discovery and acquainted with preoperation intelligence reports that had placed the 272nd Viet Cong Regiment in the area, Lieutenant Colonel Bowie journeyed back to brigade headquarters to coordinate with his air and artillery support and ensure that each were made aware of the trench and the location of his perimeter.[14] Company A, searching that same day to the west of the battalion perimeter, found a Viet Cong camp with four to five small huts, still-warm food, and several underground stoves for cooking.

Lieutenant Colonel Bowie, having decided to redeploy the 2/28 to the west the following morning, dispatched three patrols and a four-man listening post on the evening of March 4. As Bowie plotted his next move and prepared for another night in the field, elements of the 9th Viet Cong Division lurked nearby. News of the VC's proximity to the 2/28 perimeter filtered through after midnight, when the Brigade S2 (intelligence) sergeant radioed Bowie to inform him that a Viet Cong regiment had been reported northeast of Bau Bang.[15] That regiment was in all likelihood the 272nd.

In the early morning hours that followed, the 272nd converged, evidently undetected, on the 2/28. Then, at 6:15 AM on March 5, an American patrol northwest of the 2/28 perimeter witnessed an unforgettable scene:

> At 0615 hours Lt Hibbs' patrol saw a group of civilians (mostly women and children) coming down Route RED (sketch) from the east. They were moving slowly. Some of the women were carrying weapons and

almost all of the children were carrying ammunition. When they got to within 100 meters of the patrol they halted. Then from the north along Route BLUE (sketch) Lt. Hibbs saw an estimated VC company double timing toward his position. (Note: It was still dark at this time but Lt Hibbs had a Starlight Scope on his weapon.) When the VC got to within 50 meters of the patrol they halted. The VC obviously had been running for a long time as they began to cough and spit when they halted. From behind this group of VC a bald headed man in a white robe came forward with 2 or 3 other men, and they walked down Route BLUE and turned east on Route RED to join the civilians who were waiting. The bald man began to talk to the civilians.[16]

Undoubtedly sprinting south for an attack on the 2/28 perimeter, the double-timing Viet Cong company had run into a trap. While the robed man interacted with the Vietnamese civilians, Lieutenant Hibbs adjusted the position of his two Claymore mines and readied his patrol for an ambush. The robed man eventually left the civilians to rejoin the VC company, and together they headed down Route Blue toward the 2/28 perimeter. Lieutenant Hibbs waited until the enemy column had entered the "kill zone" before detonating the Claymores, and within seconds of the explosions, the road was filled with dead and wounded Viet Cong. Hibbs and his fellow patrolmen then leapt into action and heaved grenades at the dazed VC survivors. Spared the effects of the mine blasts, those to the rear of the VC column began returning fire, forcing Hibbs to order a retreat back to the battalion perimeter.

South of the ambush area and to the west of Route Blue, perhaps one hundred meters or so from the 2/28 perimeter, another company-sized Viet Cong force was deploying for an attack against the American camp. Hibbs' patrol, while tramping south along Route Blue, bumped unwittingly into the rear of this Viet Cong formation. Spotting the Americans, several of the VC fired on Hibbs and his patrol. "Bravo, Bravo, Bravo," the American patrolmen yelled out, believing that they might have run into Company B's lines. From all around the confused American patrol, however, voices thick with Vietnamese accents replied, "Bravo." One voice was quite unlike the others.

"Bravo over here," it said, in excellent English. Hibbs had heard enough. "Like hell," he hollered suddenly, "those are VC!"[17] Motivated by Hibbs' unexpected announcement, the American patrol, relying on only hand grenades and M-16 rifle fire, fought their way through the VC to return to the 2/28 perimeter.

About 6:35 AM, just about the time that Lieutenant Hibbs' patrol finally reached the safety of the American perimeter, the 272nd Viet Cong Regiment unleashed a sequence of ground assaults against the now alert American battalion. The VC force that had tussled briefly with Hibbs' patrol northwest of the 2/28 attacked first, but intense small-arms fire from dug-in American infantry repelled the attack. Successive VC attacks from the northeast (6:45 AM), east (6:55 AM), and west-southwest (7:15 AM) followed. At one point the Americans judged that the Viet Cong were assaulting with a battalion from the northeast, two companies from the east, two companies from the west, and one company each from the south and southeast.[18]

Despite the fury of the Viet Cong assaults, the combined effects of American infantry, artillery, and airpower repulsed the attackers at every turn. Air Force fighters eager to unload their deadly cargo dropped 500-pound bombs and smashed up the VC attack west of the 2/28 perimeter. Air strikes were also directed against VC attacks east of the American perimeter and against the plantation village and buildings to the north, where the VC had positioned mortars in support of the ground assaults. And when Viet Cong troops attacking from the northwest relocated to "trench number 2" north of the American battalion, they were targeted and decimated with cluster bomb units.

By midday the fighting had subsided. Company A (2/28) sent a patrol south around noontime, and while reconnoitering a short time later, the patrol met and fired on a company-sized Viet Cong force digging in near "trench 3." The Viet Cong, ironically enough, were facing in the opposite direction, or to the *south*. Likely ordered to intercept an American relief force coming up from Lai Khe, the VC instead engaged the American recon patrol with a heavy volume of fire. The Americans wisely pulled back and asked for artillery fire. Prior to this encounter, Lieutenant Colonel William Lober's 1st Battalion, 16th Infantry landed northeast of the 2/28 and behind the attacking VC to block escape routes to the north and east. A small group of khaki clad Communist soldiers stood in Lober's way, but his troops overran the opposition in short order and linked up with Bowie around 2:30 PM.

General William Westmoreland characterized the March 5 engagement as a "complete rout of the enemy." Most would concur. Communist Vietnamese sources, on the other hand, viewed the battle very differently, alleging that at Bau Bang the 272nd Viet Cong Regiment had "put out of action a U.S. battalion in a brilliant mobile raid."[19] The numbers, however, favored Westmoreland. American forces suffered 15 KIA and light material losses beyond the destruction of one F-100 fighter. In contrast the Viet Cong lost dozens of soldiers killed (a minimum of 199 KIA) and incurred serious losses in captured and destroyed equipment.[20] Colonel Cam, furthermore, could not have been comforted by the fact that elements of his 9th Viet Cong Division had raided a dug-in American force for the second time in less than two weeks and for the second time had been thoroughly defeated.

Cam, though, had little time to dwell on the 272nd's setback in the Lo Ke Rubber Plantation. On March 7 the Americans set Operation Silver City, a two-brigade thrust into the southwestern segment of War Zone D, in motion. The 173rd Airborne Brigade and the 1st Brigade, 1st Infantry Division invaded the Communist war zone to raze the headquarters of the B2 Front's Military Region 7 and draw the handful of enemy main-force units in the area to battle. Silver City would presumably force the Viet Cong to either give battle or suffer, without a fight, the loss of some of their war-sustaining supply caches and facilities in War Zone D.[21]

Keenly aware of War Zone D's allure as a target, COSVN Headquarters issued instructions, before the start of Operation Silver City, incidentally, for the establishment of a "unified forward command headquarters" to aid in the defense of the vital jungle sanctuary. Specifically the forward command was created in February 1966 to "unify command" over the 9th Viet Cong Division, the Phu Loi Battalion, and the guerrilla and full-time forces of the Military Region 7 Headquarters (Eastern Military Region Headquarters). Cam served as commander of the newly established forward headquarters and Hong Lam, the commander of Military Region 7, filled the post of deputy commander.

Along with the establishment of the aforementioned forward command, Colonel Cam contends that he and others sketched out "a basic battle plan coordinating the operations of our three types of troops (main force, local force, guerrilla) to defend War Zone D in the event the enemy launched an attack into this sanctuary area."[22] If so, the plan was rather circumspect with regard to what warranted defending and when to mount counterattacks, because the Viet Cong did not do much of either during the initial stages of Silver City. Colonel Glotzbach's 1st Brigade and Brigadier General Paul Smith's 173rd Airborne Brigade rummaged through the dense, triple canopied jungle in the area, scaling hills one moment and descending into unexplored ravines the next, unopposed save for the occasional firefight. Cam's troops had clearly chosen to avoid American units.

The tempo changed suddenly on March 14. Tasked with finding and destroying the headquarters of Military Region 7, General Smith's 173rd Airborne Brigade had crossed the Song Be River five days before, on March 9. Across the waterway first, the 1st Battalion, 503rd Infantry seized LZ 8 east of the river on March 10. The next day helicopters airlifted the 2nd Battalion, 503rd Infantry onto LZ 8, and by March 14, elements of Lieutenant Colonel John Walsh's battalion were advancing on Objective George, the reported location of the headquarters of Military Region 7. Sergeant Albert Guarusco, a member of Walsh's battalion support platoon, had just exited a ravine and a large bomb crater near George when he noticed a Viet Cong soldier moving in his direction about forty yards away. Guarusco fired on the soldier and then, moments later, on two more VC. The Viet Cong vanished into a trench.

Though not quite noon, the situation escalated rapidly. "All hell broke loose," recalled Sergeant Marvin Chapman. "Bullets flew in all directions. Grenades headed for us and exploded in the trees."[23] Guarusco and the rest of the battalion support platoon had unknowingly meandered out ahead of Company B, one of the companies designated by Walsh to lead the move on George, and straight into a major Viet Cong redoubt. Settled into well-constructed entrenchments and bunkers, the Viet Cong hit the American platoon with grenades, small-arms, and .50-caliber machine-gun fire. Companies B and C eventually reinforced the first Americans on the scene, and with these new arrivals and the addition of even more Viet Cong defenders, the battle grew in scale. Jungle and secondary scrub in the battle area restricted observation to 10 meters in some places, but the poor visibility did not deter the VC from attempting to outflank the Americans, and vice versa.

As the fighting dragged on without a reprieve, the casualties on both sides increased steadily. Wounded American paratroopers were transported from the front lines to a bomb crater to the rear and then evacuated by air. Much to the dismay of Lieutenant Colonel Walsh, American air and artillery support had to be restrained during the extraction or evacuation process. On the other side, the extraction process was, needless to say, rudimentary; the surviving VC had to haul some of their dead and wounded to a village south of the battle area.

Sensitive to the mounting American casualty count and the now rapidly diminishing daylight, Walsh ordered his troops to pull back. The taking of Objective George would have to be postponed until the following day. Walsh then arranged for air and artillery to pound the dug-in Viet Cong. On March 15 the 2/503, after a brief scuffle with a game VC "stay behind" force, secured George and located, in all probability, the headquarters complex of Military Region 7. Exploring George, the paratroopers found tunnels, bunkers, numerous huts, a makeshift hospital, documents running the gambit from rosters to training plans, and medical supplies.[24] The Viet Cong had abandoned, if not the headquarters of Military Region 7, then certainly some sort of a major military-political headquarters.

Desperately in need of a landing zone for aerial resupply, Walsh then swung his battalion south and seized Landing Zone Zulu-Zulu on the afternoon of March 15. The Viet Cong had planted long sharpened poles on Zulu-Zulu to discourage helicopter landings, but the Americans disposed of them and established a battalion perimeter. In the morning elements of Walsh's battalion would resume sweeping the area. Unbeknown to Walsh, Colonel Cam had plans for the following day as well, and during the night, his 271st Viet Cong Regiment surrounded the unsuspecting American battalion. Cam intended to compress and crush the American formation, and he amassed a force of almost two thousand men to achieve that objective.

At 7:15 AM on the morning of March 16, a heavy Viet Cong machine gun northwest of Walsh downed an incoming American resupply helicopter to ignite the battle. Intermittent to start, the volume of VC fire triggered by this initial burst of machine-gun fire rose sharply as machine guns and automatic weapons ripped the American perimeter.[25] Soon hordes of Viet Cong infantry, many donning plastic camouflaged helmets and wearing either black or green uniforms, began attacking the American perimeter from all sides. Mortars, .50-caliber machine guns, 57-mm recoilless rifles, and possibly a 75-mm howitzer supported the attacks. Rushing forward, the Viet Cong zeroed in on company tie-in points. When American defensive fire stalled an attack in one sector of the perimeter, the Viet Cong simply launched an attack in another. The VC hoped that these attacks, which were frequently launched against a distant or opposite sector of the perimeter, would exploit potential weak points created when the defending forces were shifted from one area of the perimeter to cope with attacks in another.

All morning long the 271st Viet Cong Regiment and accompanying forces bled in a grisly bid to annihilate the American battalion. Dozens of Viet Cong soldiers were mowed down by smalls-arm fire while charging the American lines. As the dead and dying crumpled to the ground, other VC raced forward to collect the bodies and drag them to the rear. Viet Cong snipers were blasted out of the surrounding trees by well-placed volleys from American M-79 grenade launchers. Ringing the American perimeter with a wall of fire, exploding bombs and artillery shells killed and maimed many in the VC assault force. Communist troops attempted to confuse the Americans by yelling, in English, "Cease fire, cease fire " and "1st Battalion here, cease fire," but these attempts failed to elicit anything other than more American defensive fire.

Around noontime the bloodletting and the battle finally ended after several major Viet Cong thrusts had been shattered. In defeat the Viet Cong had suffered horrendously—303 KIA by *body count*—at Zulu-Zulu. Astonishingly, given the ferocity of the engagement, the Americans lost only 7 KIA.[26] The VC attack, not the American perimeter, had been crushed in no uncertain terms.

Whatever the extent of General Westmoreland's strategic misjudgments in focusing on Communist main-force units and the big-unit war first, the battle for Zulu-Zulu (and others like it) strongly suggested that the relationship between his strategy and the American military's big-unit capabilities was not nearly as incongruous as the one between the Communist faction advocating big-unit war and the *Viet Cong's* big-unit capabilities.

THE DEBUT OF THE 5TH VC DIVISION

Le Xuan Chuyen seemed like the consummate Communist Vietnamese military professional. The son of Le Van Ray and Tran Thi Yem, Chuyen was born in 1929 in the Le Thuy District of Quang Binh Province, North Vietnam. On August 9, 1945, he joined the Viet Minh and was assigned to the Le Truc Battalion in Quang Binh Province. Promoted repeatedly, Chuyen rose through the ranks to command a battalion in 1953 and then, in 1960, the 66th Regiment of the 304th Division. Later on, in July 1964, Lieutenant Colonel Chuyen infiltrated into South Vietnam, where he eventually became the assistant chief of staff and chief of operations of the 5th Viet Cong Division.

Previously progressing along a strictly upward trajectory, Chuyen's Communist military career cratered unexpectedly in 1966. In March of that year, Chuyen was abruptly reassigned to the Central Office for South Vietnam. Ill at the time, he traveled to the house of an acquaintance in Binh Thuyan Province for medical treatment. Chuyen married in April and he began angling, through his wife's cousin, a man connected to the South Vietnamese military, for a way to desert. The COSVN assignment and the "political stand" of the Viet Cong had evidently upset Chuyen profoundly, and on August 2, 1966, after a number of months, he reported to South Vietnamese authorities and officially deserted.[27]

Le Xuan Chuyen's de facto desertion in March naturally concerned the leadership of the 5th Viet Cong Division. They worried that Chuyen would divulge the whereabouts of the division's "troop billeting" areas and "rear services" storage area, intelligence that would all but invite an enemy attack on those locations. To be sure Comrade Nguyen Hoa, the commander of the 5th Viet Cong Division, could ill afford to lose the 84th Rear Services Group because the group had been supplying units from his division. There were additional concerns that battle plans for the 274th and 275th Viet Cong Regiments would be compromised. A Communist history of the 5th Viet Cong Division recounted the divisional response to these concerns as well as the general mission for the upcoming rainy season: "In the face of this situation, Division Headquarters directed all units to hastily move all bases and supply caches and warehouses and to actively combat enemy sweeps to defend the food supplies and storage warehouses of the 84th Rear Services Group in areas east and west of Route 20. At the same time, the division's units were directed to continue to carry out their assigned missions during the rainy reason and to cooperate with Ba Ria local armed forces to launch surprise attacks against Australian troops as they deployed to replace U.S. troops in carrying out the enemy's pacification program in Ba Ria."[28]

Toward the end of March, the Americans went on the offensive as the leadership of the 5th Viet Cong Division had feared. Major General William DePuy, the new commander of the 1st Infantry Division, unfurled Operation Abilene in Phuoc Tuy Province southeast of Saigon. DePuy's mission, though *not* inspired by any intelligence obtained from Chuyen, called for locating and smashing units of the 274th and 275th Viet Cong Regiments, along with any Communist base camps and sanctuary areas his forces encountered along the way. An introductory blow rather than an independent spoiling action, Abilene was launched to prevent a Communist effort against Saigon from the east as part of a larger American campaign to preempt the expected Communist attacks in III Corps as the rainy season approached.[29]

Keeping abreast of American military activities, the headquarters of the 5th Viet Cong Division determined that American forces "might be preparing to conduct a sweep operation that would push into the main base area of the division's 4th Regiment [274th Regiment] at Tam Bo Stream and destroy the 84th Rear Services Group's food supply caches in the Hac Dich Area."[30] Hoa and his staff responded accordingly. On April 5 the division ordered the redeployment of the 274th Viet Cong Regiment from the southern Kiet Stream area to Tam Bo to defeat the projected American sweep operation. The 274th moved out quickly and after a three-day march reached its "assembly area" at Tam Bo Stream on April 10.

Founded in War Zone D, the 274th Viet Cong Regiment entered service in February 1965. Comrade Dang Ngoc Si commanded the 274th in April 1966, but initially the regiment was commanded by Tran Minh Tam. The 274th was at one time composed of two infantry battalions, the 800th Battalion, or "D800" Battalion, and the 308th Battalion, as well as a weapons company and a reconnaissance company. Incorporated into a brand-new regiment, the 800th was designated the "1st Battalion" and the 308th the "3rd Battalion." The 265th Battalion hiked up from central Nam Bo and joined the 1st and 3rd Battalions in September 1965.[31]

On April 10, the day the 274th arrived at Tam Bo Stream, regimental elements made contact, albeit briefly, with American forces. At approximately 4:45 PM Company C of the 2nd Battalion, 16th Infantry (1st Infantry Division) noticed and fired on three Viet Cong soldiers advancing from east to west across a wide clearing. Although one of the three VC managed to escape, the Americans killed one while the third man, a squad leader, was critically wounded and questioned. The wounded man, before expiring, indicated that he belonged to a reconnaissance detachment from the D800 Battalion and had been ordered to locate American units in the area. Documents retrieved from the bodies of the two dead VC confirmed that they were indeed members of the D800 Battalion.[32] That night the 5th Viet Cong Division deployed more reconnaissance teams and moved into position.

Earlier in the day, Nguyen The Tryuen, the bespectacled former commander of the 271st Viet Cong Regiment, replaced Hoa as the commander of the 5th Viet Cong Division. Truyen, who had grown up in Saigon despite being born in the North, learned of the preparations the 274th had undertaken to counter the imminent American sweep operation. Not an inexperienced commander, Truyen processed this information quickly before collecting his thoughts. Fight a good battle, he advised the 274th Viet Cong Regiment, and kill scores of Americans. Since this would be the 5th Viet Cong Division's first battle against American troops, it was incumbent upon the 274th to fight well and provide insights on fighting the Americans so that the division "could learn valuable lessons about fighting against American troops that could then be disseminated to the other units of the division and to the local armed forces units fighting on the Ba Ria–Long Khan battlefield."[33] Dang Ngoc Si's troops, as they squinted in the shadows on the eve of battle, were probably more interested in staying alive than evaluating American forces.

The fighting on April 11 started innocuously enough. While negotiating thick jungle approximately forty miles east of Saigon, Company C (2/16) sparred with small groups of Viet Cong snipers, beginning with a 12:45 PM encounter involving 3rd Platoon and four VC snipers. For the next hour and a half, the combatants played a deadly game of cat and mouse. The Viet Cong, in classic guerrilla fashion, would shoot at the Americans and then disengage. Assuming the role of the cat, the Americans would return fire and give chase.

The chase ceased at 1:45 PM, when Company C folded into a perimeter. Prudent in retrospect, the move afforded the commander of the American company time to summon a Med Evac and plan for a possible attack on the suspected Communist basing area to the west. Sometime around 3:00 PM, after a clearing had been hacked out of the jungle canopy, an Air Force rescue helicopter appeared and began airlifting Company C's dead (two) and wounded (fifteen) out of the battle area.

As Company C paused to regroup and tend to their wounded, the 274th Viet Cong Regiment geared up for an assault. Company C's pursuit had left the unit dangerously close to battle positions held by the 274th's "primary attack unit," the 1st (D800) Battalion. Near enough, in fact, that Regimental Commander Dang Ngoc Si and his staff agreed that the time had come to shift to a mobile offensive operation. "Seizing this opportunity to destroy the enemy, the 4th Regiment Command Group decided to change tactics from fighting a defensive battle from fortified positions to launching a maneuver attack to completely annihilate the American battalion," stated a history of the 5th Viet Cong Division, albeit overestimating the size of the American force. "At 1400 hours 1st Battalion was ordered to advance to the northwestern flank to encircle the enemy Battalion. Our 1st and 2nd Battalions pushed their forces forward right up to the concentration of enemy troops. The units would launch coordinated attacks, accompanied by the explosions of the regiment's heavy weapons, which fired a preparatory barrage."[34] Maneuvering through the dense undergrowth with great stealth, Si's troops surrounded Company C.

Promptly at 4:00 PM, the Viet Cong opened fire. Round after round of small-arms and recoilless rifle fire cut through the vegetation, while a VC mortar team pitched fourteen 60-mm rounds into the American perimeter. Encircled and taking fire, Company C attempted a breakout to the northwest and a follow-up push to the southeast. Neither of these platoon-sized thrusts, however, achieved much headway against the incoming curtain of Viet Cong fire, some of it from VC snipers perched high up in the trees. In between the firefights and the infantry assaults on the American perimeter, individual and sometimes pairs of Viet Cong soldiers would run from one position to another in the hopes of drawing fire from American troops. Those who moved to fire on the Viet Cong, exposed as they were running from point to point, immediately became quarry for the tree-bound snipers.[35]

Transitioning finally to an all out assault, the 274th began attacking the American perimeter in waves and with units from all three of its battalions.[36] The first attack, directed against the western flank of the American position, failed to gin up sufficient momentum and was foiled by Company C's 3rd and 4th Platoons. Driven back in this sector, the Viet Cong committed more light and heavy machine guns to the attack. To the northwest, a .50-caliber machine gun grazed the 3rd and 4th Platoons, while from the north, west, and south, the Viet Cong sliced into the American lines with .30-caliber machine-gun fire. Despite this boost in supporting firepower, the second Viet Cong assault fell back under the weight of American small-arms and artillery fire. Then, shortly before dark, a Vietnamese voice, the very same voice American soldiers from the 3rd and 4th Platoons had overheard directing the Viet Cong throughout the battle, "rallied" the VC for a third and final assault. This time a thunderous barrage of artillery fire, coupled with tear gas, a heavy dose of smalls-arm fire, and some hand-to-hand combat beat back the Viet Cong attack.

Thwarted by a tenacious enemy infantry company skillfully supported by artillery fire, Si's troops broke off the battle around 7:30 PM. "In the division's first face-to-face battle against U.S. troops, 4th Regiment had won a clear victory and had been able to hold its fighting positions," boasted the history of the 5th Viet Cong Division. "Although it suffered a number of casualties, the regiment had shattered the enemy sweep conducted by one U.S. battalion that had outstanding artillery and air support. This initial victory against U.S. troops at Tam Bo built confidence among our cadres and soldiers."[37] Communist hyperbole notwithstanding, the 274th had fought well on April 11. The regiment demonstrated a fair degree of tactical competence in the attack, and its troops killed 35 and wounded 71 Americans. Moreover, the Viet Cong suffered a relatively light 41 confirmed KIA, though American estimates placed the actual number of VC dead and wounded in the neighborhood of 100–150.[38] On the other hand, two Viet Cong base camps, almost certainly those of the 274th Viet Cong Regiment, were discovered on April 12 and "marked" for American air and artillery strikes.

PART IV
EPILOGUE

13

The Big-Unit War and the Road to Tet

In 1966 the chorus of voices in Hanoi expressing discontent with the strategy of reunifying the nation through military ends—and high-intensity, big-unit ends at that—grew larger and arguably louder. The North-firsters, a faction that had always feared the damaging impact of American military might on the still systemically fragile state of socialist development in North Vietnam, found new allies in the disaffected supporters of the high-intensity military approach to subjugating South Vietnam. As Communist military casualties mounted and the likelihood of a quick military victory waned, these one-time proponents of the hardline strategy aligned with the North-firsters in pushing for a negotiated end to American involvement in the war. The hardliner approach also prompted criticism from disgruntled elements within the North Vietnamese military establishment.[1] General Giap, though politically somewhat neutered, weighed in throughout 1966 to reproach Thanh for overemphasizing big-unit battle and neglecting the methods of protracted struggle. Giap was certainly not averse to big-unit war per se, but he preached greater discretion in its employment and greater balance between big-unit war and guerrilla war.

Proponents of the high-intensity, big-unit war strategy questioned in turn the resolve and judgment of the dissenters. Le Duc Tho, in an article written in early 1966, alleged that "a small number of comrades" had arrived at "an incorrect assessment of the balance of power between the enemy and us and of the enemy ruses" and that these comrades "entertain subjectivism and pacifism, slacken their vigilance, and fail to get ideologically ready for combat." Tho continued on, accusing a "number of organizations and comrades" of insufficiently comprehending the "idea that the North is the large rear and the South a large frontline [and] still fail to reflect fully the duty of the rear toward the frontline."[2] General Thanh likewise rebuked the dissidents in a July article. An unabashed militant and Hanoi's foremost man on the ground in the South, Thanh scolded the supposed tendency of some of his critics to "overestimate the enemy and underestimate ourselves."[3] Thanh's rebuttal was not an isolated event, either. As a matter of fact, Thanh defended his preferred strategy frequently, and he even insinuated that his detractors in North Vietnam—far from the fighting—could scarcely appreciate fully the situation on the ground in the South.

In May 1966, amid the ongoing strategic debates in Hanoi, the Combat Operations Department of the NVA General Staff submitted a military plan for the summer of 1966. Curiously optimistic, the plan proposed more of the same—high-intensity, big-unit war complemented by harassing guerrilla war—for Communist forces in South Vietnam:

> The battle plan for the summer of 1966 was to concentrate our forces, seize the offensive initiative, aggressively counterattack against the enemy, and annihilate an important portion of the American and puppet troop strength. We would firmly seize the opportunity to intensify our combat operations in coordination with military proselytizing operations to annihilate and shatter the puppet army; support the urban struggle movement; take another step toward defeating the enemy's plan to seize the initiative by creating political disruption within the puppet army and causing their morale to collapse; strive to expand a number of our mountain jungle base areas and disrupt the enemy's pacification and population resettlement program; create a favorable strategic posture for us to prepare to defeat American forces, even though they outnumbered our own forces; make powerful attacks against enemy roads, other lines of communications, and rear bases to slow the pace of the enemy's plan to increase his own troop strength; and overcome the weather problem

in order to continue to send additional forces to the battlefield and to build up our logistics stockpiles so that we would be ready to mount large attacks as soon as the dry season begins.[4]

That summer Colonel Cam's 9th Viet Cong Division intended to "seize the offensive initiative" with a major rainy season campaign in the Binh Long Province area north of Saigon. Initially Cam anticipated rolling out the offensive in May with the stated objectives of "destroying a part of the enemy forces and joining the local armed forces in developing guerrilla warfare and expanding the liberated areas."[5] However, in early May a U.S. Special Forces–led CIDG patrol killed an officer with the 271st Viet Cong Regiment southeast of Loc Ninh. On the deceased man's body, the patrol found a map and a plan for an attack on Loc Ninh and the U.S. Special Forces camp near the town.[6] All three of Colonel Cam's regiments were to conduct the assaults along with a North Vietnamese unit, presumably Comrade Nguyen Van Kien's reinforcing 16th NVA Regiment. Shortly thereafter, on May 17, an ARVN MIKE Force unit and elements of the 2nd Battalion, 9th ARVN Regiment collided with two Communist battalions, quite likely from the 271st and 273rd Viet Cong Regiments, west of An Loc.

Fearing an imminent enemy offensive, General William DePuy, then commander of the U.S. 1st Infantry Division, moved three infantry battalions and an artillery battalion to the Loc Ninh area on May 19 and 20. DePuy's forces quickly commenced Operation El Paso I, but the Viet Cong refused to give battle, prompting DePuy to order a withdrawal on the twenty-fourth. Subsequent intelligence suggested that the Communists had postponed the assault on Loc Ninh but intended to proceed with a major summer offensive to interdict Route 13 and attack key towns in Binh Long Province. The history of the 9th Viet Cong Division confirms that Colonel Cam's original operational plan for the summer had been altered in response to the arrival of significant American forces in the area: "However, while we were making preparations, the enemy managed to learn about our intention. They sent additional troops to the area where our new campaign was expected to be launched. The enemy took up positions in large concentrations and organized defenses to stop us. The 9th Division Party Committee and Command promptly changed their operation plan, this time aiming to be extremely flexible in using forces and fighting methods. For example, a small force might be used as a primer to start the fighting; if the enemy came out, we would fight a major battle by ambushing their convoys."[7]

According to the revised plan, the 272nd Viet Cong Regiment was to ambush American troops on Route 13. The 272nd reached its staging area on May 25 and immediately began studying the terrain, selecting ambush sites, digging combat positions, and constructing fortifications. For added protection, some of the fortifications were built using sandbags and fifty-five-gallon diesel drums filled with dirt. Assault and departure lines were carefully sited some two hundred to five hundred meters from Route 13, and the troops practiced battle tactics. Satisfied with its preparations, the 272nd then settled in and waited.

On June 8 the Americans finally "came out." Captain Ralph Sturgis' Troop A, 1st Squadron, 4th Cavalry Regiment had received orders on June 7 to head north to An Loc and reinforce it in the event of a Viet Cong attack. Augmented with a detachment of South Vietnamese soldiers, Sturgis' convoy—composed of seven M-48 tanks, twenty-five M-113 APCs, two flame thrower tracks, and at least one additional vehicle—departed Phu Loi at approximately 8:30 AM on the morning of the eighth.[8] In the afternoon, as elements of the convoy advanced through the hamlet of Tau O in wooded territory south of An Loc, the VC disabled the lead M-48 tank. The long awaited ambush had begun.

Troops from the ambushing 272nd opened up on the American column with small arms, recoilless rifles, and mortars, but the attacking companies failed to coordinate either their fire or their movement effectively. As a result some of the American vehicles maneuvered into something akin to a perimeter, and with the assistance of artillery and air strikes, the small American and South Vietnamese force routed the carefully laid, regiment-sized ambush. Following the nearly four-hour engagement, the Americans policed the battlefield and discovered 105 dead Viet Cong soldiers, among them a battalion commander. The retreating battalions of the 272nd were also suspected of having carried away an estimated 200–250 of their dead comrades. Conversely the defenders suffered only 33 battle deaths (14 American, 19 South

Vietnamese). "One hundred thirty-five Americans and South Vietnamese," announced one historian of the war, "had handily stopped a force of some twelve hundred enemy regulars."[9]

Ap Tau O illustrates why the American triad of mobility, firepower, and combined arms competency was such an anathema to the Communist big-unit war strategy. Since the onset of hostilities, American mobility had proved problematic for Communist big-unit commanders at the tactical level. During Operation Texas, for example, the 2nd NVA Division history admitted that Marine air mobility had neutralized "at least to a certain extent, our favored tactics of maneuver attacks and mobile ambushes." At Ap Tau O, however, American mobility had a direct and tangible effect on Communist operational planning. The timely deployment of 1st Infantry Division forces to the Loc Ninh area in May had in fact compelled Colonel Cam to change his original "operational plan" before it could be fully implemented in favor of the "flexible methods" that perhaps led to some suspect intelligence before the ambush at Ap Tau O. Indeed one prisoner confessed that the VC had been expecting a South Vietnamese resupply convoy, not a "hard skinned" armored convoy.[10]

Moreover, despite achieving tactical surprise with a numerically superior force, the Viet Cong ambush ended in utter defeat. Responsibility for this ringing setback lies of course with the tenacity and skill of the convoy but also with the two remaining planks of the American triad: firepower and combined arms competency. Forty-three U.S. Air Force sorties and copious amounts of American artillery (105-mm, 155-mm, and 8-inch) supported Troop A throughout the battle.[11] Skillfully delivered, these supporting arms strikes enhanced the defensive fire of the grossly outnumbered convoy and battered the ambushers without damaging friendly forces in the process.

Less than a week after the ill fated ambush at Ap Tau O, the Combat Operations Department of the NVA General Staff presented a draft plan for the 1966–67 winter–spring campaign to the Central Military Party Committee and the Politburo. The Standing Committee of the Central Military Party Committee and key Politburo members convened the next day, June 14, to consider the plan. Le Duan, General Giap, General Nguyen Chi Thanh, and General Van Tien Dung, chief of the NVA General Staff, were among those in attendance at the four-day (June 14–17) gathering. Firmly committed to continuing the big-unit war and regaining the initiative, and perhaps encouraged by the military-political unrest in I Corps in the spring of 1966 to launch a mini General Offensive–General Insurrection, the plan under review sought a battlefield decision in 1967: "According to the proposed plan, during the 1966–1967 winter–spring season operations we would use four 'blocs' of main force units to attack the enemy on four different battlefields: Eastern Cochin China, the Central Highlands, Region 5, and Tri Thien. These attacks would be combined with attacks and insurrections in three large cities—Saigon, Da Nang, and Hue—to destroy and shatter the puppet main force army and inflict heavy losses on U.S. forces in order to win a decisive victory on the South Vietnamese battlefield in 1967."[12]

Throughout the balance of 1966, however, Communist main-force units in South Vietnam weathered a host of hard hitting American offensives, making it exceedingly difficult to regain the initiative. In the Central Highlands, Operation Paul Revere IV (October–December 1966) inflicted considerable losses on several North Vietnamese units operating in the area. Around the same time, Operation Attleboro, which had evolved from a series of searches for Communist supply caches west of the Saigon River into a major offensive, pressured Colonel Cam's depleted 9th Viet Cong Division and resulted in the seizure of substantial quantities of Communist rice and ammunition. South of the DMZ, in Quang Tri Province, the Marines launched Operations Hastings and Prairie in the summer and autumn against NVA units that had infiltrated into South Vietnam.

At times the VC and NVA fought quite well, if almost always while suffering significant losses in the process, but they were unable to crush the ARVN or exact a high enough toll in American casualties to induce a negotiated withdrawal of American troops from South Vietnam. Understandably dismayed, proponents of a lower intensity, protracted conflict responded in party literature and over the airwaves. Liberation Radio served as one outlet for articulating the protracted war viewpoint, and on November 13, 1966, it broadcast an essay from "Cuu Long" on the virtues of guerrilla war:

> Guerrilla warfare not only defeats the enemy infantry, but is also able to fight against the motorized, armored, and air forces of the enemy. This

fact is of particular significance during a national salvation war in which the aggressors have a modern army. It has a greater meaning at a time when we fight against the U.S. expeditionary troops—the most modern army which continually boasts about the supremacy of its air force and the power of its armored force. In reality, the armored vehicles constitute an extremely useful shock force for the infantry while the air force, with its powerful fire power, can easily control the battlefield and bring pressure to bear on the adversary. . . . But tanks, armored craft, and aircraft cannot avoid insurmountable shortcomings. They can be smashed and shot down. This the guerrillas have clearly realized and they have a high determination.

Cuu Long then proposed several guidelines for developing guerrilla warfare:

The guerrilla warfare movement can be guided, built, and expanded satisfactorily if the leading and guiding echelons pay attention to the following points: ONE—First of all, they must clearly and deeply realize the role and nature of guerrilla warfare in the present people's war in South Viet Nam. They must also realize all its new developments, its possibilities, and its basic factors. In this way, they can avoid erroneous conceptions such as the idea of depending on concentrated troops and of overestimating the enemy's forces and weapons, and the incorrect views on combat villages, the use of weapons in guerrilla warfare, the building of forces, the role of the people in general and of women in particular, and the combat objectives and methods of the guerrillas.[13]

Self-serving foreign opposition to the strategy of big-unit war sans negotiations further complicated matters for the hardliners in Hanoi. Although the Soviet Union furnished much of the military hardware required to prosecute the big-unit war, Moscow urged Hanoi to negotiate with the United States. China, alternatively, counseled the North Vietnamese to stand firm against calls for negotiations. Yet the Chinese, no doubt motivated in part out of fear of increased Soviet influence in North Vietnamese affairs (purchased presumably with steadily increasing Soviet economic and military assistance), also advised the North to pursue a military strategy of low intensity guerrilla war. Stalemated on the battlefield and subjected to contradictory advice from abroad, the strategy of diplomatically obstinate big-unit war had clearly entered a critical phase.

In early 1967 the strategic climate in Hanoi shifted slightly as the "moderates" scored a partial policy victory with the passage of Resolution 13 in January. Carefully worded, the resolution pronounced that "the diplomatic struggle is not simply a reflection of the struggle on the battlefield. In the current international situation and because of the nature of the war between the enemy and ourselves, the diplomatic struggle will play an important, vigorous, and offensive role."[14] However, while certainly opening the door to negotiations with the United States, Resolution 13 also contained language indicating that big-unit war would not be jettisoned with the adoption of this new "talk-fight" strategy. Quite the contrary, Resolution 13, in addition to declaring the importance of the diplomatic struggle, ordered "an all-out effort . . . to win a decisive victory in a relatively short period of time."[15] Given that there would be no reasonable expectation of a "decisive victory" within a "relatively short period of time" via low intensity guerrilla war, the resolution plainly reaffirmed two crucial aspects of the hardliners' strategy—big-unit war and the pursuit of a quick victory.

American presidential politics and the interplay between those politics and the future of American war policy influenced the passage of Resolution 13 and the adoption of the talk-fight strategy. President Lyndon Johnson, the policymakers in Hanoi reasoned, would probably be amenable to negotiating an end to American military involvement in South Vietnam prior to the presidential elections in November 1968. The only question was, under what conditions and on whose terms? Since the Vietnam War was arguably the single greatest impediment to his presumptive reelection bid, it was only natural for these politically astute policymakers to assume that Johnson, if presented with a demonstrably deteriorating military-political situation in South Vietnam, would negotiate his way out of the conflict and quite likely on terms favorable to the Communists. Conversely Hanoi worried that if Communist forces did not act to produce a "decisive victory" for leverage in brokering a favorable settlement at the negotiating table, the Americans could opt for a decisive military operation of their own, succeed in that operation, and then proceed to negotiate a settlement favorable to Washington before the 1968 election.[16]

The fact that Hanoi expressed concern over the possibility of the war ending on *American* terms and that it felt compelled to take preemptive action to preclude that possibility strongly suggests the Communist Vietnamese believed the war was potentially in doubt. The North Vietnamese military establishment, represented in this case by the General Staff, voiced some concern about the coming year as well. Couched in somewhat ominous overtones, the April 1967 instructions issued by the leadership of the General Staff for the summer 1967 to spring–summer 1968 military plan cautioned: "The requirement for our strategic plan is that we must create a major change in the nature of the conflict in order to bring down the U.S. and their puppets. . . . If we are not able to transform the situation during the summer of 1967 to win a decisive victory, both North and South Vietnam will face many difficulties during 1968."[17] In calling for a "major change in the nature of the conflict" in 1967 and warning of "many difficulties" in 1968, the General Staff acknowledged that the war had not gone as well as planned and warned of the likely consequences if Communist forces failed to change the strategic dynamic in South Vietnam.

Needless to say, these concerns should not be interpreted as a sign of Communist desperation. Removed from the carnage of the southern battlefields, the hardliners in Hanoi could ruminate on the course of the war without the distracting immediacy of battle. Clearly they were not winning. Of this they were quite sure after failing to win a "decisive victory" despite the nearly two years of grueling big-unit battle Communist forces had waged against the American war machine. The war to date had actually been something of a meat grinder for Communist main-force units. On the other hand, the hardliners could find solace in the fact that they were not, strictly speaking, *losing* insofar as the Americans had yet to secure the strategic defeat of Communist military forces, much less the long-term viability of the "puppet" regime in Saigon. Furthermore, their faith in, and commitment to, final victory remained steadfast.

And yet Hanoi's rather sober, and historically consequential, acknowledgment that the war could conceivably end on American terms—in the absence of a "decisive" Communist military victory and in the event of a decisive American military operation, such as an invasion of North Vietnam—contradicts conventional wisdom, which maintains that the conflict was an entirely unwinnable enterprise for the United States.

Hanoi's talk-fight strategy was conceived then to prevent a favorable outcome for the United States. The VC and NVA would fight on, according to talk-fight, and Communist diplomats would negotiate a halt to American bombing and a withdrawal of American troops. For success in the talk component of the talk-fight strategy, however, the VC and NVA would have to fight big-unit battles and deliver a "decisive victory" for Hanoi's diplomats. General Tran Do, an NVA officer serving in the South and a man who had previously served as a political commissar for the renowned 312th Division at Dien Bien Phu, summarized this approach in an August 1966 speech: "Our basic intention is to win militarily. We use military victories as decisive factors to end the present conflict.... Therefore, we must gain military victories before even thinking about diplomatic struggles. And even when we are fighting diplomatically, we must go on with our war efforts; we must multiply our military victories if we want to succeed diplomatically."[18] Do's words underscore the inescapable fact that the talk-fight strategy was ultimately predicated on having success on the battlefield facilitate success at the negotiating table.

Decisive victory in the context of talk-fight entailed severely damaging American forces, shattering the ARVN, and fomenting a General Offensive–General Insurrection. The latter phase, the General Offensive–General Insurrection, would unfold in urban and rural areas with the objective of bringing down the "puppet regime" in Saigon and creating the conditions for the establishment of an outwardly (though not in reality) non-Communist, "coalition" government. That government would in turn negotiate an end to the American military presence in South Vietnam. Nevertheless, the General Offensive–General Insurrection had one important caveat: It was not to be launched until after American forces had been battered and ARVN all but crippled.[19]

In April 1967 the North Vietnamese General Staff authored a broader definition of "decisive victory," offered a time frame in which it could be achieved, and specified the battlefield goals required to achieve it. Here the

General Staff defined decisive victory as "to cause a transformation in the enemy's situation and a transformation in the nature of the war in South Vietnam, and particular emphasis was placed on three cities: Saigon, Hue, and Da Nang." The time frame was set for the summer of 1967 to the summer of 1968, and the upcoming South Vietnamese (September 1967) and American (November 1968) presidential elections were to be duly considered in the planning process. Finally, on the battlefield, the specified goals included:

> Annihilate 150,000 American troops (including the requirement of annihilating three to five U.S. brigades) and 300,000 puppet troops (including the annihilation of six or seven divisions); to make widespread attacks to erode the strength of the enemy's army so that it could not attack and could not defend itself; and to secure control of between five million and eight million people throughout South Vietnam. With regard to attack targets, the General Staff set the following goals: to liberate Dong Ha and Quang Tri; to overrun and destroy the enemy bases at Ban Me Thuot and Kontum; and to make attacks against Hue, Saigon, and many province capitals.[20]

Chief of the NVA General Staff, General Van Tien Dung was less than enthused with the plan. "The document prepared by the Combat Operations Department is inadequate and does not fully reflect our continuing problems, such as our inability to fight large battles," Dung lamented at the time. "The enemy cannot destroy us, but he can launch attacks into any of our base areas."[21] With age came even greater candor. In a 2004 article about the origins of the Tet Offensive, Dung elaborated on his earlier misgivings and issued a stunning admission:

> We thought about this until our heads ached. The plan was submitted to the Politburo and to the Central Military Party Committee, but the more we thought about it, the more uncomfortable we became. The plan was like our plan for the previous winter–spring campaign, the only difference being that the target goals were higher. The targets and the tactics, the fighting methods, were the same as before, *but the realities of the battle-*

field dictated that we could not attain those goals. We had set target goals for completely annihilating American companies and battalions, but on the battlefield American troops received massive air and artillery support, *so it was not possible to completely annihilate these units according to our requirements. We were not capable of completely destroying American units by killing or taking prisoner all of their troops and securing complete control of the battlefield* [emphasis added].

Dung's conclusion was equally eye opening: "Therefore, if we continued the war by simply gradually ratcheting up our target goals for completely annihilating enemy units in each successive plan, *our battle against the Americans would take a very, very long time, the war would become protracted, and we would not be able to seize opportunities and respond to the new possibilities that were opening up for us* [emphasis added]."[22]

Further contemplation only increased Dung's unease with the original plan. Indeed, the General confessed that in time he "became convinced that we must come up with new goals, new targets, and new methods of attack, and that we needed to revise the entire 1967–1968 winter–spring plan. I requested a meeting with Comrade Le Duan to discuss the matter." When Dung approached Le Duan with his concerns about the plan after the untimely death of General Nguyen Chi Thanh in early July, the First Secretary listened attentively and then, according to Dung, asked, "At this time, why can't we advance our strategic offensive to the ultimate step, a general offensive and general insurrection?"[23] Blunt yet unmistakably bold, Le Duan had proposed advancing to the "ultimate step" *before* the VC and NVA had shattered the ARVN and inflicted crippling losses on the Americans—the two heretofore universally accepted military prerequisites for launching a General Offensive–General Insurrection.

Together Le Duan and General Dung pushed the rather novel approach of skipping ahead to the General Offensive–General Insurrection with Le Duan insisting that the Central Military Party Committee work out a report on the matter for presentation to the Politburo. On July 18 and 19 the Politburo reviewed the plan. Though still very much in its infancy, the plan presented at the Politburo meeting involved drawing American and South Vietnamese forces away from the urban areas of South Vietnam and effectively tying them down so that a massive military-political offensive aimed at the cities of South Vietnam could bring down the "puppet regime" in Saigon. Fundamentally the plan embraced by Le Duan and General Dung envisioned ending the war quickly and climactically with one big multidimensional (military, political, and diplomatic) assault on the South Vietnamese state.

Ho Chi Minh, the venerable if titular head of North Vietnam, was not particularly enamored with the plan, while the role of General Giap in the planning process was apparently negligible. Meanwhile, in Beijing, the Chinese were hostile to any notion of abandoning the strategy of protracted war. Nonetheless, the plan gathered political momentum throughout the summer and early autumn of 1967. Toward the end of October, the Politburo—with Giap conspicuously absent in Hungary, an absence that would endure until his return to North Vietnam in February 1968—authorized the military element of the plan. Several months later in early January, and after another round of debate in the Politburo in December, the Central Committee passed Resolution 14, which authorized the entire plan (including the "General Insurrection"). The date of the offensive was then scheduled for the evening of January 30–31, the eve of the Tet or Lunar New Year.[24]

Following months of debate and maneuvering by the hardliners in Hanoi, not to mention a series of domestic arrests known as the "Revisionist Anti-Party Affair" in the second half of 1967, what began as an exchange between Le Duan and General Van Tien Dung had culminated in the formal authorization of the Tet Offensive.[25] Conceptually the Tet Offensive remained faithful to the basic premise put forth at the July Politburo review. Communist forces would lure the Americans and South Vietnamese into big-unit battle in the Central Highlands and along the Route 9–Khe Sanh Front (B5 Front). There, in rugged country away from American and South Vietnamese logistical support bases and comfortably removed from the critical urban centers of South Vietnam, powerful and well-equipped Communist main-force units would engage and pin down significant enemy forces.

These diversionary border battles, however, were designed to assist the subsequent and main effort of the Tet plan, an all-out General Offensive–General Insurrection. Consisting of military attacks against the provincial capitals and major cities of South Vietnam, including and especially Saigon, and the incitement of a massed political uprising, the General Offensive–General Insurrection was to administer the coup de grâce and topple the despised "puppet" regime. General Dung remembered the plan for the Tet Offensive in rich detail:

> The primary attack sector that was chosen was the cities, with the primary focal point targets being Saigon, Danang, and Hue. The primary attack targets would be the leadership organs and headquarters of the American and puppet forces, command centers, and logistics bases, and our goals would be to annihilate enemy forces and at the same time destroy enemy military equipment and weapons. Attacks would be made throughout all of South Vietnam, and they would be launched simultaneously and on the greatest scale possible. The time set for the attack to begin was midnight of the Tet Lunar New Year celebration, the time when the enemy's guard would be at its lowest. . . . The formula for the attack was to combine military attacks with mass uprisings in all three strategic areas [mountain jungles, rural countryside, the cities] throughout all of South Vietnam.

Dung, incidentally, also outlined the critical importance of the Route 9–Khe Sanh Front (B5 Front) to the "border battles" component of the Tet plan. According to Dung, Communist forces hoped to lure American and South Vietnamese forces up to the Route 9–Khe Sanh Front to strike "the primary blow our main force units would take on all battlefields where conditions were favorable to us." The blow, if successful, would then permit "other battlefields to attack the cities."[26]

Of what relevance was the Tet Offensive to the Viet Cong big-unit war? In short the Tet Offensive signified the failure of the VC/NVA big-unit war that preceded it. To negotiate an expeditious withdrawal of American troops from South Vietnam, the Communist Vietnamese believed they needed a "decisive victory" on the battlefield. The sooner Communist forces could produce a decisive victory, the sooner Communist diplomats could negotiate the United States out of South Vietnam. "We must fight," explained General Nguyen

Van Vinh, deputy chief of the NVA General Staff, "to win great victories with which to compel the enemy to accept our conditions."[27] Yet the VC/NVA big-unit war failed to deliver a decisive victory for Communist diplomats to exploit because it failed to meet the accepted military benchmarks *of* a decisive victory. At no point, in other words, did the VC/NVA big-unit war shatter the ARVN or batter American forces convincingly and on a grand scale. General Dung himself conceded that Communist forces "were not capable of completely destroying American units by killing or taking prisoner all of their troops and securing complete control of the battlefield." Similarly Chairman Mao may have been indirectly alluding to this rather inconvenient battlefield reality when he reminded General Giap and Pham Van Dong: "Fighting a war of attrition is like having meals: [It is best] not to have too big a bite. In fighting the US troops, you can have a bite the size of a platoon, a company, or a battalion. With regard to troops of the puppet regime, you can have a regiment-size bite."[28]

In deciding to launch the Tet Offensive, Le Duan and the hardliners had in effect concluded that the big-unit war could not inflict casualties on American units with the speed or on the scale required to achieve a quick, "decisive victory" in the South. Speaking candidly years later, General Dung admitted that if the Communists "continued the war by simply gradually ratcheting up our target goals for completely annihilating enemy units in each successive plan, our battle against the Americans would take a very, very long time, the war would become protracted, and we would not be able to seize opportunities and respond to the new possibilities that were opening up for us." Those remarks, coupled with his comments about the inability of Communist units to "annihilate" American units completely, probably explain why General Dung received Le Duan's proposal so favorably and why he backed the contentious Tet Offensive. Tet, unlike the prevailing big-unit war, dangled an enticing strategic carrot in front of the general—the opportunity for a quick decision in South Vietnam.

Many have assumed, particularly in light of the duration and eventual outcome of the Vietnam War, that Hanoi had subscribed to a simple yet ultimately successful strategy of outlasting the United States. The Communist Vietnamese, in this interpretation, were content to merely prolong the war while they patiently awaited an American withdrawal and the opportunity to return to the business of crushing South Vietnam. The hardliners, however, were more impetuous than patient. As far back as 1963 and Resolution 9, well before the wholesale commitment of American ground troops to the defense of South Vietnam, hardliners in the North Vietnamese military and political establishment had argued for a speedy decision to the conflict in South Vietnam. Politically correct, the hardliners dutifully espoused the virtues of protracted war. But in deed they directed an aggressive policy of pursuing a quick victory through big-unit war, and when that failed to deliver a "decisive victory" in a timely manner, they gambled on a General Offensive–General Insurrection without first battering the Americans or shattering the ARVN. If the big-unit war alone could not produce a quick and decisive victory, as General Dung feared, the hope was that the Tet Offensive would.

Why did the big-unit war circa 1965–67 fail to deliver a decisive victory in South Vietnam? Perhaps the most salient answer to that question resides in the hardliners' infatuation with big-unit war as the principal facet of the Communist military effort against South Vietnam. General Nguyen Chi Thanh, Le Duan, and others saw fit to pit a first-class light infantry force, the North Vietnamese Army and the elite main-force regiments of the Viet Cong, against a first-class combined-arms force, the U.S. military, in a campaign of extensive big-unit battle despite the fact that the latter was lavishly equipped and expertly trained for high-intensity, big-unit war. The results, heavy Communist losses and numerous setbacks on the battlefield, were eminently foreseeable. Why then did the hardliners advocate and indulge in a style of war that so obviously favored the strengths and capabilities of their most formidable military adversary? In the absence of a more plausible explanation, it would appear that the hardliners overestimated the military capabilities and performance of Communist main-force units and underestimated the battlefield effects of American firepower, mobility, and combined-arms competency.

14

Attitudes and Adversaries

Years before the VC/NVA big-unit war against the United States, another prominent Asian military officer, Admiral Isoroku Yamamoto, the legendary commander in chief of the Imperial Japanese Navy, warned: "It is a mistake to regard Americans as luxury loving and weak. I can tell you that they are full of spirit, adventure, fight, and justice."[1] Alas, it appears as if the Viet Cong of 1965 took little note of Yamamoto's sage counsel. Indeed a Viet Cong evaluation of American forces, dated July 3, 1965, read scornfully:

American Strong Points
- They have reached the training level of an expeditionary force
- Armed with modern weapons, lighter than French expeditionary forces, they have quick transportation, quick movement, have capability of quick reinforcement, thanks to vehicles, aircraft, boats
- Usually concentrated by groups

Weak Points Compared with French
- No spirit of combat; afraid of guerrillas, always rely on modern weapons, so they lose initiative and self-confidence (when in contact, they call fire for support and reinforcement); sometimes artillery must conduct fire support for the whole period of operation.[2]

Imaginatively dubbed the "Prussians of Asia," the Vietnamese people have a rich warrior tradition and the performance of the main-force Viet Cong between August 1965 and May 1966 for the most part did little to dishonor or diminish the legacy passed down by their forebears. In fairness, however, a lack of combat enthusiasm was not entirely unheard of among the Viet Cong over the course of the war. One young main-force private said, for example, "Of every ten fighters, about three or four were too scared to fight."[3] Moreover, approximately 150,000 VC of all description defected to the South Vietnamese between 1963 and November 1969.[4] Defections or desertions afflicted even the elite main-force regiments. In November 1966, to cite one specific instance, the desertion rate in the 2nd Viet Cong Regiment prompted its parent unit, the 3rd NVA Division, to relocate it north into Quang Ngai Province.[5]

Nor were the Viet Cong inoculated from war fatigue and that unique but eminently understandable brand of pacifism brought on by heavy combat. According to unit documents recovered by the U.S. military, troops of the 271st Viet Cong Regiment had exhibited "a lack of determination to seek and fight the enemy . . . weariness and the inclination to enjoy some rest . . . lack of a sense of responsibility and lack of a sense of discipline" following the battles of November 1966–March 1967.[6]

However, while proud of their own service and battlefield performance, some Viet Cong veterans have expressed frustration with and even contempt for the American combat method of introducing external supporting arms into an ongoing infantry skirmish. Again, to the average Viet Cong frontline soldier, battles were to be a contest of competing infantry forces with victory a function of valor, perseverance, and skill, not the weight and accuracy of outside supporting fires. For the Viet Cong, firepower was more or less exclusively *organic*, or the weaponry a formation could carry with it into battle. American infantry formations, on the other hand, could readily summon external supporting arms to supplement their own organic firepower.

Insofar as some Viet Cong were concerned, then, American soldiers and Marines declined a fair fight and depended on external arms for their margin of victory. General Thanh himself spoke of American "over-reliance on material and technical power."[7] The none-too-subtle inference here is clear: The quality of American soldiery did not match the quality of American technology.

The belief that the American infantryman relied too heavily on supporting arms as opposed to his supposed preeminence in individual quality reflects the "no spirit of combat" assessment found in the July 1965 Viet Cong memo, not to mention the declaration that American troops were "afraid of fighting at close quarters and hand-to-hand combat" contained in the 9th Viet Cong Division history.[8] For some former Viet Cong, neither victory nor the passage of time has softened this dismissive attitude. "When I talked to some of those guys [1st Viet Cong Regiment veterans] over there in Vietnam while researching my book on STARLITE, they were pretty cocky about it," said historian and Marine veteran Otto Lehrack. "It goes back to them knowing that they had to fight without artillery and helicopters and all of the stuff we had. They thought they were every bit as good as we were and maybe even better."[9] Sedgwick Tourison, a U.S. Army intelligence specialist who interrogated VC/NVA prisoners and defectors, reported similar findings. "They felt that man-to-man they were more than a match for Americans," Tourison wrote, "at least as far as being soldiers and demonstrating both courage and perseverance."[10]

A progeny of the peasant class like so many soldiers of the Viet Cong, General Van Tien Dung set about comparing American infantry to the PLAF. Dung submitted a bevy of reasons from the unfamiliarity of the American soldier to the climate and terrain of South Vietnam, to the length of the American logistical umbilical cord, to the "irrationality" of the equipment and organization of American troops, to explain why he considered the Viet Cong (and NVA) soldier superior to the American soldier. Dung then concluded:

> All the above-cited reasons explain why the American servicemen, when deprived of the fire support provided by aircraft, armoured cars and artillery, are not better, even worse, than the puppet soldiers in many respects. They want to be light and swift but they are in fact heavily equipped and slow. They think they are strong but they are actually weak. American papers are right in saying that the G.I.s are "play boy" soldiers while the Liberation Armed Forces are regarded as "valiant troops having a real strength and the discipline of a hard-trained army." . . . Though inferior in fire-power, they [Liberation Armed Forces] are superior in number, in fighting spirit, and military ability.[11]

Similarly scathing, General Vuong Thua Vu openly proclaimed what was only obliquely hinted at by others—that the Americans were cowards. "Their basic fighting methods are the following: Seek ways to quickly get away from liberation troops and determine enemy and friendly lines in order to call for help from air and artillery units," Vu, a North Vietnamese Army general, wrote. "This is a very monotonous and outmoded fighting method of a *cowardly* [emphasis added] but aggressive army."[12] Undoubtedly some VC and NVA soldiers shared Vu's opinion. Phat Diem was but one. Wounded twice at Dong Ha, Diem condescendingly averred that American soldiers "weren't brave" and were "afraid to leave their base, their helicopters, their artillery."[13]

Are Vu, Diem, and other like-minded soldiers and officers of the VC and NVA justified in their beliefs? Were American infantrymen reluctant warriors, and perhaps even cowardly, when removed from their firepower? Were VC and NVA soldiers innately superior for having campaigned without such firepower and at closer ranges if they could manage it?

In order to address these questions objectively, tactical context and related expediencies must be properly understood. Fighting against a military superpower, the Viet Cong and NVA often faced a stark choice: close with American infantry units, thereby negating some of the effects of American air and artillery assets, or permit tactical separation and suffer the ensuing effects of American supporting arms. Determining if the average VC *preferred* close-quarters fighting, and some have implied that he did, is immaterial to this discussion. Survival for the VC or NVA soldier, regardless of his personal preference, was often a straightforward and irreducible proposition—get as close to American troops as possible or risk getting blown to pieces by American firepower. Small wonder most Viet Cong and NVA opted to close with American ground forces.

The Viet Cong, apart from self-preservation and personal preference, may have been influenced by rank opportunism as well. At the end of 1965, Lieutenant Colonel George S. Patton published an article containing results from a questionnaire he had circulated to 147 Americans and Vietnamese who had served in Vietnam or were otherwise connected to the struggle. Patton, along with inquiring about Viet Cong motivation, petitioned the respondents to speak to the VC's "willingness to close with and destroy the enemy."[14]

Frederick E. Nolting Jr., who had served as U.S. Ambassador to Vietnam, addressed the matter directly: "While this question can be answered better by those who have been in combat, my own impression is that the VC were generally willing to 'close' only when the tactical situation was very favorable to them, otherwise not."[15] A high-ranking American military officer agreed with and expanded on Nolting's estimation. "This willingness varies directly with the Viet Cong's tactical chances for success," stated the officer. "Viet Cong units will not normally close unless chances for success are in their favor. Therefore, this willingness is closely related to the judgment and experience of small unit leaders."[16]

Irrespective of the reason or reasons—by edict of General Thanh, personal preference, opportunism, self-preservation—one thing is clear: The Viet Cong and NVA did not hesitate to grab the Americans by their belts. Confronted with this tactic, the U.S. military had little recourse but to try to reconcile the need for firepower support with the desire to avoid friendly fire casualties. American infantry units locked in close quarters combat could ask for supporting fires but they did so with a grim understanding—the closer the enemy, the riskier the proposition. American units in heavy contact could decide against requesting supporting fire, of course, but that decision could potentially consign their troops to battle against a numerically superior Communist enemy in potentially unfavorable tactical circumstances. One study, for instance, found that over 40 percent of U.S. engagements involved the ambush or encirclement (and surprise) of a moving American unit or a situation in which an American unit encountered VC/NVA forces in dug-in or fortified positions.[17] Each of these situations placed American units at a distinct tactical disadvantage. Without the equalizing effects of supporting firepower, the situation on the ground in Vietnam could become critical for American troops in a very short period of time. Thus, while there were options, there were no easy answers to the question of balancing the need for fire support and troop safety.

To further complicate matters, one internal U.S. Army analysis asserted that the NVA actually possessed an advantage in organic firepower over comparable American infantry units. Findings from a U.S. Army draft titled "Debriefing of Senior and Designated Officers Returning from Field Assignments,

Report of," reported that "weapon for weapon, a regular NVA unit outguns a U.S. infantry unit in organic firepower, due primarily to the enemy RPG weapon family."[18] Some analysts writing after the war pointed to the NVA's extensive use of light machine guns and to the reliability of VC/NVA automatic weapons as possible sources of this advantage.[19] In any case, one NVA officer, in an opinion that was quite conceivably shared by some members of the similarly equipped main-force Viet Cong, certainly noticed a difference in infantry firepower: "The American infantry units are weak, *their firepower is poor* [emphasis added] and their equipment is poor. An example of this is that an American unit cannot take or destroy a machinegun position in a properly prepared bunker except by calling for air or artillery; however, the NVA can destroy any American bunker with its B40 or B41 (RPG) rockets."[20]

Obviously it would be foolhardy to misconstrue the opinion of one NVA officer as incontrovertible proof that the American infantrymen in Vietnam had the misfortune of fighting against an enemy blessed with superior organic firepower. Indeed, although indicating that the "frequency of close combat" reaffirmed "commanders' desires for an increased number of machine guns in the platoon," an April 1966 U.S. Army evaluation of firepower concluded that "maneuver battalions as presently organized are capable of producing enough firepower in this environment."[21] Moreover, advancements in helicopter based fire support improved as the war progressed to the point where delivering supporting fires as close as 10 meters from friendly forces was not unimaginable. It also bears mentioning that some *American* veterans of the conflict reject outright the notion of NVA or VC organic firepower superiority.

Nonetheless, since the average American infantry unit probably possessed only limited intelligence as to the exact size, firepower capability, and status—NVA or VC, and if VC what type of VC—of the force opposing it when requesting fire support, and were perhaps ignorant of the exact tactical terms of the engagement, the American practice of leaning on external fire support is certainly defensible. Political and cultural sensitivities, it might also be said, practically demanded its use. "In Vietnam," wrote retired Major General Robert H. Scales Jr., "more than in any other war in American history, the preservation of soldiers' lives was the overriding tactical imperative."[22]

The 1st Infantry Division while under the command of Major General William DePuy produced a regulation in 1966 that, in addition to instructing small-unit leaders on how best to fight in Vietnam, was inherently oriented toward preserving lives.[23] This regulation coached the lieutenant in combat to preserve the cohesion and viability of his unit when the shooting started until reinforcements showed up, and to minimize casualties by resisting any unnecessary urge to, according to Scales, "assault or outflank the enemy position." The lieutenant was also advised to withdraw his unit from the VC/NVA's "close embrace." Pulling back from the enemy's embrace was regarded as necessary to ease the job of delivering close-in fire support. After pulling back, American infantry were to stand by while that support softened or smashed the enemy force.[24]

Predictably the VC/NVA grew familiar with this American technique. Colonel Cam, who fought extensively against American forces as commander of the 9th Viet Cong Division, described it rather accurately in his memoirs: "They [Americans] usually tried to achieve separation between their forces and ours to provide a fire support zone in which their heavy fire support weapons could inflict casualties on their opponents."[25] And, not unexpectedly, Cam and other Communist field commanders implored their troops to maintain close contact with American forces as much as possible to reduce the number of firepower induced casualties.

The use of regulations espousing the tactic of pulling back and putting in firepower implied that if cultural proclivities and the experiences of World War II and Korea cultivated an American preference for firepower over maneuver, Vietnam formalized it to some extent. So much so, in fact, that American commanders were asked to justify or account for *not* requesting firepower. Nothing epitomizes this top-down fealty to firepower more than the "force feed fire support system" of the U.S. 25th Infantry Division in 1969, which automatically harnessed all manner of firepower in support of a friendly unit in contact with little regard for tactical context.[26]

These norms reflected the fact that, tactically, American infantry units were to find and fix the enemy so that *firepower* could destroy him. Colonel Sidney B. Berry of the 1st Infantry Division articulated the concept clearly in 1968: "Commanders at all levels should seek the enemy with minimum forces and then use maneuver units to block the enemy's withdrawal and supporting firepower to destroy him. They should seek to avoid heavy infantry attack on, or engagement in, enemy fortified positions. The key to success . . . is the massive use of supporting firepower."[27]

Colonel Harold A. Dye had communicated a similar vision of the role of infantry and firepower in a 1967 article for *Military Review*. "The best support is given to the infantry when the infantry finds the enemy and helps maneuver the fires of the artillery," Dye wrote, "so that the artillery does the job of destroying." Dye believed that the traditional mission of the infantry to "close with and destroy the enemy" should be reviewed, and he suggested that a better mission might be to locate the enemy and let the artillery destroy him.[28] A contemporary of Colonels Berry and Dye, Lieutenant Colonel George Shuffer speculated that firepower had already replaced infantry maneuver as the principle instrument of combat power. "In fact, once a battle is joined in Vietnam," Shuffer inveighed, "firepower outweighs maneuver as the decisive element of combat power."[29]

To be sure, plenty of American company commanders, particularly early in the war against an as yet unfamiliar foe, opted for tactical maneuver first. These commanders responded to enemy contact more traditionally by ordering some of their forces to flank the enemy position or force. Far too often, however, the element dispatched to flank the enemy would move out only to become pinned down by well-sited and previously undisclosed enemy positions or units. Wary of additional maneuvering in the midst of an ongoing firefight, yet unable to advance, the company commander had few options at that point other than summoning outside supporting fires to jumpstart the advance or cover a withdrawal. Short of that, his only other recourse was to curl his unit into a taut defensive perimeter, return fire, and hope supporting artillery, or perhaps a roving gunship or two, could lay some rounds on the enemy force and alter the situation.

Traditional maneuvers, however, sometimes resulted in significant tactical success. On May 21, 1966, for example, Companies B and C of the 1st Battalion, 8th Cavalry Regiment encountered elements of the 22nd NVA Regiment (3rd NVA Division) in the jungle-covered uplands east of the Vinh Thanh Valley. When the NVA withdrew around sundown to hillside defensive positions, the American air cavalrymen pursued the retreating North Vietnamese. Fighting well into the night, Company B and a platoon from Company C maneuvered forward, assaulted the enemy bunkers, and overran the NVA position. The 1st Cavalry Division used maneuver to great effect elsewhere as well. During Operation Wallowa in October 1967, two companies from Lieutenant Colonel Edward Pierce's 1st Battalion, 7th Cavalry Regiment provided a base of fire while a third swung to the west of Ha Tay to link up with armored cavalry elements. The bold maneuver secured the hamlet and netted the American force a bounty of documents from the hastily departed headquarters of the 3rd NVA Regiment (2nd NVA Division). The following Spring, Captain Jay Vargas and the Marines of Company G (2 Battalion, 4th Marines) braved a violent squall of enemy small-arms, mortar, and artillery fire to eliminate, using fire and maneuver, one NVA bunker and fighting position after another in and around the village of Dai Do.

Similarly Marines from India Company (3rd Battalion, 5th Marines) and Lima Company (3rd Battalion, 1st Marines) employed fire and maneuver to record a pair of spectacular tactical victories in the hotly contested Que Son Valley in 1967. While patrolling the valley in June, Marines from Lieutenant Kenny Moore's flank security element observed a force of about fifty NVA soldiers, outfitted with two machine guns, preparing an ambush. Rather than rely on supporting arms to destroy the NVA formation, the Marines used two machine guns of their own to provide a base of fire and two platoons of infantry to envelop the enemy. In the ensuing action, the Marines crushed the would-be ambush, killing some thirty NVA and capturing twenty or so more all without suffering a single casualty. Weeks later Lima Company, commanded by Captain Joe Gibbs, mounted a classic infantry assault during Operation Cochise in August. Gibbs' Marines stormed a hill occupied by North Vietnamese troops and killed several dozen of them, some in hand-to-hand combat. Marine casualties were again astoundingly light. No Marine was killed nor did any sustain wounds requiring a medical evacuation in the rout of the NVA position.[30]

American infantry, as the aforementioned examples clearly demonstrate, were neither unwilling nor incapable of fighting and fighting well in a traditional role with traditional tactics (fire and maneuver). On balance, however, the remarks of Berry, Dye, and Shuffer echoed the received wisdom of the day for limiting American casualties and succeeding in a military campaign based on attrition. Whereas some American commanders objected to and even deviated from that basic premise, for many more firepower availed itself as the best means of providing expeditious infantry reinforcement, preventing friendly casualties, and killing the enemy. Infantry actions without substantial fire support could never hope to attrite the VC and NVA fast enough or hold the number of friendly casualties low enough to gratify the existing political climate.[31] The U.S. military needed to divine a way to do both, and firepower, for better or worse, was it. Consequently, like the Viet Cong and NVA soldier tutored to *grab* the enemy "by their belts," the American infantryman was also held somewhat hostage to the style of fighting his superiors deemed appropriate.

Assessing the merits of any nation's soldiery also depends on, among other things, the nature of the government and society for whom it served. The same holds true for assessing the American infantryman in Vietnam. Washington was casualty averse; Hanoi and its command mechanisms in South Vietnam were anything but. Was the average Viet Cong and NVA soldier aware that his American adversary utilized firepower, though sometimes immoderately, as a means to conserve American life rather than as a means of compensating for a timorous and ineffectual infantry force?

Perhaps not, in which case he would have been at pains to explain the often excellent performance of American infantry units under assault at night, when darkness complicated the delivery of supporting fires, or the performance of 4th Infantry Division troops over a nine-day period near the Cambodian border in May 1967. Of the 367 NVA soldiers counted on the various battlefields—good for a highly favorable 6:1 kill ratio—most were slain by American small-arms fire, not American aircraft or artillery.[32] Likewise the majority of VC killed during the Battle of Hill 65 in November 1965 were killed by American small-arms fire and not by American supporting arms. That same Viet Cong or NVA soldier might also have been surprised to learn that air- and ground-delivered "harassment" and "interdiction" fires accounted for most of the enemy ordnance expended in South Vietnam, and that close air support, often the most feared weapon available to American troops in contact, was provided in "less than 8 percent of the total ground contacts."[33]

Nor was the Communist Vietnamese military man loath to use supporting fires when supporting arms were available. At Dien Bien Phu, the most renowned of the French Indochina War and arguably the greatest triumph of Giap's distinguished military career, volley after volley of Viet Minh artillery fire battered the French garrison, prompting a physician on site to consult his watch during one particularly intense barrage and exclaim, "They're firing sixty shells a minute!"[34] Along the DMZ North Vietnamese Army gunners followed in the footsteps of their Viet Minh predecessors. On one occasion, the evening of March 20, 1967, elements of the 164th NVA Artillery Regiment, deployed near the banks of the Ben Hai River, shelled Marine positions at Gio Linh with nearly five hundred 105-mm artillery rounds.[35] The North Vietnamese buildup of mortars, rockets, and larger caliber (130-mm and 152-mm) artillery in the DMZ only increased in importance, and by July 1967 NVA artillery was capable of providing *direct* fire support to the troops of the 101D NVA Regiment (325C NVA Division) and 803rd NVA Regiment fighting in the Con Thien area south of the DMZ. NVA artillery fire, in fact, produced no less than half of the casualties (159 KIA, 345 WIA) the Marines sustained in the nearly two weeks of heavy fighting (Operation Buffalo, July 2–14) around Con Thien. Marine supporting arms, incidentally, accounted for over 500 of the reported 1,290 NVA killed.[36]

In 1972, and then again in 1975, the North Vietnamese used massed artillery and Soviet supplied tanks in major ground offensives against South Vietnam. Thereafter a newly reunified Vietnam utilized supporting arms extensively in its 1978–79 invasion of Cambodia. Prolonged artillery preparations, naval gunfire, armored thrusts, and air strikes delivered by American fighter-bombers captured after the fall of Saigon were all employed without hesitation to facilitate offensive operations against the outgunned and outnumbered forces of the Khmer Rouge. In mid-January 1979, for instance, two days of air strikes and a three-hour naval bombardment preceded a major Vietnamese attack on Koh Kong City and Koh Kong Island. Earlier in the invasion, air strikes were summoned to hold off Khmer Rouge forces after they had mauled a Vietnamese naval infantry detachment attempting to advance on Sihanoukville Port.[37] It is extremely doubtful, however, that any Communist Vietnamese officer involved in the Cambodian invasion would judge the soldiers of the Khmer Rouge superior to his own simply because the latter had to fight without the firepower support available to Vietnamese troops.

Neither, for that matter, were America's allies averse to calling on extensive firepower to support their troops in combat. At the Battle of Long Tan in August 1966, the preeminent big-unit battle waged by Australian arms in South Vietnam, artillery fire in particular proved instrumental to the survival of D Company, 6RAR (6th Battalion, the Royal Australian Regiment) and the subsequent victory recorded by Australian forces. Severely outnumbered and under heavy assault by Viet Cong forces in the Long Tan rubber plantation southeast of Saigon, Major Harry Smith, D Company's commander, requested air and artillery support and pulled back his hard-pressed platoons into a defensive position, much like an American company commander would do in similar circumstances.

The monsoon-like conditions that prevailed throughout the battle prohibited the delivery of close air support for Smith's gallant troopers, but fire from American 155-mm and ANZAC (Australian and New Zealand Army Corps) 105-mm artillery batteries at the Australian Task Force base five kilometers away bombarded the Communist force, the 275th Viet Cong Regiment (5th Viet Cong Division) and the 445th VC Local Force Battalion, with some 3,440 rounds (3,198 rounds of 105-mm and 242 rounds of 155-mm ammunition).[38] Hours of near-continuous fire from these allied batteries at Nui Dat, coupled with the courage of Smith's men and the appearance of Australian infantry reinforcements mounted in armored personnel carriers, in the end defeated the Viet Cong ground assault against D Company.[39] "The artillery fire support and the arrival of the APCs," wrote Professor Jeffrey Grey, author of an essay chronicling the Australian and New Zealand experience in Vietnam, "had undoubtedly saved D Company."[40]

Such displays of supporting firepower were not, according to Professor Grey, anomalous to the Australian experience in South Vietnam. "In keeping with the advantages enjoyed by all the allied forces in Vietnam, soldiers in the task force often expended prodigious quantities of ammunition, especially in set-piece assaults against bunkers," Grey continued. "They could call on a full suite of fire support options, including helicopter gunships, field, medium, and heavy artillery, fixed wing air support and, on occasion, naval gunfire offshore."[41] Artillery fire, air strikes, and tanks were in fact routinely summoned by Australian troops to destroy Communist bunker positions. Timely and accurate artillery fire, furthermore, supported ground operations in 1967, when on occasion Australian troops fought notable battles with VC/NVA formations.[42] Ian Kuring, who served with the Australian army in Vietnam, recognized that this Australian access to a "full suite of fire support options" afforded Australian troops a tactical edge akin to the one enjoyed by American infantry: "The great advantage for the Australian platoon was that it carried a radio which could be used to request a variety of quick response fire support to assist the immediate battle, followed up by reinforcement, medical evacuation and resupply. In almost all cases, the enemy did not have this advantage."[43]

Needless to say, access to supporting fires and the use thereof does not and should not impugn the valor, tenacity, and skill of the Australian soldier in Vietnam. It does, however, place the relationship between the American soldier and American supporting firepower in context.

So, too, does the relationship the South Korean soldier maintained with *his* supporting firepower in South Vietnam. Keen, professional soldiers by all accounts, the South Koreans were nevertheless, in the opinion of General Westmoreland, "sensitive about keeping casualties down, which resulted in a deliberate approach to operations involving lengthy preparations and heavy preliminary fire."[44] General Creighton Abrams, Westmoreland's successor at MACV, also discerned in the Korean approach a marked fondness for unhurried, deliberately planned actions backed by generous firepower. "There were some things in which the Koreans, based purely on their professionalism, probably exceeded any of our allied forces in South Vietnam," Abrams noted. "An example of this would be when they decided to surround and attack a hill. A task of this sort would take one month of preparation time during which a lot of negotiating would have to be done to get the support of B-52s, artillery and tanks."[45]

Affirming the observations of Westmoreland and Abrams, one South Korean commander, and of the famed South Korean 9th ("White Horse") Infantry Division no less, openly admitted that the "concentration of firepower on successive objectives" had been something of a hallmark of his unit. Pleasantly outspoken, the commander added that enemy forces "should be neutralized within the ring of encirclement with continuous bombardment to prevent organized resistance."[46] Firepower unquestionably assisted the 9th Infantry Division and other South Korean units in registering body counts and kill ratios on par with that of American forces. The August 1966 battle for LZ 27V near the Cambodian border illustrates this point. During that particular engagement, a company of South Korean soldiers supported by a platoon of American tanks turned back repeated NVA attempts to overrun the landing zone. Nearly two hundred North Vietnamese soldiers, compared to just seven South Koreans, perished in the abortive assault. The body count at LZ 27V, however, might not have been so absurdly one-sided if not for the gunfire of American tanks within the company perimeter or the substantial artillery support the South Korean company commander received from American and South Korean bases.[47]

Firepower, furthermore, conserved South Korean lives as it had American lives. South Korean units conducting Operation Hong Kil Dong, a major initiative in Phu Yen Province in July and August 1967, operated under an umbrella of artillery fire, helicopter gunships, and robust air support (244 tactical sorties) during the weekslong offensive. The chief South Korean forces involved, elements of the Capital Division and the 9th Infantry Division, even utilized devastating B-52 bombing strikes ("arc lights") prior to opening the third and final phase of the operation. Indeed, several weeks into the operation, General Yu Byung Hyun, commander of the Capital Division, encouraged his subordinates to be circumspect in their use of fire support in order to avert fostering a "psychological dependence on the part of the [ground] units."[48] Yu's remark reflected the Korean perception that they, unlike the firepower-loving, gung-ho Americans, waged a more deliberate war predicated on energetic pacification activities and infantry-intensive search-and-destroy operations. Dispensing firepower so unreservedly throughout Hong Kil Dong paid off, however. While claiming an enemy body count of 638 KIA, the South Koreans reported friendly losses of just 27 KIA and 68 WIA.[49]

Not long after Hong Kil Dong, South Korean and South Vietnamese forces encountered Communist units in hamlets west of Tuy Hoa. Sensitive to the potential for significant civilian casualties, the Koreans and South Vietnamese abstained from using overwhelming firepower to oust the enemy. Eventually the allies succeeded in recapturing the hamlets but not without heavy losses. Not long afterward, when Communist forces reoccupied the hamlets, the allies summoned air and artillery strikes to avoid a repeat of the previous costly fighting.[50]

Again, it should not be inferred that South Korean units lacked the skill set or the necessary aggression to succeed in infantry combat. Rather, it indicates that, much like the Australians, South Korean forces were not opposed to applying firepower, and sometimes quite lavishly, in support of ground operations.

Wholly apart from fire support and firepower considerations, the terms or conditions of a soldier's service must also be considered. Communist soldiers campaigned more or less indefinitely, with only victory or death commuting their battlefield service. "I only knew that as long as I lived," said one main-force private, "I would have to fight the war."[51] American soldiers and Marines rotated out after either twelve or thirteen months, respectively. Would a Viet Cong soldier have behaved in a substantively different manner if he, too, served a fixed tour and then rotated out? Would a Viet Cong short timer, to use an American military colloquialism, have "played it safe" toward the end of his service time, as some Americans did? Each of these considerations must be weighed against any indictment of the performance and behavior of American infantry in Vietnam.

Question marks, finally, surround the legacy of the VC/NVA's "Grab their belts to fight them" tactic for reducing the effect of American firepower and defeating American infantry. The conventional narrative of the war implies that Communist forces learned how to fight the U.S. military in the Ia Drang Valley. If the VC and NVA could shorten the distance separating friend from foe and transform the subsequent engagement into an infantry-only affair, fewer casualties and more Communist victories would supposedly follow. Yet from the Ia Drang Valley to the onset of Vietnamization, Communist units more often than not suffered profoundly disproportionate casualties when battling American forces. The Viet Cong, in particular, were very nearly rendered hors de combat as a war-impacting fighting force in 1968 and 1969. Moreover, despite the much ballyhooed "Grab their belts to fight them" dictum, the number of American combat deaths resulting from "indirect attacks by fire" increased dramatically between 1967 and 1969. Communist rockets and mortars eventually eclipsed "direct contact" as the "largest source" of American military casualties.[52]

Why were Communist casualties so disturbingly high if Communist tactical adaptations drawn from the Viet Minh experience against the French had mitigated American advantages in firepower? The answer is simple. Either the Communist Vietnamese never proffered a truly appropriate response to the U.S. military's program of integrated arms warfare or they did and in the follow-on *infantry* clashes the average American infantryman, swapping lead with his VC/NVA counterpart in dense, triple-canopied jungle or across a flood-swollen rice paddy, deserves a far more memorable tribute than history has afforded him.

Notes

Introduction
1. Douglas Pike, *PAVN: People's Army of Vietnam* (Novato, Calif.: Presidio Press, 1986), 216–17.
2. Quote from Dale Andrade and Lieutenant Colonel James H. Willbanks, USA (Ret.), "CORDS/Phoenix: Counterinsurgency Lessons from Vietnam for the Future," *Military Review*, March–April 2006, 10.
3. See Douglas Pike, *War, Peace, and the Viet Cong* (Cambridge, Mass.: MIT Press, 1969), 112–13.
4. See Dale Andrade, "Why Westmoreland Was Right," *Vietnam*, April 2009, 30.
5. Quote from Michael Lee Lanning and Dan Cragg, *Inside the VC and the NVA: The Real Story of North Vietnam's Armed Force* (New York: Ballantine Books, 1992), 263.

Chapter 1. Origins, Infrastructure, and Organization
1. Trinh Nhu et al., *Lich Su Bien Nien Xu Uy Nam Bo Va Trung Uong Cuc Mien Nam, 1954–1975* [Historical chronicle of the Cochin China Party Committee and the Central Office for South Vietnam, 1954–1975] (Hanoi: Ho Chi Minh National Political Studies Institute, Party History Institute, 2002), 180.
2. Quoted passage from ibid.
3. Quoted words from Mark Moyar, *Triumph Forsaken: The Vietnam War, 1954–1965* (New York: Cambridge University Press, 2006), 83.
4. Quote from Ho Chi Minh Trail History, 30–31, May 1979, Folder 04, Box 04, Douglas Pike Collection: Unit 03—Technology, The Vietnam Archive, Texas Tech University.
5. See Item 83, Interrogation of an officer in the 60th Battalion, 1st Viet Cong Regiment, 83–84, n.d., Folder 15, Box 01, United States Department of State Collection, The Vietnam Archive, Texas Tech University.

6. See Origin and Evolution of the Current War, 83–84, January 1, 1968, Folder 05, Box 10, Douglas Pike Collection: Unit 01—Assessment and Strategy, The Vietnam Archive, Texas Tech University.
7. See ibid. Note: Lao Dong Party and the Vietnamese Workers' Party are one and the same, the Vietnamese Communist Party.
8. See Diary of Infiltrator, 13, December 1966, Folder 01, Box 04, Douglas Pike Collection: Unit 03—Technology, The Vietnam Archive, Texas Tech University.
9. For information on the Orient Group, see Nhu et al., *Lich Su*, 259.
10. For deployment of northern military cadres, see Pike, *PAVN*, 45. With respect to the accuracy of this pronouncement, competing claims can be found in the Communist Vietnamese literature.
11. *Van Kien Dang Toan Tap, Tap 21, 1960* [Collected party documents, vol. 21, 1960] (Hà N i: National Political Publishing House [NXB Chính Tr Qu c Gia, 2003]), 1014.
12. Guenther Lewy, *America in Vietnam* (New York: Oxford University Press, 1978), 17–18.
13. Quote in ibid., 16.
14. *Van Kien Dang Toan Tap, Tap 22, 1961* [Collected party documents, vol. 22, 1961] (Hà N i: National Political Publishing House [NXB Chính Tr Qu c Gia, 2003]), 653.
15. Military History Institute of Vietnam, *Victory in Vietnam: The Official History of the People's Army of Vietnam, 1954–1974* (Lawrence: University of Kansas Press, 2002), 68.
16. For history and origins of COSVN and the Cochin China Party Committee, see Nhu et al., *Lich Su*, 41, 43, 240; additional insights provided by Merle Pribbenow, correspondence with author, November 5, 2009.
17. *Van Kien Dang Toan Tap, Tap 22, 1961*, 263–64.
18. Quoted passage from Sedgwick D. Tourison, *Talking with Victor Charlie: An Interrogator's Story* (New York: Ivy Books, 1991), 29.
19. Merle Pribbenow, correspondence with author, May 28, 2008.
20. Ellen Baker, "Tran Van Tra," in *Encyclopedia of the Vietnam War*, ed. Stanley I. Kutler (New York: Scribner's, 1996), 545.
21. For Tra's quote and his study in the USSR, see "Happiness in a Person's Life," an interview Tran Van Tra gave to *Xua Va Nay* [Yesterday and today], n.d., in Colonel General Tran Van Tra, *Goi Nguoi Dang Song* [To the living] (Ho Chi Minh City: Youth Publishing House, 1996), 58.
22. Quoted words from Interrogation of Lt. Colonel Le Xuan Chuyen, a former operations officer of the Viet Cong 5th Division, 01 August 1966, Folder 001, Box 30, Douglas Pike Collection: Unit 05—National Liberation Front, The Vietnam Archive, Texas Tech University.
23. Information on Thanh's background comes from Merle Pribbenow, correspondence with author, May 28, 2008.

24. Ho Chi Minh quote from Nhu et al., *Lich Su*, 454.
25. For estimate, see George L. MacGarrigle, *The United States Army in Vietnam, Combat Operations: Taking the Offensive, October 1966 to October 1967* (Washington, D.C.: U.S. Army Center of Military History, 1998), 21.
26. Merle Pribbenow, correspondence with author, June 17, 2008.
27. For quoted words, see Lanning and Cragg, *Inside the VC and the NVA*, 94.
28. See Gordon Rottman and Howard Gerrard, *Viet Cong Fighter* (London: Osprey, 2007), 31. The three-man cell structure was not exclusive to main-force Viet Cong.
29. See Lieutenant General Phillip Davidson, *Vietnam at War: The History, 1946–1975* (Novato, Calif.: Presidio Press, 1988), 280.
30. Quote from Lanning and Cragg, *Inside the VC and the NVA*, 267.
31. Lanning and Cragg, *Inside the VC and the NVA*, 117.
32. Pike, *War, Peace, and the Viet Cong*, 123–24.
33. See Lanning and Cragg, *Inside the VC and the NVA*, 128.
34. Quoted passages from Item 83.
35. See ibid., 83–1.
36. See Diary of infiltrator, 1.
37. See ibid., 5–6.
38. Quote from Lanning and Cragg, *Inside the VC and the NVA*, 56.
39. Ibid., 59.
40. Cited in ibid.
41. Percentage figures found in Otto J. Lehrack, *The First Battle: Operation Starlite and the Beginning of the Blood Debt in Vietnam* (Havertown, Pa.: Casemate, 2004), 36.
42. Moyar, *Triumph Forsaken*, 333.

Chapter 2. On the Field of Battle

1. Quote from James W. McCoy, *Secrets of the Viet Cong* (New York: Hippocrene Books, 1992), 166.
2. For details about the development of General Thanh's essays and the cited lessons, see Bui Tin, "Fight for the Long Haul: The War as Seen by a Soldier in the People's Army of Vietnam," in *Rolling Thunder in a Gentle Land*, ed. Andrew West (London: Osprey, 2006), 61–62.
3. MACV intelligence report excerpt cited in Lanning and Cragg, *Inside the VC and the NVA*, 210–11.
4. Note: The planning process described corresponds most closely to an attack on an enemy *base* or *static* target, though it is generally an applicable guide for all attacks. For an excellent account of the planning process, from committee debate to recon efforts and so on, see Lanning and Cragg, *Inside the VC and the NVA*, 209–14.
5. Quote from ibid., 212.
6. See Colonel Jack Samson, "Viet Cong Tactics: 'Ten against one,'" *Military Review* 47, no. 1 (January 1967): 89.

7. Quote from Department of Defense, *Know Your Enemy: The Viet Cong*, DoD Gen-20 (Washington, D.C.: U.S. Government Printing Office, 1966), 18.
8. Quote from Otto Lehrack, interview with author, November 18, 2007.
9. George M. Nipe Jr., *Decision in the Ukraine: Summer 1943, II SS and III Panzerkorps* (Winnipeg: J. J. Fedorowicz, 1996), 39.
10. Quoted words from *Handbook for US Forces in Vietnam*, April 1967, Folder 01, Box 01, Paul Lasker Collection, The Vietnam Archive, Texas Tech University.
11. For an expanded look of "one slow, four quicks" and the stages of a VC raid on an enemy base type facility, see McCoy, *Secrets of the Viet Cong*, 241–42, and Lanning and Cragg, *Inside the VC and NVA*, 213.
12. Colonel Hoang Ngoc Lung, *Strategy and Tactics*, Indochina Monographs (Washington, D.C.: U.S. Center of Military History, 1980), 126.
13. See Notes from the Underground: The Mystique of a Viet Cong, 20, February 16, 1962, Folder 04, Box 01, Douglas Pike Collection: Unit 05—National Liberation Front, The Vietnam Archive, Texas Tech University.
14. For terrain criteria, see Lanning and Cragg, *Inside the VC and the NVA*, 215; and McCoy, *Secrets of the Viet Cong*, 169.
15. For information on ambush planning, shape, and force structure, see Lanning and Cragg, *Inside the VC and the NVA*, 216; and McCoy, *Secrets of the Viet Cong*, 172–74, 258–62.
16. Quotes from Notes from the Underground, 20.
17. Major Charles M. Johnson and Jack Shulimson, *U.S. Marines in Vietnam: The Landing and the Buildup, 1965* (Washington, D.C.: History and Museums Division Headquarters, U.S. Marine Corps, 1978), 108.
18. First Lieutenant Nicholas H. Grosz Jr. quote from ibid.
19. For a full account of the ambush at Ky Phu, including VC and Marine casualties, see Johnson and Shulimson, *U.S. Marines in Vietnam*, 108–9; "USMC 1965 Lessons Learned, Operation Harvest Moon, Dec.," January 27, 1966, Folder 01, Bud Harton Collection, The Vietnam Archive, Texas Tech University.
20. For quoted VC tactic and targeting of American commanders and radio operators, see ibid. See also Shelby L. Stanton, *The Rise and Fall of an American Army: U.S. Ground Forces in Vietnam, 1965–1973* (New York: Ballantine Books, 2003), 84.
21. Tin, "Fight for the Long Haul," 63.
22. Figure cited in Major General David Ewing Ott, *Field Artillery, 1954–1973*, Vietnam Studies (Washington, D.C.: Department of the Army, 1975), 17.
23. Quote from Johnson and Shulimson, *U.S. Marines in Vietnam*, 125.
24. Ibid. A full account of the Chu Lai and Marble Mountain sapper attacks can be found on pages 125–26.
25. For a thorough list of sapper "tools of the trade," see R. Fox, *Air Base Defense in the Republic of Vietnam, 1961–73* (Washington, D.C.: Office of Air Force History, 1979), 38.

26. Quote cited in David W. P. Elliot and Mai Elliot, *Documents of an Elite Viet Cong Unit: The Demolition Platoon of the 514th Battalion*, pt. 3, *Military Organization and Archives*, RAND Corporation Study RM-5850-ISA/ARPA (Santa Monica, Calif.: RAND Corporation, May 1969).
27. Tin, "Fight for the Long Haul," 63.
28. See Ott, *Field Artillery*, 17.
29. See "Viet Cong Sappers," January 1969, Folder 03, Box 15, Douglas Pike Collection: Unit 05—National Liberation Front, The Vietnam Archive, Texas Tech University.
30. McCoy, *Secrets of the Viet Cong*, 281.
31. See Ott, *Field Artillery*, 15.
32. For a generalized look at sapper training, see McCoy, *Secrets of the Viet Cong*, 276–77; and Fox, *Air Base Defense*, 46–47.
33. See Major General Robert H. Scales Jr. (Ret.), *Firepower in Limited War*, rev. ed. (Novato, Calif.: Presidio Press, 1995), 134.
34. See McCoy, *Secrets of the Viet Cong*, 314–46.
35. Quoted passage from Robert N. Ginsburgh to W. W. Rostow, memo, with attached report, "Operations of U.S. Marine Forces Vietnam, 08 November 1967," 52, Folder 11, Box 08, Larry Berman Collection (Presidential Archives Research), The Vietnam Archive, Texas Tech University. Note: The F-4C Phantom was a multiservice, multipurpose tactical jet fighter. The A-1E Skyraider was a U.S. Air Force jet used in close support.
36. See "Operations of U.S. Marine Forces Vietnam, 08 November 1967," 54. Note: I CTZ refers to I Corps Tactical Zone. The South Vietnamese divided South Vietnam into four tactical corps (from north to south): I Corps Tactical Zone, II Corps Tactical Zone, III Corps Tactical Zone, and IV Corps Tactical Zone. In I Corps, III Marine Amphibious Force handled American operations. In II Corps, I Field Force (U.S. Army) oversaw American operations. In III Corps, II Field Force (U.S. Army) handled American operations. In mid-1966 there were no major American units operating in IV Corps. U.S. Army and Air Force aviation assets supporting the South Vietnamese in IV Corps worked "under the supervision" of the "local senior" American military advisor. For American command structures, see MacGarrigle, *United States Army in Vietnam*, 13.
37. See ibid., 205–6.
38. See United States Army, Vietnam, Rpt., USARV, 5 Feb 70, sub: History of the 273 VC Regiment, July 1964–December 1969, 31.
39. Quoted passage from Viet Cong Base Camps and Supply Caches, 20 July 1968, 1–2, Folder 02, Box 01, Douglas Pike Collection: Unit 05—National Liberation Front, The Vietnam Archive, Texas Tech University.
40. For triangular VC camps, see United States Army, Vietnam, History of the 273 VC Regiment, 31.
41. Quote from Scales, *Firepower in Limited War*, 77.

42. This requirement did not, of course, pertain to the more semipermanent bases. See Lanning and Cragg, *Inside the VC and the NVA*, 203.
43. Ibid., 207.
44. Quote from McCoy, *Secrets of the Viet Cong*, 190.
45. For VC movement, movement between camps, and counterintelligence protocol, see Lanning and Cragg, *Inside the VC and the NVA*, 204–5.
46. See United States Army, Vietnam, History of the 273 VC Regiment, 32. Note: The 273rd VC Regiment had never billeted in local villages during the time period covered in the intelligence study. Regarding the "rainy seasons," from Phan Rang (Ninh Thuan Province, former S. Vietnam) north up to the Red River Delta (N. Vietnam), the rainy season extends from September to January, while the dry season runs from March to August. From Phan Rang south, through the Mekong Delta, the rainy season runs from May to October, while the dry season runs from November to April. See Cuu Long Giang and Toan Anh, *Nguoi Viet, Dat Viet* [The land and people of Vietnam] (Saigon: Kim Lai Printers, 1967), 31.
47. See Viet Cong Base Camps and Supply Caches, 10.
48. For greater detail on "prepared battlefields" and "maneuvering forces battle," see McCoy, *Secrets of the Viet Cong*, 174–81.
49. Quote from Colonel General Dang Vu Hiep, with Senior Colonel Le Hai Trieu and Colonel Ngo Vinh Binh, *Ky Uc Tay Nguyen* [Highland memories], pt. 4 (Hanoi: People's Army Publishing House, 2000), 36–37.
50. Information on origins of slogan and Battle of Vinh Huy also from Merle Pribbenow, interview with author, November 7, 2008.
51. Quote from David Chanoff and Doan Van Toai, *Portrait of the Enemy* (New York: Random House, 1986), 155.
52. See Lieutenant Colonel George M. Shuffer Jr., "Finish Them with Firepower," *Military Review* 47, no. 12 (December 1967): 15.

Chapter 3. Generating Friction

1. Anthony Beevor, *Stalingrad: The Fateful Siege, 1942–1943* (New York: Viking Penguin, 1998), 141.
2. Lanning and Cragg, *Inside the VC and the NVA*, 110.
3. See Department of the Army, "Viet Cong Boobytraps, Mines, and Mine Warfare Techniques," 10, May 1967, training circular, Folder 07, Box 09, Glen Helm Collection, The Vietnam Archive, Texas Tech University.
4. Account found in McCoy, *Secrets of the Viet Cong*, 342.
5. See Department of the Army, "Viet Cong Boobytraps," 55–56.
6. For an excellent review of VC road mining techniques, see ibid., 54–55.
7. Eric Bergerud, *Red Thunder, Tropic Lightning: The World of a Combat Division in Vietnam* (Boulder, Colo.: Westview Press, 1993), 118.
8. John Pimlott, *Vietnam: The Decisive Battles* (New York: Macmillan, 1990), 78.
9. See Maurice Maltoff, ed., *American Military History* (Washington, D.C.: U.S. Army Center of Military History, 1980), 647.

10. Quote from Bergerud, *Red Thunder, Tropic Lightning*, 118–19.
11. Statistic cited in Adam Lind, "Mines," in *Encyclopedia of the Vietnam War*, ed. Stanley I. Kutler (New York: Scribner's, 1996), 338.
12. For the VC's use of "multiple" booby traps and how it worked, see Department of the Army, "Viet Cong Boobytraps," 34.
13. For cited casualty figures, see Mark Woodruff, *Unheralded Victory: The Defeat of the Viet Cong and North Vietnamese Army, 1961–1975* (New York: Presidio Press, 1999), 255, 365.
14. Cited in Military History Institute of Vietnam, *Victory in Vietnam*, 463. (For the date of release and other details regarding the "10 ways," see 177.)
15. Casualty figure cited in John A. Nagle, *Learning to Eat Soup with a Knife: Counterinsurgency Lessons from Malaya and Vietnam* (Chicago: University of Chicago Press, 2002), 200.
16. Quote from Eric Bergerud, interview with author, August 26, 2007.
17. Quoted passage from Bergerud, *Red Thunder, Tropic Lightning*, 123–24.

Chapter 4. Strategic Debates and Decisions

1. Pike, *PAVN*, 48.
2. At the time of the Battle of Bau Bang in November 1965, Cam was a senior colonel.
3. For conversation, see Colonel General Hoang Cam and Nhat Tien, *Chang Duong Muoi Nghin Ngay: Hoi Uc* [The ten-thousand-day journey: A memoir] (Hanoi: People's Army Publishing House, 2001), 90–93.
4. For quoted words, see Tra, "Happiness in a Person's Life," 58–59.
5. Lt. General Le Van Tuong, "The keen strategic vision and the modest but profound attitude of General Nguyen Chi Thanh," in Military History Institute of Vietnam, *Dai Tuong Nguyen Chi Thanh: Na Chinh Tri Quan Su Loi Lac* [General Nguyen Chi Thanh: An outstanding military political figure], ed. Ha Huu Khieu (Hanoi: People's Army Publishing House, 1997), 148.
6. Quote from Tra, "Happiness in a Person's Life," 58.
7. See Lien-Hang T. Nguyen, "The War Politburo: North Vietnam's Diplomatic and Political Road to the Tet Offensive," *Journal of Vietnamese Studies* 1, nos. 1–2 (February/August 2006): 11.
8. For an excellent analysis of the decision-making process and environment in North Vietnam circa 1955–59, see ibid., 7–11.
9. Quoted words from Merle Pribbenow, "General Vo Nguyen Giap and the Mysterious Evolution of the Plan for the 1968 Tet Offensive," *Journal of Vietnamese Studies* 3, no. 2 (Summer 2008): 3.
10. For a detailed look at Hoang Minh Chinh's report, his insights on the attitudes present at the Ninth Plenum, and other arguments and opponents of the "China-line," see Nguyen, "War Politburo," 15–17, 45.
11. See Pribbenow, "General Vo Nguyen Giap," 20.
12. Quotes from the "Vietnamese Public Security" history cited was found in ibid., 21.

13. See Nguyen, "War Politburo," 17; Pribbenow, "General Vo Nguyen Giap," 20.
14. Quoted words from Moyar, *Triumph Forsaken*, 325. Note: The Politburo was made up of a small number of the Central Committee's top officials and made most of the critical decisions.
15. For the plan, including the General Offensive–General Insurrection against Saigon, see Pribbenow, "General Vo Nguyen Giap," 3–4. Note: The proposed enterprise was code named Plan X.
16. Military History Institute of Vietnam, *Victory in Vietnam*, 137.
17. Davidson, *Vietnam at War*, 293.
18. Quote from in Moyar, *Triumph Forsaken*, 359.
19. Numerous sources were consulted for the biographical material on Le Duan, including Le Duan biography: 1976, Folder 13, Box 05, Douglas Pike Collection: Unit 08—Biography, The Vietnam Archive, Texas Tech University; William Duiker, *The Communist Road to Power in Vietnam* (Boulder, Colo.: Westview Press, 1981), 138, 189; Pribbenow, "General Vo Nguyen Giap," 7.
20. Quote found in Moyar, *Triumph Forsaken*, 488.
21. Le Duan quotes from Pribbenow, "General Vo Nguyen Giap," 4.
22. Military History Institute of Vietnam, *The Resistance War against the U.S. to Save the Nation, 1954–1975: Military Events*, ed. Senior Colonel Tran Hanh (Hanoi: Military History Institute of Vietnam, 1988), 69.
23. General William Westmoreland, *A Soldier Reports* (Garden City, N.Y.: Double Day, 1976), 140.
24. Quotes from Moyar, *Triumph Forsaken*, 415.

Chapter 5. Van Tuong

1. Quote from Marilyn Young, *The Vietnam Wars, 1945–1990* (New York: Harper Collins, 1991), 161.
2. Senior Colonel Nguyen Quang Dat and Senior Colonel Tran Hanh, *Mot So Tran Danh Trong Khang Chien Chong Phap, Khang Chien Chong My, 1945–1975 (Tap I)* [A number of battles during the resistance wars against the French and the Americans, 1945–1975 (vol. 1)] (Hanoi: Military History Institute of Vietnam, 1991), 24–25.
3. Quote from Johnson and Shulimson, *U.S. Marines in Vietnam*, 69.
4. Ibid., 70.
5. Quote from ibid.
6. Dat and Hanh, *Mot So Tran Danh Trong Khang Chien Chong Phap*, 26.
7. Military History Institute of Vietnam, *Resistance War against the U.S.*, 80.
8. See Lehrack, *First Battle*, 42–43, 45, 52.
9. See Dat and Hanh, *Mot So Tran Danh Trong Khang Chien Chong Phap*, 26.
10. A Vietnamese history of the 2nd NVA Division, to which the 1st VC Regiment was attached after Starlite, indicates that the regiment consisted of the 40th, 60th, 90th Battalions and the 400th Combat Support (Heavy Weapons) Battalion. American sources typically list the 45th Weapons Battalion,

but the VC/NVA practice of changing the names of units to confuse allied intelligence could account for the discrepancy. See Vu Anh Tai, Le Minh Tan, and Phan Van Tich, editorial direction, 2nd Division Party Committee and Division Headquarters, *Su Doan 2, Tap I* [2nd Division, vol. 1] (Da Nang: Da Nang Publishing House, 1989), 16.

11. See Dat and Hanh, *Mot So Tran Danh Trong Khang Chien Chong Phap*, 36.
12. Quoted words from ibid., 25.
13. Lehrack, *First Battle*, 58. Note: With respect to Marine sources other than Vo Thao, the Marine Corps official histories say only that Colonel Dulacki's G-2 (intelligence) section received "corroborative information" from an additional source.
14. For terrain features, see Dat and Hanh, *Mot So Tran Danh Trong Khang Chien Chong Phap*, 22.
15. Tai, Tan, and Tich, *Su Doan 2, Tap I*, 16.
16. See Lehrack, *First Battle*, 42.
17. Casualty figures for the 361st Company cited in ibid., 41.
18. For general battle details, see Woodruf, *Unheralded Victory*, 17–19; Pimlott, *Vietnam*, 40–47; and Otto J. Lehrack, *No Shining Armor: The Marines at War in Vietnam* (Lawrence: University of Kansas Press, 1992), 33–52.
19. For a definitive account of Huan's delaying action against Company K and its ultimate success, see Lehrack, *First Battle*, 75–76.
20. Johnson and Shulimson, *U.S. Marines in Vietnam*, 81.
21. For a thorough account of the An Cuong (2) fighting, see Lehrack, *First Battle*, 91–92, 97–100; and Johnson and Shulimson, *U.S. Marines in Vietnam*, 75.
22. Note: Lehrack and the Marine Corps official history state that Company H (2/4) touched down amid the defensive areas of the 60th VC Battalion. Colonels Nguyen Quang Dat and Tran Hanh report that a company from the 6th VC Battalion defended the "grassy hill" south of the Marine helicopter landing. Thus it's reasonable to assume the 6th and 60th VC Battalions were one in the same.
23. Note: Nguyen Quang Dat and Tran Hanh state that the two platoons involved came from the 1st Company, 6th VC Battalion. See Dat and Hanh, *Mot So Tran Danh Trong Khang Chien Chong Phap*, 29. VC/NVA expert Merle Pribbenow believes that the 6th VC Battalion was in fact the 60th VC Battalion (Merle Pribbenow, correspondence with author, June 9, 2008).
24. For Lance Corporal Ernie Wallace's exploits, see Lehrack, *First Battle*, 127.
25. The withdrawal of Company H began around 2:00 PM. For a thorough recounting of the fighting around Nam Yen (3) on August 18, see Johnson and Shulimson, *U.S. Marines in Vietnam*, 75–76; and Lehrack, *First Battle*, 86–89, 107–9, 123–29.
26. Casualty figures for Company E cited in Lehrack, *First Battle*, 90.
27. For casualty figure and an account of VC activity against Companies E and G, see Johnson and Shulimson, *U.S. Marines in Vietnam*, 72–73.

28. The battle study authored by Dat and Hanh described the ambush as having been conducted by the 1st Company of the 4th Battalion. Much like the situation in which the 6th VC Battalion is almost certainly the same unit under a different name as the 60th VC Battalion, it is reasonable to conclude and the evidence suggests the so described 4th VC Battalion is indeed the 40th. See Dat and Hanh, *Mot So Tran Danh Trong Khang Chien Chong Phap*, 34.
29. Ibid.
30. For Sergeant Mulloy's exploits, see Lehrack, *First Battle*, 132–33.
31. Marine casualties cited in Johnson and Shulimson, *U.S. Marines in Vietnam*, 79.
32. VC ambush casualties cited in ibid. For a thorough account of the VC ambush and subsequent fight, see Johnson and Shulimson, *U.S. Marines in Vietnam*, 76; and Lehrack, *First Battle*, 130–33.
33. Marine intelligence source casualty figure cited in Johnson and Shulimson, *U.S. Marines in Vietnam*, 238.
34. VC and Marine official casualty figures cited in Lehrack, *No Shining Armor*, 51; and Johnson and Shulimson, *U.S. Marines in Vietnam*, 80.
35. Quote from Colonel Harry G. Summers, *Historical Atlas of the Vietnam War* (New York: Houghton Mifflin, 1995), 102.
36. Ontos are tracked vehicles brandishing six coaxially mounted 106-mm recoilless rifles, four .50-caliber "spotting" rifles, and one .30-caliber machine gun.
37. Quote from Neil Sheehan, *A Bright and Shining Lie: John Paul Vann and America in Vietnam* (New York: Random House, 1988), 537.
38. Dat and Hanh, *Mot So Tran Danh Trong Khang Chien Chong Phap*, 37.
39. Tai, Tan, and Tich, *Su Doan 2, Tap I*, 17.
40. Dat and Hanh, *Mot So Tran Danh Trong Khang Chien Chong Phap*, 38.
41. Ibid., 41.
42. Lehrack, *No Shining Armor*, 39.
43. For a comprehensive analysis of VC/NVA antiairmobile doctrine, see McCoy, *Secrets of the Viet Cong*, 224–29.
44. Instructions found in Lieutenant General Julian J. Ewell and Major General Ira A. Hunt, *Sharpening the Combat Edge: The Use of Analysis to Reinforce Military Judgment*, Vietnam Studies (Washington, D.C.: Department of the Army, 1974), 116.
45. Robert Mason, *Chickenhawk* (New York: Viking Press, 1983), 78.
46. Quote from Lehrack, *No Shining Armor*, 41. Note: The U.S. Navy and Marine Corps A-4 Skyhawk was an attack bomber.
47. Quote from Lanning and Cragg, *Inside the VC and the NVA*, 245.
48. Cited in Stanton, *Rise and Fall*, 50.
49. Colonel David Hackworth, *Steel My Soldiers' Hearts* (New York: Touchstone Book, 2002), 157.

Chapter 6. An Ninh and the Ia Drang Valley

1. General Donn A. Starry, *Mounted Combat in Vietnam*, Vietnam Studies (Washington, D.C.: Department of the Army, 1989), 5.

2. Communist taunts from Bernard Fall, *Street without Joy* (Mechanicsburg, Pa.: Stackpole Books, 1994), 206.
3. For the definitive account of the ambush of GM 100 and its ordeal, see ibid., 185–250.
4. Quoted words from Nguyen Tri Huan et al., *Su Doan Sao Vang* [The Yellow Star Division] (Hanoi: People's Army Publishing House, 1984), 17.
5. Given the "dual hierarchy" of the Communist command system, Military Region 5 Headquarters presided over military operations in the same area as Region 5 Headquarters oversaw party and civilian matters. Roughly Region 5 was the northern half of South Vietnam. A more precise definition can be found in succeeding chapters.
6. Huan et al., *Su Doan Sao Vang*, 14.
7. For official recognition dates of the 1st, 2nd, and 3rd NVA Divisions, see Military History Institute of Vietnam, *Victory in Vietnam*, 156.
8. For appointments of commanders, see Military Encyclopedia Center of the Ministry of Defense, *Tu Dien Bach Khoa Quan Su Viet Nam* [Military encyclopedia of Vietnam], chief ed. Senior Colonel Tran Do (Hanoi: People's Army Publishing House, 1996), 561 (An), 563–64 (Nang), and 316 (Cuong). Additional bio info provided in Merle Pribbenow, correspondence with author, August 27, 2008.
9. See Huan et al., *Su Doan Sao Vang*, 15.
10. For information on reorganizations of the 2nd VC Regiment, see Captured Documents (Combined Document Exploitation Center): Organization and Personalities of Regiment 2, Division 3, 10 December 1966, Folder 2635, Box 0042, 2, Vietnam Archive Collection, The Vietnam Archive, Texas Tech University. Note: Communist sources refer to the "93rd" Battalion as the "1st Battalion" and the "95th" as the "2nd." This can be gleaned from AAR, Operation Masher/White Wing, 1st Cavalry Division (Ambl), April 29, 1966, 11, which refers to the "1st Bn, Quyet Chien Regt. (AKA 93rd Bn, 2nd VC)," and the fact that Captured Documents (Combined Document Exploitation Center): Organization and Personalities of Regiment 2, Division 3, identifies a "Senior Captain Nhue" as commander of the 95th Battalion and a "Senior Captain Ngoan" as political officer, while Huan et al., *Su Doan Sao Vang*, 71, identifies a "Battalion Commander Nguyen Tai Nhue" and a "Battalion Political Officer Nguyen Ngoc Ngoan" as commanding the "2nd Battalion."
11. Quoted passages from Huan et al., *Su Doan Sao Vang*, 26–27.
12. See Colonel (Ret.) Thomas E. Faley, "Mutual Surprise at An Ninh," *Screaming Eagle*, January/February 1998, 15–19, item found in "Mutual Surprise at An Ninh Paratroopers vs Viet Cong," January–February 1998, Folder 03, Box 01, Gary Jestes Collection, The Vietnam Archive, Texas Tech University.
13. For the planning of Operation Gibraltar, see AAR, Operation Gibraltar, 2nd Battalion, 502nd Infantry, October 8, 1965, 1; and Faley, "Mutual Surprise at An Ninh," 16.

14. Elements of the 94th VC Battalion could conceivably have been present as well, but the 3rd NVA Division history discusses only the 95th's participation in the battle. See Huan et al., *Su Doan Sao Vang*, 26–35.
15. Quoted passage from ibid., 32. Note: The 3rd NVA Division history calls the hamlet around where the fighting occurred Thuan Ninh.
16. Quote from ibid., 30.
17. Quote from Faley, "Mutual Surprise at An Ninh," 17.
18. See ibid. Note: There is some ambiguity as to the number of Company B platoons that landed with the second lift.
19. For helicopter figure, see John M. Carland, *The United States Army in Vietnam, Combat Operations: Stemming the Tide, May 1965 to October 1966* (Washington, D.C.: U.S. Army Center of Military History, 2000), 42.
20. See Faley, "Mutual Surprise at An Ninh," 17.
21. See AAR, Operation Gibraltar, 4.
22. Quote from Faley, "Mutual Surprise at An Ninh," 18.
23. Tactical air strikes became "available" at 9:04 AM. See Tony Mabb, "Vietnam Eagles," *Screaming Eagle*, November/December 2002, 34, item in The Screaming Eagle, November/December 2002, Folder 03, Box 02, Gary Jestes Collection, The Vietnam Archive, Texas Tech University.
24. The casualty figures from the American side can be gleaned from numerous sources, though Faley notes that the thirteen dead and twenty-eight wounded pertain strictly to Smith's force, not the "outside forces" such as helicopter crews. See Faley, "Mutual Surprise at An Ninh," 19. VC figure taken from Carland, *United States Army in Vietnam*, 43.
25. Quote from Faley, "Mutual Surprise at An Ninh," 19.
26. From AAR, Operation Gibraltar, 7, 8.
27. Numerous sources for Operation Gibraltar and the fighting on September 18 near An Ninh were consulted, including AAR, Operation Gibraltar; Faley, "Mutual Surprise at An Ninh," 15–19; Mabb, "Vietnam Eagles," 33–35; Carland, *United States Army in Vietnam*, 42–43; and Stanton, *Rise and Fall*, 48–51.
28. Quoted words from Huan et al., *Su Doan Sao Vang*, 35.
29. Quoted words and concerns from "The Ia Drang Campaign 1965: A Successful Operational Campaign or Mere Tactical Failure?" 23, monograph by Lieutenant Colonel Peter J. Schifferle Armor, May 6, 1994, Folder 01, Box 02, Elias A. Cuevas Collection, The Vietnam Archive, Texas Tech University.
30. For the general goals of the North Vietnamese campaign, see Merle Pribbenow, "The Fog of War: The Vietnamese View of the Ia Drang Battle," *Military Review*, January–February 2001, 93; Lt. Gen. Nguyen Dinh Uoc, director of Military History Institute of Vietnam (Ministry of Defense), "Chien Dich Play Me" [Plei Me campaign], presentation given at Pleiku–Ia Drang Veterans 40th Anniversary Commemoration, November 10–13, 2005, Washington, D.C.
31. Quote cited in Lieutenant General Hal G. Moore (Ret.) and Joseph L. Gallo-

way, *We Were Soldiers Once . . . and Young: Ia Drang—The Battle that Changed the War in Vietnam* (New York: Random House, 1992), 49.
32. See Pribbenow, "Fog of War," 93.
33. Quote from Moore and Galloway, *We Were Soldiers Once*, 36.
34. Quote from ibid., 62.
35. Merle Pribbenow, interview with author, December 1, 2008.
36. For the definitive account of NVA surprise at Ia Drang and the absence of 66th Regiment and 9th Battalion commanders, see Pribbenow, "Fog of War," 94.
37. Quote from Moore and Galloway, *We Were Soldiers Once*, 76.
38. Quote from ibid., 145.
39. Piecing together the exact forces involved in the attack is somewhat difficult. Phoung's quote firmly places the H-15 in the morning attack (though not which assault, 6:50 or 7:15), and accounts cite the presence of black pajama–clad troops fighting in the 7:15 AM attack (see Woodruff's *Unheralded Victory*, 94). Specialist Will Parish, attached to Delta, recalled seeing enemy troops in uniforms like those associated with the NVA. See Will Parish, interview with author, October 22, 2007.
40. First quote from Parish interview, October 22, 2007; second quote from Will Parish, interview with author, September 7, 2008.
41. AAR, Ia Drang Valley Operation, 1st Battalion, 7th Cavalry, November 14–16, 1965, December 9, 1965, 14.
42. For Thanh quote and COSVN Military Party Committee view of Ia Drang, see "Chien Thang Play Me–Ia Drang (tu 19–10 den 20–11–1965): Don Phu Dau Quan My o Tay Nguyen" [The Plei Me–Ia Drang victory (from 19 October to 20 November 1965): A stunning first blow against American troops in the Central Highlands], Folder 01, Box 01, Merle Pribbenow Collection, The Vietnam Archive, Texas Tech University.

Chapter 7. The B2 Front

1. Quoted words from Tra, "Happiness in a Person's Life," 58.
2. For a concise breakdown of Communist military administration of South Vietnam, see Carland, *United States Army in Vietnam*, 5. Note: In April 1966 the B4 Front was formed and it covered all of Thua Thien and Quang Tri Provinces. In July 1966 the B5 Front was formed and it covered the northern half of Quang Tri Province to the DMZ (the B4 Front thus covered Thua Thien and the southern half of Quang Tri Province).
3. Colonel General Tran Van Tra, *Vietnam: History of the Bulwark B2 Theater*, vol. 5, *Concluding the 30-Years War*, trans. Foreign Broadcast Information Service, Joint Publications Research Service 82783, Southeast Asia Report 1247 (Ho Chi Minh City: Van Nghe Publishing House, 1982), 2–3.
4. See draft of "The Big Red One" (chapters 1–5), 5, n.d., Folder 64, Box 01, William E. LeGro Collection, The Vietnam Archive, Texas Tech University.

5. "Flexible boundaries" quote and working definition of the geographic configuration of War Zones C and D provided by Merle Pribbenow, correspondence with author, July 21, 2008.
6. War Zones C and D descriptions contained in Military Encyclopedia Center of the Ministry of Defense, *Tu Dien Bach Khoa Quan Su Viet Nam*, 148.
7. For concise geographic description of Iron Triangle, see Lieutenant General Bernard William Rogers, *Cedar Falls–Junction City: A Turning Point*, Vietnam Studies (Washington, D.C.: Department of the Army, 1989), 16.
8. For quoted words and area definition, see Carland, *United States Army in Vietnam*, 32. For a more detailed definition of the Zone, see MacGarrigle, *United States Army in Vietnam*, 349.
9. For the code names of the 9th VC Division, the ceremony held by the Nhung Stream, and unit composition, see Pham Quang Dinh, ed., *Su Doan 9* [9th division] (Hanoi: People's Army Publishing House, 1990), 46–48. Note: September 2 was North Vietnam's National Day, the day when Ho Chi Minh declared Vietnam's independence from the French in 1945.
10. Ibid., 46. Note: In *Su Doan 9* the 271st, 272nd, and 273rd VC Regiments are known as the 1st, 2nd, and 3rd Regiments of the 9th Division. During the war, the designations 271st, 272nd, and 273rd were used and will be used here because the American/Western reader is most familiar with them.
11. Ibid., 51.
12. For claim that Cam's regiment captured de Castries, see ibid., 49. Note: Cam's entry in Military Encyclopedia Center of the Ministry of Defense, *Tu Dien Bach Khoa Quan Su Viet Nam*, makes no such claim.
13. For the date of departure, see Cam and Tien, *Chang Duong Muoi Nghin Ngay*, 77. For additional biographical info on Cam, see Dinh, *Su Doan 9*, 49; and Military Encyclopedia Center of the Ministry of Defense, *Tu Dien Bach Khoa Quan Su Viet Nam*, 357–58. Note: Cam was a native of the village of Cao Son, the district of Ung Hoa, and the province of Ha Tay.
14. See Colonel Ho Son Dai, ed., *Lich Su Su Doan Bo Binh 5 (1965–2005)* [History of the 5th Infantry Division (1965–2005)] (Hanoi: People's Army Publishing House, 2005), http://www.quansuvn.net/index.php?topic=155710/ (accessed Aug. 29, 2005).
15. See ibid. Note: The Communists refer to a "Ba Ria" Province, which had different boundaries then but covered roughly the same general area as the South Vietnamese "Phuoc Tuy" Province.
16. For biographical info on Hoa, see Military Encyclopedia Center of the Ministry of Defense, *Tu Dien Bach Khoa Quan Su Viet Nam*, 559.
17. See Dai, *Lich Su Su Doan Bo Binh 5*. Note: These units reflect the initial composition of the 5th VC Division. Also, the 274th and 275th Viet Cong Regiments are referred to as the 4th and 5th Regiments of the "5th Division" in the histories of the division. Again, the 274th and 275th designations are used because of American/Western familiarity.

18. Note: The VC/Communists had some of their own names for provinces in South Vietnam, and the land boundaries did not always exactly correspond to their South Vietnamese counterparts.
19. Nhu et al., *Lich Su*, 175.
20. Westmoreland had other assets at his disposal in terms of firepower, and there were a number of ARVN units in the B2 Front area of operations. The 173rd Airborne Brigade and the 1st Infantry Division were Westmoreland's chief ground-maneuver forces in November/December 1965 around Saigon.

Chapter 8. Cong Truong 9 Enters the Fray

1. For background and operational concept of Operation Hump as well as 3rd Battalion, 271st VC Regiment intentions on November 8, see Carland, *United States Army in Vietnam*, 76–78. Note: The area of operations for the 1st/503rd was inside Tan Uyen District, Bien Hoa Province.
2. Quote from Dinh, *Su Doan 9*, 8–9.
3. See ibid., 8, 9–10.
4. See ibid., 12.
5. Note: The term "Nam Bo" is not easily defined for the Western reader. Merle Pribbenow offers the best definition: "Nam Bo, or Cochin China, is divided up into three parts. Eastern Nam Bo generally equates with what the South Vietnamese Army called III Corps/Military Region 3. Central Nam Bo was the upper half of the Mekong Delta, and Western Nam Bo was the lower half of the Mekong Delta." From Merle Pribbenow, correspondence with author, September 7, 2008.
6. See Dinh, *Su Doan 9*, 36.
7. The close-quarters nature of the fighting caused supporting American artillery fires to be used primarily "in depth" rather than in close support. See "Battlefield Reports: United States Army Vietnam," January 18, 1968, Folder 11, Box 08, Glenn Helm Collection, The Vietnam Archive, Texas Tech University, 26.
8. See Carland, *United States Army in Vietnam*, 79. Note: Many sources were consulted for the Hill 65 battle, including Carland, *United States Army in Vietnam*, 76–79; "Battlefield Reports: United States Army Vietnam," 20–27; Edward F. Murphy, *Dak To: America's Sky Soldiers in South Vietnam's Central Highlands* (New York: Presidio Press, 2007), 20–22; and George Ball, Company A veteran, interview with author, September 15, 2008. Note: Since it is extremely difficult to pin down which, if any, combat support units participated in a given engagement, only the named and corroborated VC units will typically be mentioned.
9. Note: Dinh, *Su Doan 9* refers to the ambush at Dat Cuoc, while most American veterans know it as the battle at Hill 65. For the most part the battle names or references used will be those most recognized by Americans and other English speakers.

10. In regards to VC casualties caused by small-arms fire, see "Battlefield Reports: United States Army Vietnam," 26.
11. See Captured Documents (Combined Document Exploitation Center): Achievements of Cong Truong 9, 13, February 1967, Folder 0880, Box 0049, Vietnam Archive Collection, The Vietnam Archive, Texas Tech University.
12. See Su Doan, 56–57. Note: In the 9th Division history, the 2nd Regiment is written as "2d" and the 3rd Regiment as "3d." Both have been changed to "2nd" and "3rd" to maintain continuity with how American units have been written. Also, the 1st Regiment is the 271st, the 2nd is the 272nd, and the 3rd is the 273rd.
13. Note: A "troop" is the equivalent of a "company" in the infantry, and "squadron" is the equivalent of "battalion." A "battery" is the equivalent of a "company."
14. For a detailed account of Shuffer's deployment practices on November 10 and 11, see Carland, *United States Army in Vietnam*, 80–81; AAR, Operation Bushmaster I, 3rd Brigade, 1st Infantry Division, December 31, 1965, Annex B, 1.
15. See Dinh, *Su Doan 9*, 57.
16. Cam and Tien, *Chang Duong Muoi Nghin Ngay*, 148.
17. Ibid.
18. For 272nd's battle honors and designation, see Dinh, *Su Doan 9*, 45. Slogan from a captured 272nd regimental history: PLAF 9th Division–272d A Regiment, 2 (original text), May 15, 1967, Folder 06, Box 02, Douglas Pike Collection: Unit 05—National Liberation Front, The Vietnam Archive, Texas Tech University. Note: Kham commanded 272nd during Dong Xoai operations, but it is not immediately clear from the Communist Vietnamese literature whether he commanded the regiment at Bau Bang.
19. Communist sources are mum on the role of the Phu Loi, but the American AAR for the operation claims the VC battalion was encountered. See AAR, Operation Bushmaster I, 2.
20. For quoted words and formation of the 273rd, see Dinh, *Su Doan 9*, 13.
21. For VC preparations, see Carland, *United States Army in Vietnam*, 81–82; Dinh, *Su Doan 9*, 57.
22. For proximity of VC force and its movement, see Starry, *Mounted Combat in Vietnam*, 62; also see Carland, *United States Army in Vietnam*, 83.
23. M-113 APCs featured a .50-caliber machine gun and two M-60 machine guns.
24. Quoted words from Cam and Tien, *Chang Duong Muoi Nghin Ngay*, 150.
25. Battery C fired fifty-five rounds using two-second delay fuses. See AAR, Operation Bushmaster I, Annex B, 2.
26. See ibid.
27. See Carland, *United States Army in Vietnam*, 84; AAR, Operation Bushmaster I, Annex B, 2. Both Annex B (pp. 1–2) of AAR, Operation Bushmaster I and Carland (80–84) were used as resources for the battle, as were a number of others, including Starry, *Mounted Combat in Vietnam*, 60–63; Dinh, *Su Doan*

9, 56–59; Cam and Tien, *Chang Duong Muoi Nghin Ngay*, 145–50; and Senior Colonel Nguyen Viet Ta et al., *Mien Dong Nam Bo Khang Chien (1945–1975), Tap II* [The resistance war in eastern Cochin China (1945–1975), vol. 2] (Hanoi: People's Army Publishing House, 1993), 211–12.

28. For 273rd casualties, see United States Army, Vietnam, History of the 273 VC Regiment, 8.
29. For total American and VC casualties, see Carland, *United States Army in Vietnam*, 84; and AAR, Operation Bushmaster I, Annex B, 2. Vehicle losses from Starry, *Mounted Combat in Vietnam*, 63.
30. Exchange from Cam and Tien, *Chang Duong Muoi Nghin Ngay*, 151.
31. See ibid., 152.
32. For Thanh quote and his feelings about American infantry, see Senior Colonel Hoang Dong, "Dong Gop Quan Trong Ve Tu Tuong Quan Su Cua Dong Chi Nguyen Chi Thanh" [The important contributions of the military ideas of Comrade Nguyen Chi Thanh], in Military History Institute of Vietnam, *Dai Tuong Nguyen Chi Thanh: Na Chinh Tri Quan Su Loi Lac* [General Nguyen Chi Thanh: An outstanding military political figure], ed. Ha Huu Khieu (Hanoi: People's Army Publishing House, 1997), 211.
33. See PLAF 9th Division–272d A Regiment, 30.
34. Dinh, *Su Doan 9*, 59.
35. David M. Glantz, *Zhukov's Greatest Defeat: The Red Army's Epic Disaster in Operation Mars, 1942* (Lawrence: University of Kansas Press, 1999), 324.
36. See Vietnam Interview 99 (VNI-99), "Battle of Trung Loi," November 20, 1965, 1, U.S. Army Center of Military History, Washington, D.C. (Vietnam interviews hereafter cited as VNI with the corresponding number).
37. NCO stands for noncommissioned officer.
38. See AAR, Operation Bushmaster I, Annex C, 1.
39. The number of gun crews and the exact turn of events are not altogether clear. The AAR mentions a VC recoilless rifle gun crew getting to the road, but each time "they tried to load the weapon," the Company C command group killed them. It also states the weapon never fired a round until the command group ran out of ammo (see AAR, Operation Bushmaster I, Annex C, 1). The U.S. Army official history, though, mentions that the "Americans" killed the "original" gun crew and a team came forward "to take its place." It then states a third crew took over and "resumed firing" (see Carland, *United States Army in Vietnam*, 87).
40. See AAR, Operation Bushmaster I, Annex C, 1.
41. For VC casualty estimate, see Carland, *United States Army in Vietnam*, 87.
42. The operation that began in earnest on December 1 was called Operation Bloodhound/Bushmaster II (official dates of operation listed as November 26–December 9). For details on the origin of operation, see AAR, Operation Bloodhound/Bushmaster II, 3rd Brigade, 1st Infantry Division, December 30, 1965, 2–3; and Carland, *United States Army in Vietnam*, 88.

43. For the 2/2's proximity to the Communist camp and Shuffer's assessment of the 272nd VC Regiment's reason for being there, see Shuffer, "Finish Them with Firepower," 12–13; for the Communist side, see Dinh, *Su Doan 9*, 60.
44. See Cam and Tien, *Chang Duong Muoi Nghin Ngay*, 157.
45. For use of bugles and the effects of the automatic weapons volleys, see VNI-137, "The Battle of Ap Nha Mat," December 5, 1965, 3.
46. See Shuffer, "Finish Them with Firepower," 13.
47. See Carland, *United States Army in Vietnam*, 89.
48. For American efforts to keep the VC from closing in for hand-to-hand combat, see Shuffer, "Finish Them with Firepower," 13.
49. See Carland, *United States Army in Vietnam*, 91–92.
50. VC KIA figure and American figures from AAR, Operation Bloodhound/Bushmaster II, 7.
51. Quoted words from Lt. General Tran Do, "Dai Tuong Nguyen Chi Thanh Tren Chien Truong Mien Nam" [Senior General Nguyen Chi Thanh on the battlefields of South Vietnam], in Military History Institute of Vietnam, *Dai Tuong Nguyen Chi Thanh: Na Chinh Tri Quan Su Loi Lac* [General Nguyen Chi Thanh: An outstanding military political figure], ed. Ha Huu Khieu (Hanoi: People's Army Publishing House, 1997), 92.
52. See Dinh, *Su Doan 9*, 61–63. Note: Bracketed introductions by the author.
53. See Cam and Tien, *Chang Duong Muoi Nghin Ngay*, 159.
54. See ibid., 158.
55. For document name, see ibid. The 9th VC Division history calls the document "Some experiences regarding U.S. troops' tactics and our Main-Force troops' way to fight U.S. troops." See Dinh, *Su Doan 9*, 63.

Chapter 9. The Die Is Cast

1. Quote from Westmoreland, *Soldier Reports*, 142.
2. William Duiker, *The Communist Road to Power in Vietnam*, 2nd ed. (Boulder, Colo.: Westview Press, 1995), 266.
3. Quote from Davidson, *Vietnam at War*, 327.
4. Quoted words from Westmoreland, *Soldier Reports*, 145.
5. Cited in Military History Institute of Vietnam, *Victory in Vietnam*, 171.
6. See Duiker, *Communist Road to Power*, 2nd ed., 267. Note: The Twelfth Plenum ended with a resolution. Lao Dong Party (Communist Party in Hanoi, same as Vietnamese Workers' Party) Resolution 12 codified this strategy.
7. See Communist Strategy as Reflected in Lao Dong Party and COSVN Resolution, 1959–1969, 3, Folder 26, Box 07, Douglas Pike Collection: Unit 06—Democratic Republic of Vietnam, The Vietnam Archive, Texas Tech University.
8. See Joint Chiefs of Staff History of Vietnam War (II): 1965–1967—Less than War but No Peace: The Situation in January–February 1966, 29–11, July 1, 1970, Folder 02, Box 01, Joint Chiefs of Staff History of the Vietnam War, 1965–1967, The Vietnam Archive, Texas Tech University.

9. See Interrogation of Lt. Colonel Le Xuan Chuyen, 55-4 to 55-5.
10. For an excellent and concise analysis of the opposition in late 1965–early 1966 to the Communist war strategy, see Nguyen, "War Politburo," 20–21.
11. Quote from Pribbenow, "General Vo Nguyen Giap," 10.
12. See Duiker, *Communist Road to Power*, 2nd ed., 270.
13. Quote from Pribbenow, "General Vo Nguyen Giap," 10.
14. For details on "Regular Force Strategy," see Pike, *War, Peace, and the Viet Cong*, 123, 135–37.
15. Pike, *PAVN*, 342.
16. For quoted words and discussion of Giap's role, see Pribbenow, "General Vo Nguyen Giap," 6.
17. Military History Institute of Vietnam, *Victory in Vietnam*, 175.
18. Quote from Duiker, *Communist Road to Power*, 2nd ed., 265.
19. For details of Le Duan's letter, see ibid., 266–67.
20. For Thanh's views on U.S. strategic weaknesses and his own advised strategic approach, see ibid., 273.
21. Quote from the Crimp Document, 9, 01 January 1963, Folder 03, Box 03, Douglas Pike Collection: Unit 02—Military Operations, The Vietnam Archive, Texas Tech University.
22. Quoted words from Notes from the Underground, 9.
23. Quote from Lanning and Cragg, *Inside the VC and the NVA*, 171.
24. General Van Tien Dung, *After Political Failure, the U.S. Imperialists Are Facing Military Defeat in South Vietnam* (Hanoi: Foreign Languages Publishing House, 1966), 15.
25. Ibid., 34.
26. Duiker, *Communist Road to Power*, 2nd ed., 274.
27. "Stalingrad" comparison found in ibid., 407.
28. Military History Institute of Vietnam, *The Saigon–Gia Dinh Offensive Theater (1968)* (Hanoi: n.p., 1988), 87.
29. Quote from Origin and Evolution of the Current War.
30. For quoted words and appreciation of allied strategic intentions for 1966, see Nhu et al., *Lich Su*, 525–26.
31. For quoted words and basic military goals for 1966, see ibid., 526.
32. For three missions, see ibid., 526–27. See the same for "combat formula" and strategic plans for 1966.
33. Ibid., 527.
34. Quote from Huan et al., *Su Doan Sao Vang*, 57. For a similar accounting of the resolution, see Tai, Tan, and Tich, *Su Doan 2, Tap I*, 41.
35. For quoted words and the January 16, 1966, order, see Military History Institute of Vietnam, *Victory in Vietnam*, 178.
36. Quoted passages from Tai, Tan, and Tich, *Su Doan 2, Tap I*, 42–43.
37. Quoted passages from Huan et al., *Su Doan Sao Vang*, 57–58.
38. For quoted passage, quoted words, and an overview of JCS "strategic concept"

military tasks, see Joint Chiefs of Staff History of Vietnam War (II): 1965–1967—The War on the Ground—Strategy and Operations—1966, 33-4, July 1, 1970, Folder 03, Box 01, Joint Chiefs of Staff History of the Vietnam War, 1965–1967, The Vietnam Archive, Texas Tech University.
39. Quote from Andrew J. Birtle, "PROVN, Westmoreland, and the Historians: A Reappraisal," *Journal of Military History* 72 (October 2008): 1247.
40. Quote found in ibid., 1227.
41. Quoted words from Joint Chiefs of Staff History of Vietnam War (II): 1965–1967—The War on the Ground—Strategy and Operations—966, July 1, 1970, 33-3.
42. See Carland, *United States Army in Vietnam*, 158–61, 355.
43. For the "Combined Plan," Westmoreland priority areas, and an excellent review of U.S. planning for 1966, see Carland, *United States Army in Vietnam*, 152–60.

Chapter 10. An Inauspicious Beginning

1. Some accounts say the 506th operated with some "impunity" for a "year or more." See Colonel Thomas E. Faley (Ret.), "Operation Marauder: Allied Offensive in the Mekong Delta," *Vietnam*, February 1999, 34–40.
2. Since all of the units clearly didn't possess all of the weapons mentioned, it must be assumed that the two VC battalions possessed the lion's share of the aforementioned heavy and better equipment.
3. For VC defensive fortifications and intelligence on VC units in the area, their strength, and their weaponry, see AAR, Operation Marauder I, 173rd Abn Brigade (Sep), n.d., 3–4.
4. For the action at LZ Wine, see ibid.; and Carland, *United States Army in Vietnam*, 168–69.
5. For an excellent English language account of the 267th's initial opposition and the ordeal of Companies A and B, see Faley, "Operation Marauder," 37. Note: It is possible that some local force units were attached to and fought with the 267th.
6. See Tourison, *Talking with Victor Charlie*, 146.
7. The 173rd Airborne Brigade suspected that this line of thinking encouraged the VC to hold on in their redoubts. See AAR, Operation Marauder, 22.
8. For *New York Times* quote, see Faley, "Operation Marauder," 38.
9. See ibid.
10. For VC KIA count, see Carland, *United States Army in Vietnam*, 169.
11. Tourison, *Talking with Victor Charlie*, 148.
12. For VC name for Ho Bo Woods area, see Tourison, *Talking with Victor Charlie*, 153. The Ho Bo Woods were situated in northeast Hau Nghia Province and southwest Binh Duong Province.
13. Region 4, for the Viet Cong, corresponded to the Saigon–Cho Lon–Gia Dinh area.

14. Quoted from "Department of the Army Operations Report 1–66: Lessons Learned," 12, March 22, 1966, Folder 07, Box 03, Glen Helm Collection, The Vietnam Archive, Texas Tech University.
15. For VC KIA total reported by the 173rd Airborne Brigade, see ibid., 11. The 173rd's casualties during Crimp were 23 KIA, 103 wounded. Note: The 3rd Brigade, 1st Infantry Division ended its involvement in the operation on January 12.
16. For quoted words, see Carland, *United States Army in Vietnam*, 173.
17. For quote, see Tom Mangold and John Penycate, *The Tunnels of Cu Chi: The Untold Story of Vietnam* (New York: Random House, 1985), 50–51.
18. Quote from Major Robert Doughty, "Evolution of U.S. Army Tactical Doctrine, 1946–76," *Leavenworth Papers*, no. 1, August 1979, Combat Studies Institute, United States Army Command and General Staff College, Fort Leavenworth, Kans., http://carl.army.mil/resources/csi/Doughty/doughty.asp (accessed January 13, 2010).
19. Quote from Michael Maclear, *The Ten Thousand Day War, Vietnam: 1945–1975* (New York: St. Martin's Press, 1981), 162.
20. Quoted words from Lewy, *America in Vietnam*, 60.
21. Quote from David Charnoff and Doan Van Toai, *Portrait of the Enemy* (New York: Random House, 1986), 155.
22. Viet Cong Oath of Honor can be found in Lanning and Cragg, *Inside the VC and the NVA*, 327.
23. Quote from Jack Shulimson, *U.S. Marines in Vietnam: An Expanding War, 1966* (Washington, D.C.: History and Museums Division Headquarters, U.S. Marine Corps, 1982), 30.
24. Quote and likelihood of Communist advance knowledge of Double Eagle from Lewy, *America in Vietnam*, 61.
25. For a concise and excellent overview of the two Marine operations and the VC response, see Edward F. Murphy, *Semper Fi: From Da Nang to the DMZ Marine Corps Operations, 1965–1975* (New York: Presidio Press, 2003), 45–48. Note: The Marines reported over three hundred enemy KIA during Double Eagle and over one hundred during Double Eagle II.
26. See Carland, *United States Army in Vietnam*, 201.
27. See Huan et al., *Su Doan Sao Vang*, 67. Note: The 1st Cavalry Division operation was originally named Masher but was later changed to White Wing. Also, South Vietnamese and South Korean forces supported Masher/White Wing.
28. For the move into the An Loa Valley, see AAR, Operation Masher/White Wing, 8–9. For the 1st Cavalry Division campaign plan, see Carland, *United States Army in Vietnam*, 203.
29. Quoted passage from Huan et al., *Su Doan Sao Vang*, 69.
30. Moore blocked each of the Kim Son's exits with ambush positions and then sent "beater" troops supported by artillery fire through the narrow valleys to

flush the VC/NVA and push them into the established positions. Unable to produce much contact with this technique, Moore then decided to cover the valley with smaller unit patrolling. See Carland, *United States Army in Vietnam*, 209.

31. See Shelby Stanton, *Anatomy of a Division: The 1st Cavalry Division in Vietnam* (New York: Ballantine Books, 2005), 74.
32. For casualty count and synopsis of the fighting, see Carland, *United States Army in Vietnam*, 209–10; Stanton, *Anatomy of a Division*, 73–74.
33. See Captured Documents (Combined Document Exploitation Center): Interrogation Report of Dang Doan (alias Dang Son, Lao Dong Party name Dang Nguyen), Concerning Effects of Leaflets on VC Cadres and Soldiers, 2–3, 01 February 1967, Folder 0091, Box 0091, Vietnam Archive Collection, The Vietnam Archive, Texas Tech University. Note: Lieutenant Colonel Doan has also been listed as "Dong Doan."
34. Quoted exchange from Tourison, *Talking with Victor Charlie*, 178. Note: The G-2 was an intelligence officer at division or a higher level. The G-2 Section was the military intelligence division.
35. An artillery battery was airlifted into LZ Coil as well. For the circumstances that prompted the operation and the operational plan, see AAR, Operation Eagles Claw, 2nd Brigade, 1st Cavalry Division, March 16, 1966, 1–3; and Carland, *United States Army in Vietnam*, 210–11.
36. See AAR, Operation Eagles Claw, 3.
37. Quoted words from Huan et al., *Su Doan Sao Vang*, 75. For American assumptions about the unit encountered by Meyer's troops, see AAR, Operation Eagles Claw, 3.
38. The VC/NVA had broken contact by 6:00 PM. See AAR, Operation Eagles Claw, 3. Note: The history of the 3rd NVA Division mentions heavy fighting between February 16 and 20, including an engagement fought by the "2nd Battalion" on February 18, but provides a less definitive narrative on what units of the 2nd VC Regiment may or not have been involved on the 17.
39. Quote from AAR, Operation Masher/White Wing, 16.
40. See ibid.
41. Quote from Huan et al., *Su Doan Sao Vang*, 71.
42. For the 2nd Brigade estimation that the 93rd and 95th VC Battalions, and quite possibly the regimental headquarters, suffered severe damage, see AAR, Operation Eagles Claw, 2. For VC and American casualty figures, see AAR, Operation Masher/White Wing, 17. Note: The 1st Cavalry Division estimated that the VC suffered over 900 wounded and close to an additional (besides the body count number) 398 killed.

Chapter 11. Winter–Spring Battles: Region 5

1. For background on Tho, see Glen Gendzel, "Le Doc Tho," in *Encyclopedia of the Vietnam War*, ed. Stanley I. Kutler (New York: Scribner's, 1996), 284–85.

2. For a complete examination of Tho's letter and the ideas expressed therein, see Duiker, *Communist Road to Power*, 2nd ed., 267–69.
3. Quote from ibid., 268.
4. For quoted words, see Pribbenow, "General Vo Nguyen Giap," 3; for context and resolution itself, see 2–3.
5. See Kieu Tam Nguyen, chief ed., *Chien Truong Tri-Thien-Hue Trong Cuoc Chien Tranh Chong My Cuu Nuoc Toan Thang* [The Tri-Thien-Hue battlefield during the Victorious Resistance War against the Americans to save the nation] (Hue: Thuan An Publishing House, 1985), 109.
6. Cited in Shulimson, *U.S. Marines in Vietnam*, 51.
7. For VC defensive works and fire discipline, see Stanton, *Rise and Fall*, 117.
8. Quote from Shulimson, *U.S. Marines in Vietnam*, 52. For details on the peninsula battle between the 810th VC Battalion and Task Unit Hotel, see Shulimson, *U.S. Marines in Vietnam*, 51–52; and Stanton, *Rise and Fall*, 118–19.
9. See Command Chronology, 6, 01 February 1966, Folder 002, U.S. Marine Corps History Division Vietnam War Documents Collection, The Vietnam Archive, Texas Tech University.
10. VC and Marine casualty figures cited in Shulimson, *U.S. Marines in Vietnam*, 52.
11. For faulty allied intelligence and the impact on Sullivan, see Shulimson, *U.S. Marines in Vietnam*, 65–67.
12. Ibid., 67.
13. See U.S. Military Assistance Command, Office of Information, "FLWG Is the Official MACV Communiqué # 080-66 as of 1700H, 21 March 1966," 6, Folder 19, Box 06, Douglas Pike Collection: Unit 02—Military Operations, The Vietnam Archive, Texas Tech University.
14. Quote cited in Shulimson, *U.S. Marines in Vietnam*, 69; see 65–69 for the definitive account of the fighting at Ap Chinh An.
15. For casualty count, see ibid., 69.
16. For the units involved in Operation Kings and an account of the action, see ibid., 78–79; and Murphy, *Semper Fi*, 67–69.
17. Quoted passage from Shulimson, *U.S. Marines in Vietnam*, 79.
18. Tom "Doc" Stubbs, FMF corpsman (and veteran of the battle), interview with author, June 23, 2008.
19. Cited in Shulimson, *U.S. Marines in Vietnam*, 100.
20. Marine Corps sources indicate another eighty-three may have been killed. See ibid.
21. Sources for the May 21 battle include author interviews with 1/9 Marine veterans Tom Stubbs and Gary Hutchinson; and Shulimson, *U.S. Marines in Vietnam*, 100. The Hutchinson interview was conducted on June 27, 2008.
22. Quoted words from Bui Minh Hai and Vu Van Sum, *Quang Ngai: Lich Su Chien Tranh Nhan Dan 30 Nam (1945–1975)* [Quang Ngai: A history of 30 years of people's war (1945–1975)] (Ho Chi Minh City: Nghia Binh Province Joint Publishing House and the Nghia Binh Province Military Headquarters, 1988), 278.

23. Lieutenant Colonel P. X. Kelley: Letter to Director of Marine Corps History, n.d., review of draft manuscript, History of the U.S. Marine Corps, Part III (s), in possession of General P. X. Kelley (Ret.). Note: The Marines initially thought the 21st NVA Regiment was involved.
24. Ibid.
25. For the run up to Operation Texas and the allied planning, see Lieutenant Colonel P. X. Kelley: Letter to Director; and Shulimson, *U.S. Marines in Vietnam*, 120–21.
26. For presence of 1st VC Regimental HQ and defending battalion in Phoung Dinh (2), plus Westmoreland's comment, see Lieutenant Colonel P. X. Kelley: Letter to Director.
27. Quoted words and passage above quoted words from Tai, Tan, and Tich, *Su Doan 2, Tap I*, 51.
28. Lieutenant Colonel P. X. Kelley: Letter to Director.
29. Marine KIA and wounded cited in ibid.
30. Shulimson, *U.S. Marines in Vietnam*, 123.
31. Types of artillery rounds used from Ken Sympson, Marine artillery officer and veteran of the battle, interview with author, June 27, 2008.
32. Sympson interview.
33. NLF claim from author interview with General P. X. Kelly (Ret.), June 26, 2008. A reference to Operation Texas and the missing VC was found in a copy of Chief, U.S. Delegation, Four Party Joint Military Commission, RVN, Message 251013Z, October 1973, provided to author by General P. X. Kelley (Ret.).
34. Quote from Shulimson, *U.S. Marines in Vietnam*, 127.
35. See Tai, Tan, and Tich, *Su Doan 2, Tap I*, 51; and Hai and Sum, *Quang Ngai*, 281.
36. Casualty figures cited found in Shulimson, *U.S. Marines in Vietnam*, 127. Sources used for Operation Texas battles include Shulimson, *U.S. Marines in Vietnam*, 120–27; Ken Sympson, *Images from the Otherland* (Jefferson, N.C.: McFarland, 1995), 175–90; AAR, Operation Texas, 2nd Battalion, 4th Marines, March 29, 1966, 8–66; and aforementioned correspondences and interviews with, and materials provided by, Ken Sympson and General P. X. Kelley (Ret.).
37. For VC deserter and the intelligence behind the Marine–South Vietnamese operation against the 1st VC Regiment, see AAR, Operation Hot Springs, 3rd Battalion, 7th Marines, April 30, 1966, 4. See also AAR, Operation Hot Springs, 2nd Battalion, 7th Marines, April 28, 1966, 3.
38. Two South Vietnamese battalions touched down in landing zones west of the objective area on April 21 as well.
39. Because of the number of VC killed at the "site of contact" along with the types and number of weapons found after the battle, the Marines believed the unit that engaged the 2/7 on April 21 was from the 1st VC Regiment's heavy weapons battalion. See AAR, Operation Hot Springs, 2nd Battalion, 7th Marines, 3–4.

40. For this incident and the concealment of VC machine guns opposing Company H, see ibid., 4.
41. For quoted words, see ibid., 6.
42. The number of ten to fifteen VC killed in the A-4 bombing runs was believed to be a conservative figure. See ibid., 2–3.
43. See AAR, Operation Hot Springs, 3rd Battalion, 7th Marines, 8.
44. For casualty figures, see ibid.
45. For casualty figures of the VC and 3/7 Marines, see ibid., 9–10, and for casualty figures of the VC and the 2/7 Marines, see AAR, Operation Hot Springs, 2nd Battalion, 7th Marines, 7.

Chapter 12. Winter–Spring Battles: The B2 Front

1. Quoted passage from Cam and Tien, *Chang Duong Muoi Nghin Ngay*, 163.
2. Quoted words from ibid., 165.
3. See ibid., 164–65. Note: In 1961 the Communist Vietnamese changed the name of the old Military Region 7, used during the war with the French, to Military Region 1 (code name T1). This was done to give the appearance of independence from Hanoi. Similarly the old Military Region 8 became Military Region 2 (code name T2) and the old Military Region 9 became Military Region 3 (T3). In 1974 all three military regions were called by their old names once more.
4. For the mission of Rolling Stone and the possible impact of its successful completion, see AAR, Operation Rolling Stone, 1st Brigade, 1st Infantry Division, March 28, 1966, 1, 16.
5. Quoted passage from Cam and Tien, *Chang Duong Muoi Nghin Ngay*, 167.
6. See AAR, Operation Rolling Stone, 1; Carland, *United States Army in Vietnam*, 180.
7. Quoted passage from AAR, Operation Rolling Stone, 1.
8. Quoted passage from Cam and Tien, *Chang Duong Muoi Nghin Ngay*, 171.
9. See Dinh, *Su Doan 9*, 64.
10. For a comprehensive look at American artillery support efforts during Rolling Stone, see AAR, Operation Rolling Stone, 11.
11. For American and VC equipment losses, see ibid., 1, 2; for American and VC personnel losses, see 14–15.
12. Quoted words and passage from Nhu et al., *Lich Su*, 531–32.
13. For operational concepts behind Operation Boston/Cocoa Beach, see AAR, Operation Cocoa Beach, 3rd Brigade, 1st Infantry Division, April 3, 1966, 4, 7; Narrative of the Battle of Lo Khe, 1, n.d., Folder 58, Box 01, William E. LeGro Collection, The Vietnam Archive, Texas Tech University.
14. See Comments of Commanding Officer of the 2nd Battalion, 28th Infantry on the Battle of Lo Khe, 1, 05 March 1966, Folder 58, Box 01, William E. LeGro Collection, The Vietnam Archive, Texas Tech University.
15. See Narrative of Lo Khe, 2; Comments of Commanding Officer of the 2nd Battalion, 28th Infantry on the Battle of Lo Khe, 1.

16. Quoted passage from Comments of Commanding Officer of the 2nd Battalion, 28th Infantry on the Battle of Lo Khe, 2.
17. For a composite account of the incident, see ibid.; and Narrative of the Battle of Lo Khe, 3.
18. See "Battlefield Reports: United States Army Vietnam," 33.
19. For Westmoreland quote, see Carland, *United States Army in Vietnam*, 178; for Communist Vietnamese quote, see Dinh, *Su Doan 9*, 64–65.
20. For VC personnel losses and American personnel and material losses, see Narrative of the Battle of Lo Khe, 6–7; for VC material losses, see AAR, Operation Cocoa Beach, 6.
21. For the operational aims and planning of Silver City, see Carland, *United States Army in Vietnam*, 181; and Colonel Thomas E. Faley (Ret.), "The Battle of Zulu-Zulu," *Vietnam*, October 1994, 18.
22. Quote from Cam and Tien, *Chang Duong Muoi Nghin Ngay*, 172.
23. Quote and account of the opening action from Faley, "Battle of Zulu-Zulu," 20.
24. For an excellent account of the assault on Objective George and the discoveries thereafter, see ibid., 20–22.
25. There is some dispute as to whether the initial VC machine-gun burst that downed the American helicopter triggered the ensuing assault prematurely and caused the initial confusion in the VC attack. For example, Faley's account states that a wounded VC soldier said after the battle that the signal to begin the battle around 8:00 AM was to be given by firing one of the VC's .50-caliber machines guns and "that the signal had been given prematurely." See ibid., 22.
26. In addition to the KIA figures, the Americans also suffered 162 WIA. For the respective losses, see Carland, *United States Army in Vietnam*, 183. American losses and a concise but excellent account of the battle can also be found in the Presidential Unit Citation earned by the 2/503 for its battle on March 16. See General Orders (GO) 40, DA, September 21, 1967.
27. For circumstances surrounding Chuyen's defection, see Interrogation of Le Xuan Chuyen, a lieutenant colonel in the North Vietnamese army and assistant chief of staff and chief of operations of the 5th Viet Cong Division, 02 August 1966, 110-4, Folder 003, Box 30, Douglas Pike Collection: Unit 05—National Liberation Front, The Vietnam Archive, Texas Tech University.
28. See Lieutenant Colonel Ho Son Dai et al., *Lich Su Su Doan 5* [History of the 5th Division] (Hanoi: People's Army Publishing House, 1995), 88. Note: *Lich Su Su Doan 5* claims that "all 20" of the 5th's "troop billeting" areas and the division's "rear storage" area were identified and attacked. The history also states that numerous battle plans of the 274th and 275th VC Regiments were disclosed and that these had to be scrapped. Since Chuyen did not formally surrender until August, it seems highly improbable that all of these events occurred before the 5th fought its first battle against American troops in April or that Chuyen could have had much to do with them if they did occur. Also,

the Communists refer to a "Ba Ria" Province, which covered roughly the same general area as the South Vietnamese "Phuoc Tuy" Province, even if the two had different boundaries.
29. The most concise examination of the goals of Operation Abilene and its role as part of a larger campaign can be found in Carland, *United States Army in Vietnam*, 306; and MacGarrigle, *United States Army in Vietnam*, 33. Note: Carland's volume, the official combat history for the U.S. Army for the time period covered, makes *no* mention of Chuyen having anything to do with the launching of Operation Abilene, and there is no evidence to suggest that he provided any information inspiring the operation or was in any way involved in it. Rather, the concerns of the 5th VC Division and the actions of the 1st Infantry Division with Abilene seem to be nothing more than coincidence. Indeed, Sedgwick Tourison Jr., in his book *Talking with Victory Charlie*, mentions interviewing Chuyen in July 1966 (see 186).
30. See Dai et al., *Lich Su Su Doan 5*, 76.
31. In addition to the three infantry battalions (1st, 3rd, and "265th"), the 274th VC Regiment contained the following combat support units: a mortar company, a recoilless rifle company, a 12.8-mm antiaircraft machine-gun company, an engineer company, a reconnaissance company, a signal company, and a transportation company. See Dai, *Lich Su Su Doan Bo Binh 5*. Note: The 274th's sister regiment, the 275th Viet Cong Regiment or "5th Regiment," was formed in May 1965. The 275th was originally the Western Nam Bo Military Region's 1st Regiment.
32. See VNI- 97, "Narrative—History of the Battle of Xa Cam My," February 21, 1967, 2. Note: The VC who escaped was also wounded by American troops.
33. See Dai et al., *Lich Su Su Doan 5*, 77.
34. Quote passage from ibid., 79.
35. See VNI-97, 4.
36. Although most American accounts identify the D800 Battalion as a participant in the April 11 battle, the history of the 5th VC Division indicates that all three battalions participated to some extent in the battle. For example, the history states, "At 1600 hours all of the regiment's mortars and recoilless rifles opened fire, pouring a heavy barrage into the concentration of American troops. 1st and 3rd Battalion units maneuvered up right next to the American position, coordinating with 2nd Battalion to totally annihilate the enemy battalion." See Dai et al., *Lich Su Su Doan 5*, 79.
37. See ibid., 80.
38. For information on VC and American casualties, see Carland, *United States Army in Vietnam*, 306; VNI-97, 5.

Chapter 13. The Big-Unit War and the Road to Tet
1. For opposition to the hardline strategy in 1966, see Nguyen, "War Politburo," 21.

2. Quotes found in "Radio Propaganda Report: North Vietnamese Party Problems and Differences," 1, March 9, 1966, Folder 34, Box 03, Central Intelligence Agency Collection, The Vietnam Archive, Texas Tech University.
3. Quote from Duiker, *Communist Road to Power*, 251.
4. Quoted passage found in *Lich Su Cuc Tac Chien, 1945–2000* [History of the Combat Operations Department, 1945–2000] (Hanoi: People's Army Publishing House, 2005), available on the Internet at Quan Su Viet Nam [Vietnamese military history], http://www.quansuvn.net/ (accessed Dec. 20, 2007).
5. See Dinh, *Su Doan 9*, 69.
6. See VNI-101, "The Campaign along National Route 13," August 7, 1966, 1.
7. See Dinh, *Su Doan 9*, 69.
8. The exact vehicle composition of Sturgis's convoy differs slightly depending upon the source. The cited composition was derived from VNI-77, "The Battle of Ap Tau O," July 5, 1967, 1.
9. Quote and casualty figures from Carland, *United States Army in Vietnam*, 313. Numerous other sources were consulted on the Battle of Ap Tau O and the events that precipitated it, including VNI-101; VNI-77; AAR, Operation El Paso II/III, 1st Infantry Division, n.d.; "ORLL," 1 May–31 July 1966, 1st Infantry Division, August 15, 1966; and Dinh, *Su Doan 9*.
10. See VNI-77, 3.
11. See ibid., 5.
12. Quoted passage found in *Lich Su Cuc Tac Chien*.
13. For quoted excerpts, see Hanoi assessment of guerrilla war in the South, 13 November 1966, Folder 17, Box 06, Douglas Pike Collection: Unit 01—Assessment and Strategy, The Vietnam Archive, Texas Tech University. Note: "Cuu Long" may or may not have been Tran Do.
14. For quoted words, see Tran Tinh, ed., *Van Kien Dang Toan Tap, Tap 28, 1967* [Collected party documents, vol. 28, 1967] (Hanoi: National Political Publishing House, 2003).
15. For quoted words from Resolution 13 and the adoption of "talk-fight" with its passage, see Pribbenow, "General Vo Nguyen Giap," 10–11.
16. See ibid., 10–12. Note: Pribbenow's account of the Communist Vietnamese rationale for the "talk-fight" strategy, the factors that influenced it, and the corresponding evolution of the Tet Offensive is the definitive exposition on the subject in English to date.
17. Quote from *Lich Su Cuc Tac Chien*.
18. Quote from Excerpts from North Vietnamese/Viet Cong documents, 1966, Folder 09, Box 05, Douglas Pike Collection: Unit 01—Assessment and Strategy, The Vietnam Archive, Texas Tech University.
19. See Pribbenow, "General Vo Nguyen Giap," 11, 15.
20. Quoted excerpts from *Lich Su Cuc Tac Chien*.
21. Quote from ibid.
22. Dung quotes from Le Lien, "Creating a Turning Point in the Resistance War

against the Americans," *Quan Doi Nhan Dan Newspaper*, December 3, 2004, http://www.quandoinhandan.org.vn/sknc/?id=1108&subject+=7/ (accessed Jan. 2, 2005).
23. General Dung and Le Duan quotes from ibid.
24. For details regarding Giap's absence from the October meeting, as well as an excellent account of the development of the new plan from its July 1967 presentation to the Politburo until its final passage in January 1968, see Pribbenow, "General Vo Nguyen Giap," 16–19. For a less contemporary study of the origins of the Tet Offensive, see Ang Cheng Guan, "Decision-making Leading to the Tet Offensive (1968)—The Vietnamese Communist Perspective," *Journal of Contemporary History* 33, no. 3 (1998): 341–53.
25. North Vietnamese internal security conducted three waves of arrests in 1967. The arrests occurred in July, October, and December. Among those targeted on national security grounds were journalists, academics, government officials, party members, military officers, and so on. For an account suggesting a strong political, rather than national security, motive for the arrests, see Nguyen, "War Politburo," 25–27.
26. Quotes from Lien, "Creating a Turning Point."
27. Quote from Excerpts from North Vietnamese/Viet Cong documents, 1966.
28. See Cold War International History Project, "Discussion between Mao Zedong, Pham Van Dong, and Vo Nguyen Giap," April 11, 1967, Virtual Archive, The Vietnam (Indochina) War (s) Collection, http://www.wilsoncenter.org/index.cfm?topic_id=1409&fuseaction=va2.document&identifier=5034C9C6-96B6-175C-96D86CF8502CADDD&sort=Collection&item=TheVietnam(Indochina)War(s)/ (accessed January 26, 2010).

Chapter 14. Attitudes and Adversaries

1. Quote from Captain Roger Pineau, "Admiral Isoroku Yamamoto," in *The War Lords: Military Commanders of the Twentieth Century*, ed. Field Marshall Sir Michael Carver (Boston: Little, Brown, 1976), 397.
2. Lehrack, *First Battle*, 45.
3. Quote from Lanning and Cragg, *Inside the VC and the NVA*, 190.
4. Figure cited in ibid., 45.
5. See MacGarrigle, *United States Army in Vietnam*, 88.
6. See David Maraniss, *They Marched into Sunlight: War and Peace, Vietnam and America, October 1967* (New York: Simon & Schuster, 2003), 158.
7. Truong Son, *A Bitter Dry Season for the Americans* (Hanoi: Foreign Languages Publishing House, 1966), 35. Note: "Truong Son" is an alias of General Nguyen Chi Thanh.
8. Quoted words at the end of sentence from Dinh, *Su Doan 9*, 62.
9. Quote from Otto Lehrack, interview with author, June 3, 2008. Lehrack, who interviewed a number of former VC for his work, *The First Battle*, first discussed this attitude in an interview with author April 21, 2008.

10. Quote from Lanning and Cragg, *Inside the VC and the NVA*, 277–78.
11. Dung, *After Political Failure*, 31.
12. Vu quote from Maraniss, *They Marched into Sunlight*, 157.
13. Phat Diem's words from William Broyles Jr., "The Road to Hill 10: A Veteran's Return to Vietnam," *Atlantic Monthly*, April 1985, http://www.theathlantic.com/past/docs/issues/85apr/broyles.htm/ (accessed April 28, 2010).
14. For more information about the survey conducted by Patton, see Lieutenant Colonel George S. Patton, "Why They Fight," *Military Review* 45, no. 12 (December 1965): 20.
15. Quote from ibid., 22–23.
16. Quote from ibid., 23.
17. Study cited in McCoy, *Secrets of the Viet Cong*, 5.
18. Quote from Woodruff, *Unheralded Victory*, 250. Title of draft/study found on 364.
19. See McCoy, *Secrets of the Viet Cong*, 220–21; and Scales, *Firepower in Limited War*, 74.
20. Quote from McCoy, *Secrets of the Viet Cong*, 213.
21. See "Evaluation of U.S. Army Combat Operations in Vietnam: Volume 4—Firepower," 28, April 25, 1966, Folder 05, Box 05, Glenn Helm Collection, The Vietnam Archive, Texas Tech University.
22. Scales, *Firepower in Limited War*, 82.
23. Ibid., 75. Note: Other American units adopted variations of this regulation thereafter.
24. For quoted words and an excellent overview of these recommended small unit leader tactics, see ibid. Note: As with everything else in Vietnam, hard and fast rules didn't always apply. For instance, if an American unit had a VC or NVA unit on the run, it may not have stopped, pulled back, and called in fire support.
25. Cam and Tien, *Chang Duong Muoi Nghin Ngay*, 158.
26. Scales, *Firepower in Limited War*, 144; in regard to having to justify *not using* fire support, see 80.
27. Quote from Carland, *United States Army in Vietnam*, 360–61.
28. For Dye quote and his ideas on infantry and artillery firepower, see Colonel Harold A. Dye, "Close Fire Support," *Military Review* 47, no. 9 (September 1967): 43.
29. Shuffer, "Finish Them with Firepower," 11.
30. For the June and August actions in the Que Son Valley, see Otto Lehrack, *Road of 10,000 Pains: The Destruction of the 2nd NVA Division by the U.S. Marines, 1967* (Minneapolis: Zenith Press, 2010), 118, 154–56.
31. For perhaps the best contribution on the use of American firepower in the Vietnam War, see Scales, *Firepower in Limited War*, 63–154.
32. See MacGarrigle, *United States Army in Vietnam*, 296.
33. For quoted words and comments about "harassment" and "interdiction" fires,

see Scales, *Firepower in Limited War*, 102, 141. Note: Close air support does not include armed helicopters.
34. Quote from Ted Morgan, *Valley of Death: The Tragedy at Dien Bien Phu that Led America into the Vietnam War* (New York: Random House, 2010), 271.
35. See Nguyen Khac Tinh, Tran Quang Hau, et al., *Phao Binh Nhan Dan Viet Nam: Nhung Chang Duong Chien Dau, Tap II* [People's artillery of Vietnam: Combat history, vol. 2] (Hanoi: Artillery Command and Artillery Party Current Affairs Committee, 1986), 125.
36. For casualty figure, see Major Gary L. Telfer, Lieutenant Colonel Lane Rogers, and V. Keith Fleming Jr., *U.S. Marines in Vietnam: Fighting the North Vietnamese, 1967* (Washington, D.C.: History and Museums Division Headquarters, U.S. Marine Corps, 1984), 104.
37. For details of the Vietnamese attack on Koh Kong City and Koh Kong Island, as well as the calling of air strikes in support of the hard-pressed Vietnamese marines, see Merle Pribbenow, "A Tale of Five Generals," *Journal of Military History* 70 (January 2006): 484, 481.
38. See Ian McNeill, *To Long Tan: The Australian Army and the Vietnam War 1950–1966* (Sydney: Allen & Unwin, 1993), 351.
39. For an excellent, firsthand account of the battle, see Lieutenant Colonel (Ret.) Harry Smith, "No Time For Fear," *Wartime*, Issue 35, 2006, http://www.awm.gov.au/wartime/35/article.asp/ (accessed May 19, 2010).
40. Quote from Professor Jeffrey Grey, "Diggers and Kiwis: Australian and New Zealand Experience in Vietnam," in *Rolling Thunder in a Gentle Land*, ed. Andrew Wiest (London: Osprey, 2006), 166.
41. Quote from ibid., 171.
42. See Ian Kuring, "Australian Task Force Operations in South Vietnam, 1966–1971," in *The Australian Army and the Vietnam War, 1962–1972: The Chief of Army's Military History Conference 2002*, ed. Peter Dennis and Jeffrey Grey (Canberra: Army History Unit; Dept. of Defence, 2002), available on the Internet at www.defence.gov.au/army/ahu/docs/The_Australian_Army_and_the_Vietnam_War_Kuring.pdf/ (accessed on May 19, 2010).
43. Quote from ibid.
44. Quote from Lewy, *America in Vietnam*, 97.
45. Quote from Lieutenant General Stanley R. Larsen and Brigadier General James L. Collins Jr., *Allied Participation in Vietnam*, Vietnam Studies (Washington, D.C.: Department of the Army, 1975), 153.
46. Quotes found in Kil J. Yi, "The Making of Tigers: South Korea's Experience in the Vietnam War," in *The Australian Army and the Vietnam War, 1962–1972: The Chief of the Army's Military History Conference 2002*, ed. Peter Dennis and Jeffrey Grey (Canberra: Army History Unit; Dept. of Defence, 2002), available on the Internet at http://www.defence.gov.au/army/ahu/docs/The_Australian_Army_and_the_Vietnam_War_Kil.pdf/ (accessed on May 20, 2010).

47. For an account of the fighting at LZ 27V, see AAR, Battle of 27V, 9–10 Aug. 1966, 1st Battalion, 69th Armor, September 8, 1966.
48. Quote from Military History Unit, Ministry of Defense (Republic of Korea), *Pawol Hangukgun Jonsa* [Military history of South Korea's participation in the Vietnam War], vol. 3 (Seoul: Republic of Korea, 1971), 158.
49. For details on Operation Hong Kil Dong, see Op Sum, Opn Hong Kil Dong, MACV-MHB, Sep 67, Historians Files, Office of the Chief of Military History, Washington, D.C.
50. See MacGarrigle, *United States Army in Vietnam*, 313–14.
51. Lanning and Cragg, *Inside the VC and the NVA*, 172.
52. For series of quoted words and casualty commentary, see Scales, *Firepower in Limited War*, 133.

Bibliography

Books

Appy, Christian G. *Patriots: The Vietnam War Remembered from All Sides*. New York: Viking, 2003.

Bergerud, Eric. *Red Thunder, Tropic Lightning: The World of a Combat Division in Vietnam*. Boulder, Colo.: Westview Press, 1993.

Birdwell, Dwight W., and Keith William Nolan. *A Hundred Miles of Bad Road: An Armored Cavalryman in Vietnam, 1967–1968*. Novato, Calif.: Presidio Press, 1997.

Carland, John M. *The United States Army in Vietnam, Combat Operations: Stemming the Tide, May 1965 to October 1966*. Washington, D.C.: U.S. Army Center of Military History, 2000.

Carver, Field Marshall Sir Michael, ed. *The War Lords: Military Commanders of the Twentieth Century*. Boston: Little, Brown, 1976.

Chanoff, David, and Doan Van Toai. *Portrait of the Enemy*. New York: Random House, 1986.

Colby, William, with James McCargar. *Lost Victory: A Firsthand Account of America's Sixteen Year Involvement in Vietnam*. Chicago: Contemporary Books, 1989.

Conboy, Kenneth, Kenneth Bowra, and Simon McCouaig. *The NVA and Viet Cong*. London: Osprey, 1991.

Davidson, Lieutenant General Phillip B. *Vietnam at War: The History, 1946–1975*. Novato, Calif.: Presidio Press, 1988.

Dennis, Peter, and Jeffrey Grey, eds. *The Australian Army and the Vietnam War, 1962–1972: The Chief of Army's Military History Conference 2002*. Canberra: Army History Unit, Department of Defence, 2002. Available on the Internet at http://www.defence.gov.au/army/ahu/docs/The_Australian_Army_and_the_Vietnam_War_Kuring.pdf/.

Duiker, William. *The Communist Road to Power in Vietnam.* Boulder, Colo.: Westview Press, 1981.

———. *The Communist Road to Power in Vietnam.* 2nd ed. Boulder, Colo.: Westview Press, 1995.

Ewell, Lieutenant General Julian J., and Major General Ira A. Hunt Jr. *Sharpening the Combat Edge: The Use of Analysis to Reinforce Military Judgment.* Vietnam Studies. Washington, D.C.: Department of the Army, 1974.

Fall, Bernard B. *Hell in a Very Small Place: The Siege of Dien Bien Phu.* New York: J. B. Lippincott, 1967.

———. *Street without Joy.* Mechanicsburg, Pa.: Stackpole Books, 1994.

Fox, R. P. *Air Base Defense in the Republic of Vietnam, 1961–73.* Washington, D.C.: Office of Air Force History, 1979.

Giap, General Vo Nguyen. *Big Victory, Great Task.* New York: Praeger, 1968.

Glantz, David M. *Zhukov's Greatest Defeat: The Red Army's Epic Disaster in Operation Mars, 1942.* Lawrence: University of Kansas Press, 1999.

Hackworth, Colonel David H. *Steel My Soldiers' Hearts.* New York: Touchstone Book, 2002.

Johnson, Major Charles M., and Jack Shulimson. *U.S. Marines in Vietnam: The Landing and the Buildup, 1965.* Washington, D.C.: History and Museums Division Headquarters, U.S. Marine Corps, 1978.

Knightley, Phillip. *The First Casualty—From the Crimea to Vietnam: The War Correspondent as Hero, Propagandist, and Myth Maker.* New York: Harcourt, Brace, Jovanovich, 1975.

Kutler, Stanley I., ed. *Encyclopedia of the Vietnam War.* New York: Scribner's, 1996.

Lanning, Michael Lee, and Daniel Cragg. *Inside the VC and the NVA: The Real Story of North Vietnam's Armed Forces.* New York: Ballantine Books, 1992.

Larsen, Lieutenant General Stanley R., and Brigadier General James L. Collins Jr. *Allied Participation in Vietnam.* Vietnam Studies. Washington, D.C.: Department of the Army, 1975.

Lehrack, Otto. *The First Battle: Operation Starlite and the Beginning of the Blood Debt in Vietnam.* Havertown, Pa.: Casemate, 2004.

———. *No Shining Armor: The Marines at War in Vietnam.* Lawrence: University of Kansas Press, 1992.

———. *Road of 10,000 Pains: The Destruction of the 2nd NVA Division by the U.S. Marines, 1967.* Minneapolis: Zenith Press, 2010.

Lewy, Guenther. *America in Vietnam.* New York: Oxford University Press, 1978.

Lind, Michael. *Vietnam the Necessary War: A Reinterpretation of America's Most Disastrous Military Conflict.* New York: Free Press, 1999.

Lung, Colonel Hoang Ngoc. *Strategy and Tactics.* Indochina Monographs. Washington, D.C.: U.S. Army Center of Military History, 1980.

MacGarrigle, George L. *The United States Army in Vietnam, Combat Operations: Taking the Offensive, October 1966 to October 1967.* Washington, D.C.: U.S. Army Center of Military History, 1998.

Maclear, Michael. *The Ten Thousand Day War, Vietnam: 1945–1975.* New York: St. Martin's Press, 1981.
Maltoff, Maurice, ed. *American Military History.* Washington, D.C.: U.S. Army Center of Military History, 1980.
Mangold, Tom, and John Penycate. *The Tunnels of Cu Chi: The Untold Story of Vietnam.* New York: Random House, 1985.
Mann, Robert. *A Grand Delusion: America's Descent into Vietnam.* New York: Basic Books, 2001.
Maraniss, David. *They Marched into Sunlight: War and Peace, Vietnam and America, October 1967.* New York: Simon & Schuster, 2003.
Marrin, Albert. *America and Vietnam: The Elephant and the Tiger.* New York: Viking, 1992.
Mason, Robert. *Chickenhawk.* New York: Viking Press, 1983.
McCoy, James W. *Secrets of the Viet Cong.* New York: Hippocrene Books, 1992.
McNeill, Ian. *To Long Tan: The Australian Army and the Vietnam War, 1950–1966.* Sydney: Allen & Unwin, 1993.
Military History Unit. Ministry of Defense (Republic of Korea). *Pawol Hangukgun Jonsa* [Military history of Korea's participation in the Vietnam War]. Vol. 3. Seoul: Republic of Korea, 1971.
Moore, Lieutenant General Harold G. (Ret.), and Joseph L. Galloway. *We Were Soldiers Once . . . and Young: Ia Drang—The Battle that Changed the War in Vietnam.* New York: Random House, 1992.
Morgan, Ted. *Valley of Death: The Tragedy at Dien Bien Phu that Led America into the Vietnam War.* New York: Random House, 2010.
Moyar, Mark. *Triumph Forsaken: The Vietnam War, 1954–1965.* Cambridge University Press, 2006.
Murphy, Edward F. *Dak To: America's Sky Soldiers in South Vietnam's Central Highlands.* New York: Presidio Press, 2007.
———. *Semper Fi: From Da Nang to the DMZ Marine Corps Operations, 1965–1975.* New York: Presidio Press, 2003.
Nagel, John A. *Learning to Eat Soup with a Knife: Counterinsurgency Lessons from Malaya and Vietnam.* Chicago: University of Chicago Press, 2002.
O'Connel, Kim A. *Primary Source Accounts of the Vietnam War.* Berkeley Heights, N.J.: Enslow, 2006.
Ott, Major General David Ewing. *Field Artillery, 1954–1973.* Vietnam Studies. Washington, D.C.: U.S. Army Center of Military History, Department of the Army, 1975.
Pike, Douglas. *PAVN: People's Army of Vietnam.* Novato, Calif.: Presidio Press, 1986.
———. *War, Peace, and the Viet Cong.* Cambridge, Mass.: MIT Press, 1969.
Pimlott, John. *Vietnam: The Decisive Battles.* New York: MacMillan, 1990.
Rogers, Lieutenant General Bernard William. *Cedar Falls–Junction City: A Turning Point.* Vietnam Studies. Washington, D.C.: Department of the Army, 1989.

Rottman, Gordon, and Howard Gerrard. *Viet Cong Fighter*. London: Osprey Publishing, 2007.

Santoli, Al. *To Bear Any Burden: The Vietnam War and Its Aftermath in the Words of Americans and Southeast Asians*. New York: E. P. Hutton, 1985.

Sheehan, Neil. *A Bright and Shining Lie: John Paul Vann and America in Vietnam*. New York: Random House, 1998.

Shulimson, Jack. *U.S. Marines in Vietnam: An Expanding War, 1966*. Washington, D.C.: History and Museums Division Headquarters, U.S. Marine Corps, 1982.

Sorley, Lewis. *A Better War: The Unexamined Victories and Final Tragedy of America's Last Years in Vietnam*. New York: Harcourt, Brace, 1999.

Stanton, Shelby. *Anatomy of a Division: The 1st Cavalry Division in Vietnam*. New York: Ballantine Books, 2003.

———. *The Rise and Fall of an American Army: U.S. Ground Forces in Vietnam, 1965–1973*. New York: Ballantine Books, 2003.

Starry, General Donn A. *Mounted Combat in Vietnam*. Vietnam Studies. Washington, D.C.: Department of the Army, 1989.

Summers, Colonel Harry G. *Historical Atlas of the Vietnam War*. New York: Houghton Mifflin, 1995.

———. *On Strategy: A Critical Analysis of the Vietnam War*. Novato, Calif.: Presidio Press, 1981.

Sympson, Ken. *Images from the Otherland*. Jefferson, N.C.: McFarland, 1995.

Telfer, Major Gary L., Lieutenant Colonel Lane Rogers, and V. Keith Fleming Jr. *U.S. Marines in Vietnam: Fighting the North Vietnamese, 1967*. Washington, D.C.: History and Museums Division Headquarters, U.S. Marine Corps Headquarters, 1984.

Tourison, Sedgwick D., Jr. *Talking with Victor Charlie: An Interrogator's Story*. New York: Ivy Books, 1991.

Truong, Nhu Tang, David Chanoff, and Doan Van Toai. *A Viet Cong Memoir: An Inside Account of the Vietnam War and Its Aftermath*. New York: Harcourt, Brace, Jovanovich, 1985.

Webb, Kate. *On the Other Side: 23 Days with the Viet Cong*. New York: Quadrangle Books, 1972.

West, Bing. *The Village*. New York: Pocket Books, 1972.

Westmoreland, General William C. *A Soldier Reports*. Garden City, N.Y.: Doubleday, 1976.

Wiest, Andrew, ed. *Rolling Thunder in a Gentle Land: The Vietnam War Revisited*. London: Osprey, 2006.

Woodruff, Mark. *Unheralded Victory: The Defeat of the Viet Cong and North Vietnamese Army, 1961–1975*. New York: Presidio Press, 1999.

Young, Marilyn. *The Vietnam Wars, 1945–1990*. New York: Harper Collins, 1991.

Communist Vietnamese Sources

Cam, Colonel General Hoang, and Nhat Tien. *Chang Duong Muoi Nghin Ngay: Hoi Uc* [The ten-thousand-day journey: A memoir]. Hanoi: People's Army Publishing House, 2001.

"Chien Thang Play Me–Ia Drang (tu 19–10 den 20-11-1965): Don Phu Dau Quan My o Tay Nguyen" [The Plei Me–Ia Drang victory (from 19 October to 20 November 1965): A stunning first blow against American troops in the Central Highlands]. Folder 01, Box 01. Merle Pribbenow Collection, The Vietnam Archive, Texas Tech University.

Dai, Colonel Ho Son, ed. *Lich Su Su Doan Bo Binh 5 (1965–2005)* [History of the 5th Infantry Division (1965–2005)]. Hanoi: People's Army Publishing House, 2005. http://www.quansuvn.net/index.php?topic=155710/.

Dai, Lieutenant Colonel Ho Son, et al. *Lich Su Su Doan 5* [History of the 5th Division]. Hanoi: People's Army Publishing House, 1995.

Dai, Ho Son, and Tran Phan Chan. *History of the Resistance War in Saigon–Cho Lon–Gia Dinh (1945–1975)* [*Lich Su Saigon–Cho Lon–Gia Dinh Khang Chien (1945–1975)*]. Ho Chi Minh City: Ho Chi Minh Publishing House, 1994.

Dat, Senior Colonel Nguyen Quang, and Senior Colonel Tran Hanh. *Mot So Tran Danh Trong Khang Chien Chong Phap, Khang Chien Chong My, 1945–1975 (Tap I)* [A number of battles during the resistance wars against the French and the Americans, 1945–1975 (vol. 1)]. Hanoi: Military History Institute of Vietnam, 1991.

Dinh, Pham Quang, ed. *Su Doan 9* [9th division]. Hanoi: People's Army Publishing House, 1990.

Dung, General Van Tien. *After Political Failure, the U.S. Imperialists Are Facing Military Defeat in South Vietnam.* Hanoi: Foreign Languages Publishing House, 1966.

Giang, Cuu Long, and Toan Anh. *Nguoi Viet, Dat Viet* [The land and people of Vietnam]. Saigon: Kim Lai Printers, 1967.

Hai, Bui Minh, and Vu Van Sum. *Quang Ngai: Lich Su Chien Tranh Nhan Dan 30 Nam (1945–1975)* [Quang Ngai: A history of 30 years of people's war (1945–1975)]. Ho Chi Minh City: Nghia Binh Province Joint Publishing House and the Nghia Binh Province Military Headquarters, 1988.

Hiep, Colonel General Dang Vu, with Senior Colonel Le Hai Trieu and Colonel Ngo Vinh Binh. *Ky Uc Tay Nguyen* [Highland memories]. Pt. 4. Hanoi: People's Army Publishing House, 2000.

Huan, Nguyen Tri, et al. *Su Doan Sao Vang* [The Yellow Star Division]. Hanoi: People's Army Publishing House, 1984.

Lich Su Cuc Tac Chien, 1945–2000 [History of the Combat Operations Department, 1945–2000]. Hanoi: People's Army Publishing House, 2005. Available on the Internet at Quan Su Viet Nam [Vietnamese military history]. http://www.quansuvn.net/.

Lich Su Su Doan Bo Binh 324, 1955–2005 [History of the 324th Infantry Division, 1955–2005]. Hanoi: People's Army Publishing House, 2005. Available on the Internet at http://www.quansuvn.net/index.php?topic=103.0/.

Lien, Le. "Creating a Turning Point in the Resistance War against the Americans." *Quan Doi Nhan Dan*, December 3, 2004. http://www.quandoinhandan.org.vn/skhc/?id=1108&subject+=7/.

Military Encyclopedia Center of the Ministry of Defense. *Tu Dien Bach Khoa Quan Su Viet Nam* [Military encyclopedia of Vietnam]. Chief editor Senior Colonel Tran Do. Hanoi: People's Army Publishing House, 1996.

Military History Institute of Vietnam. *Dai Tuong Nguyen Chi Thanh: Na Chinh Tri Quan Su Loi Lac* [General Nguyen Chi Thanh: An outstanding military political figure]. Edited by Ha Huu Khieu. Hanoi: People's Army Publishing House, 1997.

———. *The Resistance War against the U.S. to Save the Nation, 1954–1975: Military Events*. Edited by Senior Colonel Tran Hanh. Hanoi: Military History Institute of Vietnam, 1988.

———. *The Saigon–Gia Dinh Offensive Theater (1968)*. Hanoi: n.p., 1988.

———. *Victory in Vietnam: The Official History of the People's Army of Vietnam, 1954–1974*. Lawrence: University of Kansas Press, 1994.

Nguyen, Kieu Tam, chief editor. *Chien Truong Tri-Thien-Hue Trong Cuoc Chien Tranh Chong My Cuu Nuoc Toan Thang* [The Tri-Thien-Hue battlefield during the Victorious Resistance War against the Americans to save the nation]. Hue: Thuan An Publishing House, 1985.

Nhu, Trinh, et al. *Lich Su Bien Nien Xu Uy Nam Bo Va Trung Uong Cuc Mien Nam, 1954–1975* [Historical chronicle of the Cochin China Party Committee and the Central Office for South Vietnam, 1954–1975]. Hanoi: Ho Chi Minh National Political Studies Institute, Party Historian Institute, 2002.

Nhung, Dang Van, Vu Lam, et al. *Su Doan 7: Ky Su* [7th Division: A record]. Hanoi: People's Army Publishing House, 1986.

Son, Truong. *A Bitter Dry Season for the Americans*. Hanoi: Foreign Languages Publishing House, 1966.

Ta, Senior Colonel Nguyen Viet, et al. *Mien Dong Nam Bo Khang Chien (1945–1975), Tap II* [The resistance war in eastern Cochin China (1945–1975), vol. 2]. Hanoi: People's Army Publishing House, 1993.

Tai, Vu Anh, Le Minh Tan, and Phan Van Tich, editorial direction. 2nd Division Party Committee and Division Headquarters. *Su Doan 2, Tap I* [2nd Division, vol. 1]. Da Nang: Da Nang Publishing House, 1989.

Thai, Hoang Van. "Building and Employing the Strength of the Rear Area in the War of Resistance against the United States for National Salvation." *Tap Chi Cong San* 12 (December 1982): 11–19.

Tinh, Nguyen Khac, Tran Quang Hau, et al. *Phao Binh Nhan Dan Viet Nam: Nhung Chang Duong Chien Dau, Tap II* [People's artillery of Vietnam: Combat history, vol. 2]. Hanoi: Artillery Command and Artillery Party Current Affairs Committee, 1986.

Tinh, Tran, ed. *Van Kien Dang Toan Tap, Tap 28, 1967* [Collected party documents, vol. 28, 1967]. Hanoi: National Political Publishing House, 2003.

Tra, Colonel General Tran Van. *Goi Nguoi Dang Song* [To the living]. Ho Chi Minh City: Youth Publishing House, 1996.

———. *Vietnam: History of the Bulwark B2 Theater*. Vol. 5, *Concluding the 30-Years War*. Translated by Foreign Broadcast Information Service. Joint Publications Research Service 82783. Southeast Asia Report 1247. Ho Chi Minh City: Van Nghe Publishing House, 1982.

Uoc, Lieutenant General Nguyen Dinh, director of Military History Institute of Vietnam (Ministry of Defense). "Chien Dich Play Me" [Plei Me campaign]. Presentation given at Pleiku–Ia Drang Veterans 40th Anniversary Commemoration, November 10–13, 2005, Washington, D.C.

Van Kien Dang Toan Tap, Tap 21, 1960 [Collected party documents, vol. 21, 1960]. Hà N i: National Political Publishing House (NXB Chính Tr Qu c Gia), 2003.

Van Kien Dang Toan Tap, Tap 22, 1961 [Collected party documents, vol. 22, 1961]. Hà N i: National Political Publishing House (NXB Chính Tr Qu c Gia), 2003.

Articles, Papers, and Unpublished Sources

Andrade, Dale. "Why Westmoreland Was Right." *Vietnam*, April 2009, 26–32.

Andrade, Dale, and Lieutenant Colonel James H. Willbanks, USA (Ret.). "CORDS/Phoenix: Counterinsurgency Lessons from Vietnam for the Future." *Military Review*, March–April 2006, 9–23.

Barclay, Brigadier C. N. (Ret.). "The Western Soldier versus the Communist Insurgent." *Military Review* 2, no. 2 (February 1969): 86–94.

Birtle, Andrew J. "PROVN, Westmoreland, and the Historians: A Reappraisal." *Journal of Military History* 72 (October 2008): 1213–47.

Bradford, Lieutenant Colonel Zeb B., Jr. "US Tactics in Vietnam." *Military Review* 52, no. 2 (February 1972): 63–76.

Broyles, William, Jr. "The Road to Hill 10: A Veteran's Return to Vietnam." *Atlantic Monthly*, April 1985, http://www.theathlantic.com/past/docs/issues/85apr/broyles.htm/.

Comments of Commanding Officer of the 2nd Battalion, 28th Infantry on the Battle of Lo Khe, 05 March 1966. Folder 58, Box 01. William E. LeGro Collection, The Vietnam Archive, Texas Tech University.

Communist Strategy as Reflected in Lao Dong Party and COSVN Resolution, 1959–1969. Folder 26, Box 07. Douglas Pike Collection: Unit 06—Democratic Republic of Vietnam, The Vietnam Archive, Texas Tech University.

Draft of "The Big Red One" (chapters 1–5). N.d. Folder 64, Box 01. William E. LeGro Collection, The Vietnam Archive, Texas Tech University.

Dye, Colonel Harold A. "Close Fire Support." *Military Review* 47, no. 9 (September 1967): 36–43.

Faley, Colonel Thomas E. (Ret.). "The Battle of Zulu-Zulu." *Vietnam*, October 1994, 18–25.

———. "Mutual Surprise at An Ninh," *Screaming Eagle*, January/February 1998, 15–19. Item found in Mutual Surprise at An Ninh Paratroopers vs Viet Cong, January–February 1998. Folder 03, Box 01. Gary Jestes Collection, The Vietnam Archive, Texas Tech University.

———. "Operation Marauder: Allied Offensive in the Mekong Delta." *Vietnam*, February 1999, 34–40.

Guan, Ang Cheng. "Decision-making Leading to the Tet Offensive (1968): The Vietnamese Communist Perspective." *Journal of Contemporary History* 33, no. 3 (1998): 341–53.

Hanoi assessment of guerrilla war in the South, 13 November 1966. Folder 17, Box 06. Douglas Pike Collection: Unit 01—Assessment and Strategy, The Vietnam Archive, Texas Tech University.

Hauser, Lieutenant Colonel William L. "Firepower Battlefield." *Military Review* 51, no. 10 (October 1971): 21–27.

Ho Chi Minh Trail History. May 1979. Folder 04, Box 04. Douglas Pike Collection: Unit 03—Technology, The Vietnam Archive, Texas Tech University.

Ladd, Lieutenant Colonel Jonathan F. "Viet Cong Portrait." *Military Review* 44, no. 8 (August 1964): 20–25.

Loc, Major General Vinh. "Road-clearing Operation." *Military Review* 46, no. 4 (April 1966): 22–28.

Mabb, Tony. "Vietnam Eagles." *Screaming Eagle*, November/December 2002, 33–35. Item found in The Screaming Eagle, November/December 2002, November/December 2002. Folder 03, Box 02. Gary Jestes Collection, The Vietnam Archive, Texas Tech University.

Narrative of the Battle of Lo Khe. N.d. Folder 58, Box 01. William E. LeGro Collection, The Vietnam Archive, Texas Tech University.

Nguyen, Lien-Hang T. "The War Politburo: North Vietnam's Diplomatic and Political Road to the Tet Offensive." *Journal of Vietnamese Studies* 1, nos. 1–2 (February/August 2006): 4–58.

Origin and Evolution of the Current War. 01 January 1968. Folder 05, Box 10. Douglas Pike Collection: Unit 01—Assessment and Strategy, The Vietnam Archive, Texas Tech University.

Patton, Lieutenant Colonel George S. "Why They Fight." *Military Review* 45, no. 12 (December 1965): 16–23, 56–64.

Pribbenow, Merle. "The Fog of War: The Vietnamese View of the Ia Drang Battle." *Military Review*, January–February 2001, 93–97.

———. "General Vo Nguyen Giap and the Mysterious Evolution of the Plan for the 1968 Tet Offensive." *Journal of Vietnamese Studies* 3, no. 2 (Summer 2008): 1–33.

———. "A Tale of Five Generals: Vietnam's Invasion of Cambodia." *Journal of Military History* 70 (January 2006): 459–86.
"Radio Propaganda Report: North Vietnamese Party Problems and Differences." March 9, 1966. Folder 34, Box 03. Central Intelligence Agency Collection, The Vietnam Archive, Texas Tech University.
Samson, Colonel Jack. "Viet Cong Tactics: 'Ten against One.'" *Military Review* 47, no. 1 (January 1967): 89–93.
Shuffer, Lieutenant Colonel George M., Jr. "Finish Them with Firepower." *Military Review* 47, no. 12 (December 1967): 11–15.
Smith, Jack P. "Death in the Ia Drang Valley, November 13–18, 1965." *Saturday Evening Post,* January 28, 1967.
Weller, Jac. "Highway 19: Then and Now." *Military Review* 48, no. 12 (December 1968): 56–64.
Working Paper on the North Vietnamese Role in the War in South Vietnam, 20 August 1971. Folder 06, Box 17. Douglas Pike Collection: Unit 02—Military Operations, The Vietnam Archive, Texas Tech University.

Documents, Records, and Studies
Captured Documents (Combined Document Exploitation Center): 95th VC Battalion of the 2nd Regiment, 11 January 1967. Folder 0515, Box 0041. Vietnam Archive Collection, The Vietnam Archive, Texas Tech University.
Captured Documents (Combined Document Exploitation Center): Achievements of Cong Truong 9, 13 February 1967. Folder 0880, Box 0049. Vietnam Archive Collection, The Vietnam Archive, Texas Tech University.
Captured Documents (Combined Document Exploitation Center): Interrogation Report of Dang Doan (alias Dang Son, Lao Dong Party name Dang Nguyen), Concerning Effects of Leaflets on VC Cadres and Soldiers, 01 February 1967. Folder 0091, Box 0091. Vietnam Archive Collection, The Vietnam Archive, Texas Tech University.
Captured Documents (Combined Document Exploitation Center): Organization and Personalities of Regiment 2, Division 3, 10 December 1966. Folder 2635, Box 0042. Vietnam Archive Collection, The Vietnam Archive, Texas Tech University.
Chief, U.S. Delegation. Four Party Joint Military Commission, RVN. Message 251013Z, October 1973. Provided to author by General P. X. Kelley (Ret.).
Cold War International History Project. "Discussion between Mao Zedong, Pham Van Dong, and Vo Nguyen Giap." April 11, 1967. Virtual Archive, Vietnam (Indochina) War(s) Collection. http://www.wilsoncenter.org/index.cfm?topic_id=1409&fuseaction=va2.document&identifier=5034C9C6-96B6-175C-96D86CF8502CADDD&sort=Collection&item=TheVietnam(Indochina)War(s)/.
The Crimp Document, 01 January 1963. Folder 03, Box 03. Douglas Pike Col-

lection: Unit 02—Military Operations, The Vietnam Archive, Texas Tech University.

Department of Defense. *Know Your Enemy: The Viet Cong*. DoD Gen-20. Washington, D.C., U.S. Government Printing Office, 1966.

Department of the Army. "Viet Cong Boobytraps, Mines, and Mine Warfare Techniques." May 1967. Training circular. Folder 07, Box 09. Glen Helm Collection, The Vietnam Archive, Texas Tech University.

Diary of infiltrator. December 1966. Folder 01, Box 04. Douglas Pike Collection: Unit 03—Technology, The Vietnam Archive, Texas Tech University.

Doughty, Major Robert. "Evolution of U.S. Army Tactical Doctrine, 1946–76." *Leavenworth Papers*, no. 1, August 1979. Combat Studies Institute, United States Army Command and General Staff College, Fort Leavenworth, Kans. Available on the Internet at http://carl.army.mil/resources/csi/Doughty/doughty.asp/.

Elliot, David W. P., and Mai Elliot. *Documents of an Elite Viet Cong Unit: The Demolition Platoon of the 514th Battalion. Part 3, Military Organization and Activities*. RAND Corporation Study RM-5880-ISA/ARPA. Santa Monica, Calif.: RAND Corporation, May 1969.

General Orders (GO) 40, DA. September 21, 1967. Presidential Unit Citation.

Ginsburgh, Robert N., to W. W. Rostow. Memo. With attached report, "Operations of U.S. Marine Forces Vietnam, 08 November 1967." Folder 11, Box 08. Larry Berman Collection (Presidential Archives Research), The Vietnam Archive, Texas Tech University.

"The Ia Drang Campaign 1965: A Successful Operational Campaign or Mere Tactical Failure?" Monograph by Lieutenant Colonel Peter J. Schifferle Armor. May 6, 1994. Folder 01, Box 02. Elias A. Cuevas Collection, The Vietnam Archive, Texas Tech University.

The Ia Drang Valley Campaign: The Army's First Battle in Vietnam, 16 June 1989. Folder 01, Box 02. Elias A. Cuevas Collection, The Vietnam Archive, Texas Tech University.

Interrogation of Le Xuan Chuyen, a lieutenant colonel in the North Vietnamese army and assistant chief of staff and chief of operations of the 5th Viet Cong Division. August 2, 1966. Folder 003, Box 30. Douglas Pike Collection: Unit 05—National Liberation Front, The Vietnam Archive, Texas Tech University.

Interrogation of Lt. Colonel Le Xuan Chuyen, a former operations officer of the Viet Cong 5th Division, 01 August 1966. Folder 001, Box 30. Douglas Pike Collection: Unit 05—National Liberation Front, The Vietnam Archive, Texas Tech University.

Interviews Concerning the National Liberation Front of South Vietnam # TET-VC41, 03 May 1968. Folder 13, Box 10. Douglas Pike Collection: Unit 02—Military Operations, The Vietnam Archive, Texas Tech University.

Item 83. Interrogation of an officer in the 60th Battalion, 1st Viet Cong Regiment.

N.d. Folder 15, Box 01. United States Department of State Collection, The Vietnam Archive, Texas Tech University.

Kelley, Lieutenant Colonel P. X: Letter to Director of Marine Corps History. N.d. Review of draft manuscript. History of the U.S. Marine Corps, Part III (s). In possession of General P. X. Kelley (Ret.).

Le Duan biography: 1976. Folder 13, Box 05. Douglas Pike Collection: Unit 08—Biography, The Vietnam Archive, Texas Tech University.

"Notes from the Underground: The Mystique of a Viet Cong." February 16, 1962. Folder 04, Box 01. Douglas Pike Collection: Unit 05—National Liberation Front, The Vietnam Archive, Texas Tech University.

PLAF 9th Division–272d A Regiment. May 15, 1967, Folder 06, Box 02. Douglas Pike Collection: Unit 05—National Liberation Front, The Vietnam Archive, Texas Tech University.

United States Army, Vietnam. Rpt., USARV, 5 Feb 70, sub: History of the 273 VC Regiment, July 1964–December 1969.

U.S. Military Assistance Command. Office of Information. "FLWG Is the Official MACV Communiqué #080-66 as of 1700H, 21 March 1966." Folder 19, Box 06. Douglas Pike Collection: Unit 02—Military Operations, The Vietnam Archive, Texas Tech University.

Viet Cong Base Camps and Supply Caches, 20 July 1968. Folder 02, Box 01. Douglas Pike Collection: Unit 05—National Liberation Front, The Vietnam Archive, Texas Tech University.

Viet Cong Sappers. January 1969. Folder 03, Box 15. Douglas Pike Collection: Unit 05—National Liberation Front, The Vietnam Archive, Texas Tech University.

U.S Military After Action Reports (AARs)

AAR, Battle of 27V, 9–10 Aug. 1966, 1st Battalion, 69th Armor. September 8, 1966.

AAR, Ia Drang Valley Operation, 1st Battalion, 7th Cavalry. November 14–16, 1965. December 9, 1965.

AAR, Operation Bloodhound/Bushmaster II, 3rd Brigade, 1st Infantry Division. December 30, 1965.

AAR, Operation Bushmaster I, 3rd Brigade, 1st Infantry Division. December 31, 1965.

AAR, Operation Cocoa Beach, 3rd Brigade, 1st Infantry Division. April 3, 1966 .

AAR, Operation Eagles Claw, 2nd Brigade, 1st Cavalry Division. March 16, 1966.

AAR, Operation El Paso II/III, 1st Infantry Division. N.d.

AAR, Operation Gibraltar, 2nd Battalion, 502nd Infantry. October 8, 1965.

AAR, Operation Hot Springs, 2nd Battalion, 7th Marines. April 28, 1966.

AAR, Operation Hot Springs, 3rd Battalion, 7th Marines. April 30, 1966.

AAR, Operation Marauder I, 173rd Abn Brigade (Sep). N.d.

AAR, Operation Masher/White Wing, 1st Cavalry Division (Ambl). April 28, 1966.

AAR, Operation Rolling Stone, 1st Brigade, 1st Infantry Division. March 28, 1966.
AAR, Operation Texas, 2nd Battalion, 4th Marines. March 29, 66.

U.S. Military Command Chronologies, Histories, and Summaries

Command Chronology, 01 February 1966. Folder 002. U.S. Marine Corps History Division. Vietnam War Documents Collection, The Vietnam Archive, Texas Tech University.

Joint Chiefs of Staff History of Vietnam War (II): 1965–1967—Less than War but No Peace: The Situation in January–February 1966. July 1, 1970. Folder 02, Box 01. Joint Chiefs of Staff History of the Vietnam War, 1965–1967, The Vietnam Archive, Texas Tech University.

Joint Chiefs of Staff History of Vietnam War (II): 1965–1967—The War on the Ground—Strategy and Operations—1966. July 1, 1970. Folder 03, Box 01. Joint Chiefs of Staff History of the Vietnam War, 1965–1967, The Vietnam Archive, Texas Tech University.

U.S. Military Assistance Command, Vietnam. "Summary of Action for 1965." January 1, 1966. Folder 20, Box 03. Glenn Helm Collection, The Vietnam Archive, Texas Tech University.

U.S. Military Assistance Command, Vietnam. "Summary of USMACV News Events 1966." Special report from the USIS Press Branch—American Embassy, Tokyo, March 7, 1967. Folder 04, Box 06. Douglas Pike Collection: Unit 02—Military Operations, The Vietnam Archive, Texas Tech University.

U.S. Military Handbooks, Reports, Evaluations, and Lessons Learned

"Battlefield Reports: United States Army Vietnam." January 18, 1968. Folder 11, Box 08. Glenn Helm Collection, The Vietnam Archive, Texas Tech University.

"Department of the Army Operations Report 1-66: Lessons Learned," March 22, 1966. Folder 07, Box 03. Glen Helm Collection, The Vietnam Archive, Texas Tech University.

"Evaluation of U.S. Army Combat Operations in Vietnam: Volume 4—Firepower." April 25, 1966. Folder 05, Box 05. Glenn Helm Collection, The Vietnam Archive, Texas Tech University.

Handbook for US Forces in Vietnam. Military Assistance Command, Vietnam, April 1967. Folder 01, Box 01. Paul Lasker Collection, The Vietnam Archive, Texas Tech University.

"Operations Report, Lessons Learned: Report 1-68: Summary of Lessons Learned." February 1, 1968. Folder 04, Box 08. Glenn Helm Collection, The Vietnam Archive, Texas Tech University.

"ORLL [Operations Report, Lessons Learned]." May 1–July 31, 1966. 1st Infantry Division. August 15, 1966.

"USMC 1965 Lessons Learned—Operation Harvest Moon, Dec." January 27, 1966. Folder 01. Bud Harton Collection, The Vietnam Archive, Texas Tech University.

Vietnam Interviews (VNIs), U.S. Army Center of Military History, Washington, D.C.

VNI- 77. "The Battle of Ap Tau O." July 5, 1967.
VNI-99. "Battle of Trung Loi." November 20, 1965.
VNI- 97. "Narrative—History of the Battle of Xa Cam My." February 21, 1967.
VNI-101. "The Campaign along National Route 13." August 7, 1966.
VNI-137. "The Battle of Ap Nha Mat." December 5, 1965.

Author Telephone Interviews and E-mail Correspondence

Ball, Gary. USA (Ret.). September 15, 2008.
Bergerud, Eric. August 26, 2007.
Hutchinson, Gary. USMC (Ret.). June 27, 2008.
Kelley, General P. X. USMC (Ret.). Jun 26, 2008.
Lehrack, Lieutenant Colonel Otto. USMC (Ret.). November 18, 2007; April 21, 2008; June 3, 2008.
Parish, Will. USA (Ret.). October 22, 2007; September 7, 2008.
Pribbenow, Merle. Central Intelligence Agency (Ret.). May 28, 2008; June 9, 2008; June 17, 2008; July 21, 2008; August 27, 2008; September 7, 2008; November 7, 2008; December 1, 2008; November 5, 2009.
Stubbs, Tom "Doc." USN (Ret.). June 23, 2008.
Sympson, Captain Ken. USMC (Ret.). June 27, 2008.

Index

Abilene, Operation, 191
Abrams, Creighton, 225
Ackerson, Frederic, 156
Ah Ninh, 82–91
American Sky Soldiers. *See* Army Airborne Brigade, 173rd (U.S.)
American troops: escalation, 62; and road security, 43–44; strategy against Viet Cong base camps, 35
An, Nguyen Huu, 84
An Cuong, 70–71, 72
An Hoa, 165–66
An Khe, 81, 82, 85
An Lao Valley, 151–54
An Ninh, 88
An Trach, 164
Andrade, Dale, 2
Ap Bau Bang: map, 114
Ap Chinch An, 162–63
Ap Nha Mat, 120–23; map, 120
Ap Tau O, 200–201
Ap Tay Hoang, 162
Army Airborne Brigade, 173rd (U.S.), 62, 104, 109, 143, 146–47, 186, 187–89
Army Airborne Division, 101st (U.S.), 83, 86; 1st Brigade, 86; 502nd Regiment, 2nd Battalion, 91
Army Artillery Regiment, 33rd (U.S.): 2nd Battalion, Battery B, 118, 121–23; 2nd Battalion, Battery C, 110–11, 112, 113, 115
Army Artillery Regiment, 320th (U.S.): 2nd Battalion, Battery B, 86; 2nd Battalion, Battery C, 86
Army Cavalry Division, 1st (U.S.), 93, 151, 155; 5th Cavalry Regiment, 1st Battalion, 155–58; 5th Cavalry Regiment, 2nd Battalion, 155–58; 12th Cavalry Regiment, 2nd Battalion, 156
Army Cavalry Division, 7th, 1st Battalion, (U.S.), 93
Army Cavalry Regiment, 4th (U.S.): 1st Squadron, 178; 1st Squadron, Troop A, 110–13, 200
Army Cavalry Regiment, 7th (U.S.), 154; 1st Battalion, 221; 1st Battalion, 3rd Brigade, 153; 1st Battalion, Company C, 94; 1st Battalion, Company D, 94
Army Cavalry Regiment, 8th, 1st Battalion (U.S.), 220–21
Army Cavalry Regiment, 17th, 1st Battalion, Troop A (U.S.), 86
Army Infantry Division, 1st (U.S.), 104; 1st Brigade, 177, 178, 186; 2nd Brigade, 121; 3rd Brigade, 181; Big Red One, 117; instructions for fighting, 219

Army Infantry Division, 2nd (U.S.): 2nd Battalion, 120; 3rd Brigade, 2nd Battalion, 109; 3rd Brigade, 2nd Battalion, Company A, 110, 112
Army Infantry Division, 4th (U.S.), 222
Army Infantry Division, 25th (U.S.), force feed fire support system, 219
Army Infantry Regiment, 327th, 2nd Battalion, Company A (U.S.), 86
Army Infantry Regiment, 503rd (U.S.): 173rd Airborne Brigade, 1st Battalion, 144; 173rd Airborne Brigade, 2nd Battalion, 144, 145, 146
Army of the Republic of Vietnam (ARV), 16; defeatability, 59
Army of the Republic of Vietnam (ARVN) Division, 1st, 161–62
Army of the Republic of Vietnam (ARVN) Division, 2nd: 5th ARVN Airborne Battalion, 166
Army of the Republic of Vietnam (ARVN) Division, 5th: 7th ARVN Regiment, 120
Army of the Republic of Vietnam (ARVN) Regiment, 3rd: 1st Battalion, 161
Attleboro, Operation, 21, 202

B2 Front, 96–104, 175–94; description, 97, 98; Iron Triangle, 100–101; North Vietnamese Army plans, 175–76; War Zone C, 99–100; War Zone D, 100, 105, 106, 108; zones, 98–99
Ba Gia Regiment, 68
Ba Ria, 191
Bang, Trang, 146
Battle of Van Tuong. *See* Starlite, Operation
Bau Bang, 112–16, 129, 186; map, 114
Beevor, Anthony, 41
Bergerud, Eric, 46
big-unit debate, 51–63, 127–29, 132, 133, 138, 139, 189, 197–99, 202, 203–4, 210–12; clique, 52; strategic thought about, 51–63; Thanh, General, 52–53; Tra, General, 53–54; Tuong, General, 54–55. *See also* main force unit debate

big-unit war, xii, 2, 47, 129, 171–74; failure of, 212; and Tet Offensive, 210–11
Binh Dinh, 137–38, 150
Binh Duong, 176–77
Binh Long, 199
Birtle, Andrew J., 138–39
Bittrich, Lowell, 108
"black pajamas," 18
Bodley, Charles, 166
booby traps, 44–46, 78, 79; casualties, 46; effectiveness of, 46. *See also* mines
Boston/Cocoa Beach, Operation, 181–86; casualties, 186
"Bouncing Betty" mine, 42
Bowie, Kyle, 181, 183
Brodbeck, William, 120; and small battalion-sized search-and-destroy operations within tactical area of responsibilities (TAOR), 181
Brown, F. C., 17
Brown, Leslie E., 29–30
Brown, Thomas W., 93
Buffalo, Operation, 223

Call, Michael, 46–47
Cam, Hoang, 52, 102, 111, 112, 116, 120, 125–26, 175, 177, 179, 186–87, 219
Cam Xe battle, 117
Cambodia, 223–24
Carter, George, 89
Cedar Falls, Operation, 21
Central Office for South Vietnam (COSVN), 160; building up logistics reserve stockpiles mission in 1966, 136; command of forces in South Vietnam, 13–14; directive for southern branch, 11; establishment of unified forward command headquarters, 186; force-building missions in 1966, 135–36; fourth plenary conference, 180; interaction with People's Revolutionary Party, 13; military missions in 1966, 135; origins and responsibilities, 12–13; strategic military guidelines for 1966, 134–40; strategy, 124–25, 134,

204–6, 206–7, 208–9; tactics for war, 126; talk-fight strategy, 206
Chapman, Marvin, 187
Chau Nhai, 173
China, 20, 56–57, 203–4, 209; and "modern revisionism," 56–57
Chinh, Hoang Minh, 56, 57
Chu Lai, 66
Chu Pong Massif, 93
Chuan, Van Nguyen, 161
Chuyen, Le Xuan, 190
Cochin China Party Committee, 159
Cochrane, Operation, 221
"combined arms," 75
"Combined Plan for Military Operations in the Republic of Vietnam," 1966, 140
Cong Truong 9, 105–26
Cragg, Dan, 17, 33
Crimp, Operation, 146–49

Daniels, Walter, 108
Dap, Do Phu, 85
Dat Cuoc, 109, 129. *See also* Hill 65
dau tranh, 1–2
Davidson, Phillip, 59
"Denounce communists, Kill communists" policy, 103
DePuy, William, 191, 199, 219
Dexter, George, 144
Dexter, Herbert, 89
Diem, Ngo Dinh, 10, 55
Diem, Phat, 216
"digging in," 34
Do, Tran Do, 206
Doan, Dang, 154–55
Doc Lap Viet Cong Battalion, 163–64; final defeat of, 165
Don, Nguyen, 151
Dong, Pham Van, 211
Dong Thap II Regiment, 104; 267th Battalion, 143
Dong Xai Regiment, 123
Double Eagle, Operation, 149–50
Double Eagle II, Operation, 149–50
Doyle, Edward, 75
Duan, Le, 52, 55, 56, 58, 59, 129, 130–31, 201, 208–9, 211, 212; and avoiding American "limited war," 60–61; background, 59–60
Dulacki, Leo J., 65
Dung, Van Tien, 132–33, 201, 207–8, 209, 210, 211, 215
Dye, Harold A., 220

Eastern Europe, 20
El Paso I, Operation, 199
Eleventh Plenum, 60

F-100 Super Sabres, 90
Fifteenth Plenum, 7–8, 55
Finton, Pat, 80
Fisher, Joseph R., 65
"Flexible Response" strategy, xi, xii
Fourth Plenary conference, 180–81
France, 40, 131, 213

General Offensive–General Insurrection, 206, 208, 209
Giang, Dang Kim, 56, 201
Giap, Nguyen Vo, 16, 51, 130, 197; "Revolutionary Guerilla War," 58; and war philosophy, 21–22
Gibbs, Joe, 221
Gibraltar, Operation, 86–87
Gibson, Mel, 94
Glantz, David M., xi–xiii, 118
"Grab the enemy's belts to fight them" slogan, 21, 38–40, 125, 227–28
Green Beach, 68, 70
Grey, Jeffery, 224–25
Group 34, 19
Group 559, 8
Groupement Mobile 100 (GM 100), 82
Guarausco, Albert, 187
guerilla warfare, xii, 8, 33, 45, 143, 176, 181, 192, 198, 202–3; low-intensity, 204; proposed guidelines for developing, 203

Hackworth, David, 81
hand grenade, 44
Hanifin, Robert, Jr., 161
Hanoi: and relationship with Viet Cong, 51; response to American Phase II, 127–28; strategy, 51–54, 127–31

Hanson, Mark, 86
Harvest Moon/Lien Ket, Operation, 28
Hastings, Operation, 202
Hau Nghia Province, 143
Hibbs, Lt., 184–86
Hiep, Dang Vu, 39
Highland, Operation, 85
Hill 65, 105, 108, 109, 129
Hinson, Burt, 70
Ho Bo Woods, 146–49
Hong Kil Dong, Operation, 226
Hot Springs, Operation, 172–74; casualties, 174
Huan, Phan Tan, 68, 70
Hump, Operation, 105
Hyun, Yu Byung, 226

Ia Drang Valley, 91–95, 129, 227; lessons from, 130
III Corps: operations map, Oct.–Dec. 1965, 107; operations map, Jan.–Apr. 1966, 182
III Marine Amphibious Force, 64
infiltrators, 8–10

Jenkins, Brian Michael, 132
Jenkins, Michael, 72
Johnson, Lyndon B., 60, 61, 64, 91, 204; and troop escalation, 62–63
Jones, Bruce, 166
just war rationale, 131–32

Karch, Frederick, 76
Kelley, P. X., 166, 168
Kennedy, John F., xi, xii
Khiem, Ung Van, 56
Kinh Tong Doc Loc canal, 81
Kim Son Valley, 153–54
Kuring, Ian, 225

Lam, Hong, 186
Lanning, Michael Lee, 17, 33
Lao Dong Party, 9
Lehrack, Otto, 66, 215
Liberation Radio, 202–3
Linh, Nguyen Thanh, 147
Lipsman, Samuel, 75
Litton, Larry, 94

Lo Ke Rubber Plantation, 181, 183–86
Lober, William, 185–86
Loc Ninh, 199
Long, Cuu, 202–3
Long Tan, 224
Lung, Hoang Ngoc, 26
Lynch, William, 155, 157

main force unit debate, 51–55, 60, 61; and guerillas, 139
Man, Chu Huy, 39, 92, 93
Mao, Chairman, 211
Marauder I, Operation, 143–46
Marble Mountain, sapper raid of, 29–30
Marine Regiment (U.S.), 3rd: 3rd Battalion, 65, 66; 3rd Battalion, Company H, 78; 3rd Battalion, Company I, 70, 73, 75; 3rd Battalion, Company K, 70; 3rd Battalion, Company M, 73
Marine Regiment (U.S.), 4th: 2nd Battalion, 65–66, 166, 167–19, 170; 2nd Battalion, Company E, 73; 2nd Battalion, Company H, 71, 72
Marine Regiment (U.S.), 5th: 3rd Battalion (India Company), 221
Marine Regiment (U.S.), 7th: 2nd Battalion, 28, 86, 172–74; 2nd Battalion, ambush of, 28–29; 3rd Battalion, 166, 172–74
Marine Regiment (U.S.), 9th: 1st Battalion, 164; 1st Battalion, Company A, 164; 1st Battalion, Company C, 164; 2nd Battalion, 29; 2nd Battalion, Company E, 163–64; 2nd Battalion, Company H, 28–29, 164
Marines: MAG-12 sapper raid, October 27–28, 1965, 29–30
Marines (U.S.), 1st: 3rd Battalion (Lima Company), 221
Marines (U.S.), 4th: 1st Battalion, 162
Masher/White Wing, Operation, 149–58; map, 152
Mason, Robert, 80
"Massive Retaliation" strategy, xi
Mastiff, Operation, 181

Mat Khu Ho Bo. *See* Ho Bo Woods
McNamara, Robert, 62
Meyer, Edward, 156
Michelin Plantation, 120
Military Assistance Command, Vietnam (MACV), 22, 62
mines, 41–47; antipersonnel mines, 41–42; antitank mines, 43; "Bouncing Betty" mine, 42; Claymore mine, 42; command-detonated antivehicle mines, 43; directional fragmentation mine (DH-10), 42; and hand grenades, 44; improvised, 42; tactical spectrum, 42–43
Minh, Ho Chi, 209
"modern revisionism," 56–57
Moore, Hal, 93

Nakashima, Gerald, 89
Nam Bo, 176
Nang, Nguyen, 84, 136, 165
napalm, 115
National Liberation Front (NLF), establishment, 10–11
New York offensive, 162
New York Times, 145
Nha Mat, 123, 129
Nhue, Nguyen Tai, 156, 158
night defensive positions (NDP), 79
Ninth Plenum, 56–57
Nipe, George, Jr., 24–25
Nolting, Frederick, Jr., 217
nonlinear nature of the war, 41
North Vietnam: Central Committee, 8, 12; Central Committee Unification Division, 134; "decisive victory," 206–7; first infiltrators, 8–9; goals, 51; "great victory," 134; North-first contingent, 128–29; Politburo, 12, 58, 128, 130, 208–9; regroupees, 8; socialist economic development of, 55
North Vietnamese Army (NVA): battle plan for spring 1966, 136–137; battle plan for summer 1966, 198–99; battlefield reporting, 133–34; limited war, strategy against, 60–61; manpower drive, 19; and relationship with Viet Cong, 130; supporting firepower, 223–24
North Vietnamese Army (NVA) Artillery Regiment, 164th, 223
North Vietnamese Army (NVA) Division, 2nd: 1st Viet Cong Regiment, 137, 167; 3rd NVA Regiment, 221; 21st NVA Regiment, 165, 167, 171; mission, 137; spring battle plan, 165
North Vietnamese Army (NVA) Division, 3rd, 83–84, 87–88, 150; 2nd Viet Cong Regiment (Yellow Star), 83, 137; 22nd Regiment, 220–21; mission, 137–38
North Vietnamese Army (NVA) Division, 22nd, 150, 151
North Vietnamese Army (NVA) Division, 325th, 20
North Vietnamese Army (NVA) Regiment, 12th, 150
North Vietnamese Army (NVA) Regiment, 21st, 167, 171; 2nd NVA Division, 165; 11th Battalion, 171
North Vietnamese Army (NVA) Regiment, 33rd, 92
North Vietnamese Army (NVA) Regiment, 66th: 7th Battalion, 94; 9th Battalion, 93
North Vietnamese Army (NVA) Regiment, 320th, 20, 92
North Vietnamese Army (NVA) Regiment, 324th, 8
Northfirsters, 129
"A Number of Lessons about the U.S. Tactics and How Our Main Force Troops Can Fight the Americans," 1966, 126
Nye, George, 93

Objective George, 188
O'Connor, Thomas J., 30
"one slow, four quicks," 22, 26
Oregon offensive, 162
Ott, David Ewing, 31–32

Parish, Will, 94
pacification, 2, 138, 191
Patton, George S., 216

Paul Revere IV, Operation, 202
People's Army of Vietnam (PAVN), 12, 51
People's Liberation Armed Forces (PLAF), 12, 51
People's Revolutionary Party: interaction with Central Office for South Vietnam (COSVN), 13; name establishment, 11
Phu Loi Battalion, 103, 186
Phu Thu Peninsula, 161, 162
Phuoc Tuy, 191
Phuong Dinh, 167–71
Pike, Douglas, 1, 17, 51, 129–30
Plain of Reeds, 143
Plei Me campaign, 92
Politburo, 58–59
Preece, Alec, 144, 147
Prussians of Asia, 214
punji pits, 45, 78

Quang, Tran Van, 9
Quang Ngai, 137, 149
Quang Tri, 160–62
Que Son Valley, 221

Rawls, Robert E., 87
Recoil, position, 155
Red Beach, 149
Region 5, 149–58
Regular Force Strategy, 129–30
Resolution 9, 56, 160
Resolution 13, 204
Resolution 14, 209
Resolution 15, 55
reunification of Vietnam, 133, 197
Revisionist Anti-Party Affair, 209
Reynolds, Lee, 44
Richard B. Anderson, 163
Rogers, Bernard W., 147–48
Rolling Stone, Operation, 176–80; casualties, 180
Rolling Thunder, 60
Route 13, 200
Royal Australian Regiment: 1st Battalion, 105, 144, 147; 6th Battalion, 224

Saigon, 207; campaign against, 58; capture of, 61
sapper raids, 29–32; and big-unit war, 32; Chu Lai SATS field, 29–30; Marble Mountain, 30; missions, 39; most effective methods, 32; and Thanh, General, 30
Scales, Robert, Jr., 218
Sherman, David, 2
Shuffer, George, 109–11, 112, 120, 220
Si, Dang Ngoc, 191, 192, 193
Silver City, Operation, 186–89
Sino-Soviet rift, 56–57
Smith, Erskine, 178
Smith, Paul, 187
Smith, W. K. G., 91
South Korea: and firepower, 225–27
South Vietnam: Communist command/administrative areas July 1965 map, 97; draft, 20; first North Vietnamese Army regiments deployed to, 58; "liberation" of, 12; map, 3; security breaches, 148; villages, as base camps, 35–36
South Vietnamese: forces as weak link, 160; people, and U.S. objectives, 138
Soviet Union, 56, 203
Standing Committee of the Central Military Party Committee: military plan for 1966–67 winter-spring, 201–2; military plan for 1967–68 spring-summer, 205–8
stand-off attacks, 32–33; and big-unit war, 33; Danang, 33
Starlite, Operation, 28, 64–81; body count, 75; lessons from, 76–81; map, 69
Sturgis, Ralph, 200

"talk-fight" strategy, 129, 204
Tam, Tranh Min, 191
Tam Bo Stream, 191–92; casualties, 194
Tan Binh, 178
Task Force Mark, 86
Tau O, 200
technology and warfare, 130
Tet Offensive, 207–8, 209–12; and big-unit war, 210–11; border battles, 210; Route 9–Khe Sanh Front, 210

Texas, Operation, 166–71, 201; casualties, 171; map, 169
Tham, Ho Cong, 74
Thanh, Nguyen Chi, 14, 58, 59, 60, 63, 64, 95, 124, 131, 176, 198, 201, 212, 214; background, 14–15; and "grab belts" slogan, 38, 39; and sapper raids, 30–31; and strategy, 52, 55; and war philosophy, 21–22
Thao, Vo, 65
Thi, Nguyen Chanh, 65
Tho, Le Duc, 159–60, 197–98; strategy, 159–60
"three cuts, one destroy" approach. *See* Vu, Vuong Thua
three-man cells, 16
Thu, Luong Van, 88
Thua Thien, 160–62
Thuan, Pham Quoc, 109
Time magazine, 127
Timothy, James, 81, 86
Tourison, Sedgwick, 215
Tra, Tran Van, 14, 15, 96, 98, 116; background, 14; and strategy, 52–54
Tra Khuc River, 137
Trinh, Nguyen Duy, 129
Trong, Nguyen Dinh, 68
Tru, Le Huu, 68
Trung Loi, 117–20, 129
Tryuen, Nguyen The, 192
Tung, Ha Vi, 82
Tuong, Le Van, 54–55
Twelfth Plenum, 128, 134, 135, 136
Ty, Ta Quang, 117
Tyler, John, 144

United States: airmobile tactical innovation, 79; escalation, 127; external fire support, 218; firepower, 22, 124, 170, 214, 217–18, 219–20; infantry, traditional fighting, 221–22; "limited war," 60, 124, 180; mobility, 201; noise of troops, 148; overland travel, 77; and pacification, 138–39; Phase II, 139–40; preservation of lives, 218–19; presidential politics, 204; quality of forces, 214–16; response to close-quarters fighting, 217; road security, 43–44; strategy, xi–xiv, 127–32, 134, 138, 159; strong points, 213; tactical maneuver first, 220; troop movements vs. Viet Cong movements, 147–49; troop rotations, 227; use of external arms, 214–15, 218, 222, 225; weak point, 213
Utter, Leon, 28, 172

Vam Co Dong River, 143–44
Van, Bui Thanh, 105
Van Quang, Tran, 9
Van Tuong: analysis of, 133; and big-unit war, 78; casualties, 133. *See also* Starlite, Operation
Vaughen, Ezra, 89
Viet Bac Battalion, 545th, 20
Viet Cong, 7–47; ambushes, 26–29; ambushes, August 18, 1965, 28–29; ambushes, force structure, 27; anti-airmobile doctrine, 78, 79–80, 88; approval to overthrow South Vietnamese government, 7; attack planning, 22–24; base camps, defensive aspect, 34–35; and battle tempo, 147–49; big-unit war, 127; bunkers, 38; close quarters combat, 216–17; continuous movement, 35; defectors, 214; defensive war, 33–38; draft of South Vietnamese, 20; equipment, 19; evaluation of U.S. forces, July 1965, 213; field dress, 17–18; firepower, 214, 217–18; first infiltrators to south, 8–9; forces, factions of, 15–16; fortified villages, 36–37; goals, 51; "grab belts" slogan, 38–40, 116; Group 34, 18–19; Group 559, 8; guerilla units, 16; H-15 Battalion, 94, 95; hand grenades, 44; hugging tactic, 125; infantry raids, 25; local-force units, 15; main-force units, 15, 16; manpower issue, 18, 19; as military adversary, 147–48; mission, understanding of by soldiers, 24; offensive philosophy, 21; operational flexibility, 24–25; operational

planning, 22–23; and opportunism, 216–17; original nucleus, 9; peasant labor, 36; philosophy of war, 21; radios, 24; reconnaissance, 23; rehearsal for attack, 23; relationship with Hanoi, 51; superiority over U.S. forces, 214–16; temporary camps, 35–36; triad system, 16. *See also* booby traps; mines

Viet Cong Anti-Aircraft Company, 12th, 103

Viet Cong Artillery Division, 69th, 104

Viet Cong Battalion, 60th, 72

Viet Cong Battalion, 90th, 28

Viet Cong Battalion, 93rd, 154–58

Viet Cong Battalion, 95th, 86, 87, 88, 90; manpower, 86; weaponry, 86

Viet Cong Battalion, 267th, 144–46

Viet Cong Battalion, 802nd, 162, 163

Viet Cong Division, 5th, 102–3

Viet Cong Division, 9th, (Da Chien or Cong Truong 9), 101–2, 103, 109–10, 117–18, 124–25, 175, 179, 186

Viet Cong Engineer Company, 25th, 103

Viet Cong Local Company, 21st, 68

Viet Cong Local Force Battalion, 506th, 143; intelligence haul from, 146

Viet Cong Medical Company, 95th, 103

Viet Cong Mortar Company, 23rd, 103

Viet Cong Mountain Howitzer Battalion, 22nd, 103

Viet Cong Rear Services Group, 84th, 190

Viet Cong Reconnaissance Battalion, 95th, 103

Viet Cong Regiment, 1st, 19, 64–69, 75, 76, 77, 165, 167–71, 170, 172–74; 40th Battalion, 66; 45th Weapons Battalion, 66; 60th Battalion, 66, 171; advantages over Marines, 67

Viet Cong Regiment, 2nd, 83, 85, 91, 150, 151, 153, 155, 156–57, 214

Viet Cong Regiment, 271st, 112, 120, 178–79, 188–89, 199, 214; 1st Battalion, 113; 3rd Battalion, 105, 108–9, 109; history of, 105–6

Viet Cong Regiment, 272nd, 111–12, 115, 120, 121–23, 178, 183, 185, 186, 200; 4th Battalion, 117

Viet Cong Regiment, 273rd, 37, 112, 178–79; 7th Battalion, 112

Viet Cong Regiment, 274th, 103, 191–94

Viet Cong Regiment, 275th, 103

Viet Cong Regiment, 810th, 161, 162

Viet Cong Signal Company, 605th, 103

Viet Minh, 40

Viet Minh Regiment, 803rd, 82

Vinh, Nguyen Van, 210–11

Vu, Vuong Thua, 216; "three cuts, one destroy" approach, 40

Wallace, Ernie, 72

Wallowa, Operation, 221

Walsh, John, 187, 188

Walt, Lewis W., 65

War Zone D, 177, 186–87

warrior tradition, 214

weaponry, 16–17

West, Bing, 2

Westmoreland, William, 1, 57–58, 60, 62, 104, 127, 138, 140, 143, 186, 225; Phase I, 127; Phase II, 127

Williamson, Ellis W., 143

Xuan Mai Infiltration Training Center, 8, 19, 68

Yamamoto, Isoroku, 213

Yen River, 164–65

Zulu-Zulu, 188; casualties, 189

About the Author

Perhaps not surprisingly, Warren Wilkins' interest in the Vietnam War developed as an outgrowth of the boyhood conversations he enjoyed with his uncle, a proud combat veteran of the conflict. Today, Warren is affiliated with the Center for Threat Awareness (CTA) and is a contributor to CTA publications.

The **Naval Institute Press** is the book-publishing arm of the U.S. Naval Institute, a private, nonprofit, membership society for sea service professionals and others who share an interest in naval and maritime affairs. Established in 1873 at the U.S. Naval Academy in Annapolis, Maryland, where its offices remain today, the Naval Institute has members worldwide.

Members of the Naval Institute support the education programs of the society and receive the influential monthly magazine *Proceedings* or the colorful bimonthly magazine *Naval History* and discounts on fine nautical prints and on ship and aircraft photos. They also have access to the transcripts of the Institute's Oral History Program and get discounted admission to any of the Institute-sponsored seminars offered around the country.

The Naval Institute's book-publishing program, begun in 1898 with basic guides to naval practices, has broadened its scope to include books of more general interest. Now the Naval Institute Press publishes about seventy titles each year, ranging from how-to books on boating and navigation to battle histories, biographies, ship and aircraft guides, and novels. Institute members receive significant discounts on the more than eight hundred Press books in print.

Full-time students are eligible for special half-price membership rates. Life memberships are also available.

For a free catalog describing Naval Institute Press books currently available, and for further information about joining the U.S. Naval Institute, please write to:

Member Services
U.S. NAVAL INSTITUTE
291 Wood Road
Annapolis, MD 21402-5034
Telephone: (800) 233-8764
Fax: (410) 571-1703
Web address: www.usni.org